BROADWAY
LIBRARY
of
LARCENY

The Telephone Booth Indian

A. J. Liebling

WITH AN INTRODUCTION BY LUC SANTE

LIBRARY OF LARCENY
BROADWAY BOOKS
NEW YORK

PRINTED IN THE UNITED STATES OF AMERICA

BROADWAY BOOKS and B colophon and Library of Larceny and colophon are trademarks of Random House, Inc.

Visit our website at www.broadwaybooks.com

First Broadway Books trade paperback edition published 2004

Book design by Elizabeth Rendfleisch

Library of Congress Cataloging-in-Publication Data

Liebling, A. J. (Abbott Joseph), 1904–1963.
    The telephone booth Indian / A. J. Liebling; with an introduction by Luc Sante.—1st Broadway Books trade pbk. ed.
        p. cm.
    Originally published: Garden City, N.Y. : Doubleday, Doran & Co., 1942.
    ISBN 0-7679-1736-7 (pbk.)
        1. Businesspeople—New York (State)—New York—History—20th century.
    2. Entrepreneurship—New York (State)—New York—History—20th century.
    3. Swindlers and swindling—New York (State)—New York—History—20th century. I. Title.

HC108.7.L54 2004
338.04'092'27471—dc22   2004040655

10 9 8 7 6 5 4 3 2 1

Contents

Introduction

Luc Sante

Unless you think it stands for a slightly tarnished category of theatrical entertainment, you are probably under the impression that Broadway is merely a street. That street is either the original model, which begins at the foot of Manhattan and runs up to somewhere near the Canadian border, or one of its lesser replicants, the kind Wilson Pickett found in every burg, each of them invariably containing a bar, each bar containing a woman. The idea of "main stem" is still attached to Broadway, but that is the last vestige of its former glory. "Broadway" was once a culture unto itself, with its own tribes, castes, customs, and language. It was somehow connected to the entertainment industry, but its compass was broad, extending well past the theaters. It took in costumers' ateliers and actors' boardinghouses, trade-paper publishers and vaudeville agencies, flea circuses and pokerino parlors, pawnshops and cafeterias, hair salons and painless dentists that catered to chorines and voice coaches and supper-club magicians and itinerant Swiss bell–ringing troupes. It also sheltered a substantial parasitic population, of chiselers and percentage players and seekers after the main chance, of all degrees of probity or the lack thereof and at all stages on the road of life. Even dine-and-dash specialists and storm-drain fishermen and people who spent their waking hours sitting in hotel lobbies had a purpose, however occult, in that complex ecosystem.

Somehow, though, the students of Franz Boas at Columbia

did not consider the folkways of Broadway to be as worthy of their interest as those of the Trobriand Islands, and so the task of anthropological investigation was left to the newspapers. These did a decent if unscientific job of it, at least in disseminating the substance of their findings among the general population, so that the proverbial inhabitants of Oshkosh, if confronted by a green suit with a windowpane check picked out in magenta, would instantly identify it as a Broadway suit. Newspaper readers could retell jokes that had allegedly been hatched along the counter at Lindy's, and had a rough idea how many paces separated the stage door at the Winter Garden from the next-to-latest venue of a notable floating crap game. This was all glamour stuff, of course, roneotyped by Walter Winchell and airbrushed by Damon Runyon. The more subtle business, which occurred well away from the footlights and among characters less likely to own more than one hat, was left for the feature writers, who did not tend to be syndicated. It did not catch a nationwide audience until the mid to late 1930s, when several of the best of these writers fetched up at a magazine that had once primarily covered the bon ton, *The New Yorker*.

A. J. Liebling, along with his colleagues Joseph Mitchell and Meyer Berger (who was at *The New Yorker* only briefly, an interlude in a long career mostly spent at the *New York Times*), introduced into those pages all manner of flotsam and riffraff, which they refused to play for cheap laughs or moral scores, treating them instead with seriousness—not solemnity—and even respect: mitt readers, bearded ladies, street preachers, bailbondsmen, racetrack psychics, promoters of all sorts. Their study of Broadway was so intensive that, for example, Meyer Berger could not only detail the existence of an entire society of chiselers, giving an hour-by-hour breakdown of a typical nonworking day, but could go so far as to name the specific street corners on which chiselers from different parts of the country tended to forgather (Southern chiselers on 49th and Seventh, New England chiselers on 46th and Broadway.) For Berger, who hailed from Brooklyn, the study of Broadway was a chapter in a lifelong celebration of the hidden byways of New York City, which culminated in his beloved *Times* column of the 1950s, "About New York." Mitchell, from North Carolina, also devoted his life's work almost exclusively to the city, and his recurrent interest in Broadway was one facet of his poetic contemplation of urban microsocieties—fishermen, Gypsies, Bowery bums— with roots that went back at least to the Middle Ages, if not to the Paleolithic Era.

Abbott Joseph Liebling, known to one and all as Joe, was actually born in Manhattan, in 1904, but for him New York City and its inhabitants figured among a vast constellation of interests he returned to episodically over the course of his thirty-odd-year career. Although he was comfortably reared—his father, who had worked his way up from the Lower East Side, was prominent in the fur trade—he maintained an inclination toward lowlife from his youth onward, and he had a knack for finding its traces and effects everywhere, including medieval history and early French literature. After his expulsion from Dartmouth (for repeatedly cutting chapel; he later completed his degree at Columbia), he went to work for the *New York World*, and then for its successor, the *World-Telegram*, where he wrote many of the short features that are collected in his first book, *Back Where I Came From* (1938). The *World* was a first-class paper; the *World-Telegram* was decidedly not, and Liebling suffered there (anyone confused as to why a profile of the head of the Scripps-Howard Syndicate should be included in this, a book about riffraff, should know that Roy Howard was the *World-Telegram*'s founding publisher; both the profile and its placement were acts of revenge).

In 1935 he went to work at *The New Yorker*, where he first made his name with a profile of the Harlem-based deity Father Divine, written in collaboration with St. Clair McKelway. The pieces in this book, along with about half the contents of *Back Where I Came From*, were written in the period immediately thereafter, between 1936 and 1939. The first things that will strike the reader about Liebling upon starting to read *The Telephone Booth Indian* are his sense of humor, his virtuoso ear, his timing, his sense of style—and his boundless capacity for appreciation. This appreciation was first and foremost linguistic. As his *New Yorker* colleague Philip Hamburger wrote, "Tinhorn entrepreneurs who called the Club Chez Nous the Club Chestnuts sent him joyously humming, in a state of euphoria, to his typewriter." Liebling as a reporter was among other things an impresario, with a nose for linguistically gifted civilians, such as Morty Ormont, the renting agent of the Jollity Building ("whose expression has been compared, a little unfairly, to that of a dead robin"), whose phrasings and coinages make him in effect a contributor to the piece in which he figures, not simply a subject. Reflecting a modernist sensibility, Liebling the impresario saw art in outcomes rather than intentions; thus he made no special distinction between epigrammatists whose successes resulted from their imperfect command of English idiom (the boys at the I & Y Cigar Store: "Hymie is a man what knows to get a dollar") and those whose effects were calculated (the great boxing cut-man Whitey Bimstein: "I like the country. It's a nice spot").

Liebling also had an eye for the beauty of a con, and if this book has a hero, it is a man who, lying low somewhere, is present only in conversational reference: Maxwell C. Bimberg, aka Count de Pennies (who, according to Liebling's biographer, Raymond

Sokolov, was actually a promoter named Samuel J. Burger). The telephone booth Indians may be garden-variety schlemiels, the cannon fodder of swindling, but the Count is an artist. And if Broadway is a microcosm of the human condition, then the Jollity Building is a thimble-theater representation of Broadway, an entire world contained in a single, squat, shabby office building, whose tenants all have their eyes on the prize while they are struggling to assemble twenty-five cents. Most of the subjects of the other pieces can also be termed promoters, including Roy Howard and the Shubert Brothers, who are shown as merely more successful representatives of the species—and even they were arguably to be outdone over time by Tim Mara, the teenage bookie who went on to found the New York football Giants and whose family owns the team to this day. The book finally has a pleasing fullness, as a delineation of an American economic food chain based entirely on guile and palaver. The steep stratification of this edifice is something that can otherwise be found only in the pages of Balzac.

When this book, Liebling's second, was published in 1942, its author was in the middle of covering the war, accompanying the Allied forces from London through North Africa, then from the Normandy invasion to the liberation of Paris. Afterward he became *The New Yorker*'s deadly press critic, and simultaneously established himself as the greatest boxing writer of the century. He eventually published some fifteen books—the number is difficult to establish precisely because of overlaps. All of them have gone in and out of print over the years, including the one you are holding, which is enjoying something like a fourth life. A. J. Liebling died of multiple causes on December 28, 1963. As his friend Joseph Mitchell noted at the funeral, the second-hand booksellers who were then clustered together in a district on Fourth Avenue held his books in special esteem because they were in perpetual demand. "Literary critics don't know which books will last," Mitchell quoted a bookseller as saying, "and literary historians don't know. *We* are the ones who know. We know which books can be read only once, if that, and we know the ones that can be read and reread and reread."

Preface

There was once a French-Canadian whose name I cannot at present recall but who had a window in his stomach. It was due to this fortunate circumstance, however unlikely, that a prying fellow of a doctor was able to study the man's inner workings, and that is how we came to know all about the gastric juices, as I suppose we do. The details are not too clear in my mind, as I read the story in a hygiene reader which formed part of the curriculum of my fourth year in elementary school, but I have no doubt that it is essentially correct. I believed everything I read in that book, including the story of the three regiments of Swiss infantry who started to climb a mountain on a very cold day: the first regiment had been stimulated with a liberal ration of schnapps; the second had been dosed with about half an ounce of alcohol per man; the third had had only milk. The soldiers of the first regiment froze to death unanimously after marching only 223 yards; half the members of the second arrived at their destination, after losing their fingers, toes, and ears; the fellows in the third regiment not only raced to the top of the mountain feeling warm as toast, but took the mountain down boulder by boulder and threw it at a shepherd who was yodeling flat. This is a digression. What I meant to say is that the Telephone Booth Indians, a tribe first described by me in a monograph called "The Jollity Building," offer to the student of sociology the same opportunity that the fenestrated Canadian gave the inquiring physiologist. The glass side of the telephone booth which forms the Indian's habitat affords a chance to observe all his significant activities. These in turn illustrate the Economic Structure, for the Indian is a capitalist in what my Marxian friends would call a state of pre-primary acquisition. He has as yet acquired not even the nickel with which to make a telephone call, and so must wait in the booth until another fellow calls him.

The Telephone Booth Indians range over a territory approximately half a mile square, bounded longitudinally by Sixth and Eighth avenues in New York City, and in latitude by the south side of Forty-second and the north side of Fifty-second streets. This in part coincides with what is called humorously Broadway, the Heart of the World, and is in fact a sort of famine area, within which the Indians seek their scanty livelihood. Scattered about the district are a few large structures like the Jollity Building, but less imaginary, which are favorite camping grounds of the Indians because they contain large numbers of the telephone booths necessary to the tribe's survival. The Telephone Booth Indians are nomads who have not attained the stage of pastoral culture in which they carry their own shelter.* Like the hermit crab, the Telephone Booth Indian, before beginning operations, must find a habitation abandoned by some other creature, and in his case this is always a telephone booth. The numerical strength of the tribe is therefore roughly limited by the number of telephone booths in the district, as a sow's litter is by the number of her teats. Yet between the Telephone Booth Indian and the great man of the Indian's special world there is only the unessential difference between grub and worm. Instead of spending his working day looking at a coin box, the great man has from three to six telephones on his desk. In the land of the Telephone Booth Indians, according to the definition of my profound friend Izzy Yereshevsky, a successful man is one who knows how to get a

---

* Example: Cheyenne, Sea Lapps, Bedawi, owners of trailers.

dollar and the rest haven't got what to eat. All of the subjects of the sketches in this book come under one or the other heading. That is about all they have in common, but there is a good deal that some of them have in common with some of the others. Mr. Yereshevsky thinks that the Telephone Booth Indian is a key figure in our city and age. He has always refused to allow the installation of a telephone booth in the I. and Y. Cigar Store which he owns at Forty-ninth Street and Seventh Avenue. "The store is open twenty-four hours a day," he says, "so if I had a booth how would I get the guy out of it?"

The only subject of a piece in this book who does not at least make his business headquarters in the territory of the Telephone Booth Indians is Mr. Roy Howard, the publisher. He dresses like a Telephone Booth Indian's idea of a fellow who knows how to get a dollar, and he likes to use the telephone. However, the main reason that he is in this book is that we needed the 15,000 words.

The Author

The Telephone
Booth Indian

• Masters of the Midway •

One of the most distinctive periodicals published in the land of the Telephone Booth Indians is called the *Greater Show World*, a trade paper for outdoor showmen. It is edited in one room in the Gaiety Building, which is *not* a fictional edifice, by a man named Johnny J. Kline who has five typewriters in his office and usually has a sheet of copy paper in each of them. When he sits at one typewriter he is editor-in-chief, at another he is business manager, and at a third a gossip columnist. He writes under different by-lines as two other reporters at the remaining typewriters. The magazine which he gets out all by himself every month is just as big as the *New Yorker*, he reminds me whenever I see him, and he says he wonders what the hell the *New Yorker* staff does for a living. Since the advertising and editorial departments of the *Greater Show World* are lodged in adjacent wrinkles of the same brain lobe, they sometimes get telescoped, and the result is a spontaneous eulogy for an advertiser. Through the years a pair of showmen named Lew Dufour and Joe Rogers have drawn more eulogies and paid for more ads than almost anybody else. The pair never got a chance to work near Telephone Booth Indian territory until Grover Whalen opened his World of Tomorrow over in Flushing Meadows in 1939. When that happened they showed they knew how to get a dollar.

Among the shows on the World's Fair midway presented by the firm of Dufour & Rogers, one, "We Humans," illustrated the grand strategy of evolution in a somewhat macabre fashion. A reverent, three-dimensional presentation of Da Vinci's "Last Supper," with life-sized models of the apostles, trick lighting effects, and a musical background of Gregorian chants supplied by a phonograph with an electrical record-changing device, was to have been another Dufour & Rogers offering. They could not find a suitable Catholic organization to sponsor the "Last Supper," so they dropped it. Rogers says, without any intended disrespect, "The nuns would not play ball with us." Dufour, the senior partner, saw no conflict in the subject matter of the "Last Supper" and "We Humans." He is a man of a speculative and scientific temperament. "We tell the customers about evolution," he says, "but we don't advocate it." Jang, a Malay boy with a tail six inches long, was a principal in "Strange as It Seems," another Dufour & Rogers attraction. Dufour wanted to invite all the inhabitants of Dayton, Tennessee, to come to see Jang and draw their own conclusions. Rogers, however, was against the necessary outlay for postage stamps.

As the partners had already rented a midway site for the abandoned religious spectacle, they substituted a hastily erected saloon and restaurant called the Rondevoo. The Rondevoo made its chief appeal to other concessionaires and their employees—an example of Dufour & Rogers resourcefulness, because, as Rogers said, "The attendance is off, but the boys have got to be here anyhow." The Rondevoo turned out to be their most profitable stab.

In deference to Dufour's scholastic leanings, Rogers, an earthy type, sometimes calls his partner "Dr. Itch." The firm believes in diversification of investments, as Dufour puts it, or, as Rogers says, spreading its bets. When the Fair opened, the partners had five shows and one ride, the Silver Streak, ready in the amusement area. They also had one of their evolution shows in operation at the San Francisco Fair. The New York shows were "We Humans"; "Strange as It Seems," which they described as a "de luxe Congress of Strange People, Presented in an Air-Cooled Odditorium"; the Seminole Village, the title of which is self-explanatory; "Nature's Mistakes," an exhibit featuring Adonis, the Bull with the Human Skin, and "Gang Busters," an epic depiction of the dangers and fascination of crime, with reformed gangsters reenacting the St. Valentine's Day Massacre and Juanita Hansen, a reformed movie actress, lecturing on the evils of narcotics, to which she said she was once addicted. They also added "Olga, the Headless Girl, Alive," and the restaurant. This list includes about every kind of proved midway attraction except a girl show, and that omission is due not to prudery but commercial principles. A girl show for a world's fair must have a rather elaborate installation, usually a name star, and always a considerable salary list. Moreover, one nude non-freak woman is much like another, and while it is certain that one or two of the dozen girl shows at a world's fair will make money, nobody can tell in advance which ones they will be. Freaks, crime, five-legged cows, and aborigines are staple midway commodities. At Flushing the five-legged cows came through for the firm, but the human freaks lost money.

Dufour and Rogers began their joint career at the Century of Progress Exposition in Chicago in 1933 and have figured conspicuously on the midways at San Diego, Dallas, Fort Worth, Cleveland, Brussels, and San Francisco since then. Long before 1933 they had worked separately in that curious world of sixty thousand outdoor show people, the "carnies," who travel from town to town with carnivals. A stranger once asked Joe Rogers whether he had started as a barker with a carnival. "Hell, no,"

Rogers replied. "I worked my way up to that." And anyway, he might have explained, no carnie says "barker." The man who holds forth outside the show to bring the people in is the "outside talker"; his oration is known as "the opening." The fellow who guides them about inside the exhibit is an "inside talker."

Banks, as might be expected, are reluctant to lend money to carnival people, so Dufour & Rogers finance their ventures largely by selling "pieces" of them to other men in the amusement business—owners of touring carnivals, manufacturers of slot machines, and retired circus proprietors. The ease with which they promote money from this skeptical investing public is evidence of their prestige in the profession. Outdoor showmen always refer to important sums as "paper money." When concessionaires with less of it ran through their bank rolls at past fairs, Dufour & Rogers bought them out. That way the firm wound up the second summer of the Greater Texas Exposition at Dallas with thirty-eight attractions on the midway, including the "Streets of Paris." The "Streets of Paris" was a girl show, but even a girl show may prove a good investment after the original proprietor's investment has been written off the books. The competition of pale-faced indoor showmen, like some of the concessionaires at the Fair who had a Broadway background, always makes Lew and Joe feel good. "Give me the sky for a canopy," Rogers once said, "and I will take Flo Ziegfeld and make a sucker out of him. How do you like that?" The difference between what will draw in Beloit, Wisconsin, and what will draw in New York, they think, is not basic, but is chiefly a matter of flash—the old vaudeville word for "class" or "style"—in presentation. "You can buy a ham sandwich at the Automat," Dufour says, "or you can buy it at the Waldorf. What's the difference? The Waldorf has more flash."

The partners have little of that pure enthusiasm for a freak as a freak that distinguishes some of their friends. A man named Slim Kelly, for example, who managed "Nature's Mistakes" for Dufour & Rogers, once spent three months and all his capital in the lumber country around Bogalusa, Louisiana, where he had heard there was a Negro with only one eye, and that in the center of his forehead. Kelly still believes the cyclops is somewhere near Bogalusa but that he may be self-conscious. Lew and Joe feel that the chance of finding a really new kind of freak is a tenuous thing on which to maintain a business.

Joe Rogers is a hyperactive man in his early forties, with contrapuntal eyes set in a round, sleek head. He has a boundless capacity for indignation, which he can turn on like a tap. Rogers' complexion, when he is in low gear, indicates rosy health. When he is angry, it carries a horrid hint of apoplexy. During the last few weeks before a fair opens, he carries on a war of alarums and sorties with contractors, delegates of labor unions, and officials of the concession department. His theory is sustained attack.

Once, on being approached by a stranger at the Fair grounds, Joe asked the man his business. "I'm a landscape architect," the stranger said. "Oh," Rogers yelled before beginning to bargain, "so you're the muzzler who's going to rob me!" He had a particularly bitter time with the contractor on one of his buildings in Flushing, a tall, solemn, chamber-of-commerce sort of fellow whose work Rogers regarded as slow and expensive. "He is a legit guy, a businessman," Rogers moaned one day, "and he tries to sell me a soft con!" "Con," of course, is a contraction of "confidence game." A soft con is one that begins with a plaint, as, "When I made this contract I didn't know the site was so marshy." A short con and a quick con are less humiliating variants because they are aimed at catching a victim off guard rather than insulting his intelligence. "Me, a showman, a snake guy!"

Rogers continued. A snake guy is one who has exhibited snakes in a pit at a fair. The incongruity of the contractor's attempt to invert the natural order appeared to affect Rogers deeply. "Trying to cheat the cheaters!" he screamed. "I'll wrap a cane around his neck!" And he went out looking for the contractor.

Before he had gone three steps from his office in the "Strange as It Seems" building, however, he had become involved in a quarrel with two gypsies who sought employment in the Seminole Village. "Me Indian," said the first gypsy, who was swarthy enough to qualify. "You *gypsy!*" Rogers yelled. "You want to open a mitt joint in my concession! Get outa here!" A mitt joint is a booth for palm reading. Its bad feature, from the point of view of a respectable concessionaire, is the frequent disappearance of patrons' pocketbooks. This provokes beefs, which are bad for business. Rogers' life as opening day approaches is an assault in constantly accelerating tempo. Once a fair has opened, he goes to bed for twenty-four hours and wakes up thinking about the next fair on the international schedule.

Rogers was born in the Brownsville region of Brooklyn, but for the last fifteen years he has made his headquarters in the Hotel Sherman, a business and theatrical hotel in the Chicago Loop. He finds people out there more compatible. Dufour, however, lives in an apartment in Forest Hills. Between fairs the partners keep in touch by air line and long-distance telephone.

Lew Dufour is tall, sallow, and bland, and wears his dark clothes with a sort of mortuary elegance. Superficially, he does not resemble Rogers. "Mr. Dufour," a subordinate once said, "is a mental genius. Mr. Rogers is an executive genius." When Rogers fails to overwhelm an opponent in a business argument, Dufour takes up the task and wheedles him. It is a procedure used by teams of detectives to make criminals confess. As a unit, Lew and Joe are nearly irresistible. On propositions requiring dignity and aplomb, Dufour makes the first approach. At Chicago in 1934, however, Lew failed to impress General Charles G. Dawes, who was chairman of the finance committee for the Century of Progress. The partners had had a successful first season at the Fair, but the management wished to shift their "Life" show—an earlier edition of "We Humans"—to a less favorable site for the reprise of the Fair. When Dufour failed to move Dawes, Rogers leaned forward, pincered the general with his intercepting eyes, and shouted, "You can't do this to us, General! We are good concessionaires. We made a lot of money for the Fair." The general said, "How much did you make for yourselves?" "Oh," said Rogers, suddenly vague, "we made lots and lots." Rogers says he could hear the famous pipe rattling against the general's teeth from the force of the general's curiosity. "And what do you call lots of money, Mr. Rogers?" Joe's voice became a happy croon. "What I call lots of money, General, is lots and lots and *lots*." General Dawes permitted them to keep their old site. Presumably he hoped Rogers might relent someday and tell him. "I just worked on his curiosity," Joe says, "like I wanted him to come in and see a two-headed baby." The partners had made $111,000 on the "Life" show.

A favored type of investment among world's-fair concessionaires is an aboriginal village. Eskimos, Filipinos, or Ashantis usually can be hired at extremely moderate rates to sit around in an appropriate setting and act as if they were at home. The city dweller's curiosity about exotic peoples, built up by a childhood of reading adventure books, is apparently insatiable. Providing suitable food is not such a problem as it might seem once the concessionaire has learned the fact, unreported by anthropologists, that all primitive peoples exist by preference on a diet of hamburger steak. Dufour derives from this pervading passion a theory that all races of man once inhabited a common Atlantis, but Rogers does not go so far. He just says he is glad they do not crave porterhouse. Once engaged, the aborigine must be encouraged and, if necessary, taught to perform some harmless maneuver which may be ballyhooed as a sacred tribal rite, just about to begin, folks. This is ordinarily not difficult, as the average savage seems to be a good deal of a ham at heart.

Dufour & Rogers' debut as practical ethnologists was really caused by a large captive balloon that blew away from its moorings at the Century of Progress. The balloon had been one of the sights of the midway, and its taking off left a large site vacant. So Lew and Joe, who already had a couple of other shows, leased the space for a tropical village, which they called Darkest Africa. Some of the partners' acquaintances say they opened with a cast of tribesmen from South State Street, which is in the Chicago Black Belt, but Lew insists that he came to New York to engage them all. "Naturally, there was no time to go to Africa for performers on such short notice," he says, "but you would be surprised the number of real Africans there are in Harlem. They come there on ships."

By the time Dufour got back to Chicago with his company of hamburger-eating cannibals, Rogers had built the village, a kind of stockade containing thatched huts and a bar. "We had a lot of genuine junk, spears and things like that, that an explorer had brought from the bacteria of Africa," Joe Rogers says, "but this chump had gone back to Africa, so we did not know exactly which things belonged to which tribes—Dahomeys and Ashantis and Zulus and things like that. Somehow our natives didn't seem to know, either." This failed to stump the partners. They divided the stuff among the representatives of the various tribal groups they had assembled and invited the anthropology departments of the Universities of Chicago and Illinois to see their show. Every time an anthropologist dropped in, the firm would get a beef. The scientist would complain that a Senegalese was carrying a Zulu shield, and Lew or Joe would thank him and pretend to be abashed. Then they would change the shield. "By August," Joe says with simple pride, "everything in the joint was in perfect order."

The partners bought some monkeys for their village from an importer named Warren Buck and added an outside sign which said, "Warren Buck's Animals." By the merest chance, the branches and leaves of a large palm tree, part of the decorative scheme, blotted out the "Warren," so the sign appeared to read "Buck's Animals." Since Frank Buck was at the height of his popularity, the inadvertence did not cut into the gate receipts of Darkest Africa.

The concession proved so profitable that Lew and Joe decided to open a more ambitious kraal for the 1934 edition of the Fair. They chose a Hawaiian village this time. Customers expect things of a Hawaiian village which they would not demand in Darkest Africa. They expect an elaborate tropical *décor*, languorous dance music, and a type of entertainment that invites trouble with the police. The few Hawaiian entertainers on this continent will not even eat hamburger, a sure indication that theirs is a vitiated type of savagery. All such refinements increase the "nut," or overhead. There was also a rather expensive restaurant. All told, Dufour and Rogers and their friends invested a hundred thousand dollars in the venture before it opened. The central feature of the Village was a volcano seventy feet high, built of painted concrete, near the restaurant. Joe Rogers in his youth had been much impressed by a play called *The Bird of Paradise*. In the big scene of the play the heroine jumped into the smoking crater of Mount Kilauea to appease the island gods. The Dufour & Rogers Chicago volcano was "gaffed" with steampipes. "Gaff," a synonym for "gimmick," means a concealed device. The verb "to gaff" means to equip with gaffs. Lew and Joe hired a Hawaiian dancer named Princess Ahi as the star of their Village. Twice nightly the Princess ascended the volcano, during the dinner and supper shows. As the Princess climbed along a winding path in the concrete, a spotlight followed her. The steampipes emitted convincing clouds; electrical gimmicks set around the crater gleamed menacingly, and the Princess, warming with her exertions, dropped portions of her tribal raiment as she gained altitude. The volcano was visible from all parts of the midway, a great ballyhoo for the Village and, incidentally, a free show for the small-money trade. When the Princess Ahi reached the top of the mountain, she whipped off the last concession to Island modesty and dived into the crater, which was only about four feet deep and was lined with mattresses to break her fall. "She would land right on her kisser on a mattress," Joe Rogers says. The lights were dimmed; the steam subsided, and the Princess climbed out of Kilauea and came down again unobserved. Joe had to show the Princess how to dive into the crater, kisser first, instead of stepping gingerly into it. This astonished him. "She must have seen plenty other broads jump into them volcanoes at home," he says.

When interest in the Princess began to flag, the partners added Faith Bacon to their show. Miss Bacon did a dance in the N. T. G. show out at Flushing earlier that summer. "She was not a Hawaiian," Joe explains, "but she had once eaten some Hawaiian pineapple." At the Hawaiian Village, Miss Bacon did a gardenia dance, wearing only a girdle of the blooms and discarding them as she went along. This disappointed the customers, who expected her to start with one gardenia and discard petals. The partners also engaged a girl named Fifi D'Arline, who did a muff dance, using a small muff in place of an ostrich fan. She did not draw the crowds consistently, either. It was midsummer before the partners acknowledged to each other that the attendance at the 1934 renewal of the Fair consisted mainly of Chicagoans who came out to kill a day without spending any considerable sum. Lew and Joe ripped out the luxurious modernistic bar in the Village and installed a cafeteria that sold a cup of coffee for a nickel and a ham sandwich for ten cents. The cafeteria pulled the concession through. Lew and Joe made no money on the Hawaiian Village but at least were able to break even.

The Seminole Indians, Dufour & Rogers' contribution to the urban understanding of the savage, subsisted on buckets of hamburger exactly as the Kroomen and Dahomans did in Chicago. The Seminoles were not very cheerful, for long acquaintance with winter visitors to Florida had given them a peculiarly bilious view of the white man. The adult males wrestled with torpid alligators in the brackish water of a small swimming pool, and the women sold beads if visitors to the Seminole Village insisted upon it. When the Seminoles arrived at the Fair grounds, on a cold, rainy April day, they walked into a culinary crisis. The gas for their cookhouse range had not been turned on. The nonplussed Indians tried, rather ineptly, to build a campfire over which to fry their only known form of sustenance, but the World's Fair fire department raced to the midway and put out the fire. When the firemen went away the Seminoles built another fire. After several repetitions of the episode the firemen got tired and let them alone. By that time, Rogers had had the gas connected.

Another emergency arose when the World's Fair health officer insisted that the Seminole cookhouse be equipped with an electric dishwashing machine, required by Fair regulations wherever food was prepared and served. It was impossible to change regulations at the Fair, because they had all been printed in a booklet. The partners won an indefinite delay, however, by arguing that the Seminoles might accidentally mangle one of their papooses in a dishwashing machine, and so feel impelled to scalp Grover Whalen.

Joe Rogers liked the Seminoles. He understood them as intuitively as he understood General Dawes. Labor-union regulations prevented the Indians from doing any serious construction work on their village, but they did cover the tar-paper roofs of their lean-tos with palm leaves brought from Florida. They tacked overlapping layers of palm leaves to the tar paper, and in their lavish aboriginal manner used an inordinate number of tacks, which cost Dufour & Rogers money. Three or four days after the Seminoles got there, Will Yolen, the publicity man, arranged for them to make a tour of a New York department store. Yolen and the publicity department of the store hoped that some photographs of the Indians in the white man's trading post might get into the newspapers. Before the Indians went into town, Rogers, who had studied the Seminoles' mores, told his press agent to be sure that the party visited the hardware department. When the Seminoles returned, they brought plenty of tacks and even a few hammers which they had snitched en route, fulfilling their boss's expectations.

"You should have sent them to a jewelry store," said the admiring Mr. Dufour. "We could have cleared the nut before we opened."

Long before Lew Dufour and Joe Rogers became partners in the firm that once ran a half-dozen shows on the World's Fair midway, they had pursued separate careers with traveling shows. The men have been aware of each other's existence for at least twenty-five years, but until they started working together, during the Century of Progress in Chicago, their paths crossed so casually and so often that they can't remember where they first met or the occasion of the meeting.

Twenty years ago, Dufour was head of a carnival known as Lew Dufour's Exposition. The Exposition traveled in twenty-five railroad cars, and Lew's name was bravely emblazoned on each, although his equity was sometimes thinner than the paint. The carnival included a small menagerie, snakes, freaks, a girl show, several riding devices, and a goodly number of wheels on which the peasantry was privileged to play for canes or baby dolls. At the beginning of every season, the Exposition would leave winter quarters in debt to the butchers who had provided meat for the lions in the menagerie. If the weather was fair the first week out, the Exposition would make enough to go on to the second date on its always tentative route. On one occasion the organization was bogged down in mud and debt at a town in eastern Tennessee after two weeks of steady rain. The tents were pitched in a gully which had become flooded, but as in most outdoor shows, the personnel lived on the train. The sheriff came down to Dufour's gaudy private car to attach the Exposition's tangible assets. With the aid of a quart of corn liquor, Dufour talked the sheriff into lending him the money to pay off the local creditors. Then he got him to ask the creditors down to the car and talked them into lending him $1800 to haul the show as far as Lynchburg, Virginia. At Lynchburg he talked the agent of the Southern Railroad into sending the train through to Washington without advance payment. It was a mass migration of four hundred persons and six wild Nubian lions in twenty-five railroad cars, without other motive machinery than Dufour's tongue.

Shortly after that hegira, Dufour decided that while the show owners got the glory, it was the concessionaires traveling with the shows who got the money. So he became the proprietor of a "jam joint." A jam joint is a traveling auction store in which, as the climax of the "regularly scheduled sale," the auctioneer says, "Now, my friends, who will bid one dollar for this empty, worthless box?" A man in the audience says, "I will," and passes up a dollar. The auctioneer is touched. He says, "This gentleman has sufficient confidence in me that he offers one dollar for an empty box. I will not abuse his confidence. Here, mister, is the box. Open it in front of everybody." The box, it turns out, contains "a seventeen-jewel Elgin watch." "I don't want your dollar, mister," the auctioneer says. "Take this beautiful forty-five-dollar watch as a present." Then he asks how many people will give him five dollars for an empty box. A few five-dollar bills are passed up hopefully. He asks the people if they are perfectly satisfied to give him five dollars for an empty box. Sensing that it is a game, they shout "Yes!" He hands back their money and presents each of them with a "handsome and valuable gift," usually a wallet or vanity case worth about a dime, as a reward for their confidence in him. Next he calls for ten-dollar bids on an empty box. By this time the contagion of something for nothing has spread, and the countrymen eagerly pass up their bills. He asks them if they would have any kick if he kept their money and gave them nothing but an empty box. Remembering the previous routine, they shout "No!" "Nobody will have any complaint if I keep the money?" the jam guy asks. Nobody. The auditors expect him to return the money, with a present as a reward for their faith. The auctioneer assures them that he will *not* give them an empty box for their money. He will give to each and every one of them a special platinum-rolled alarm clock "worth ten dollars in itself." He makes a speech about the alarm clock. That is not all. He will give to each a beautiful Persian rug, worth twenty-five dollars, specially imported from Egypt. He makes a speech about the rug. That is not all. He adds a couple of patent picture frames "worth six dollars apiece." In short, he loads each of his confiding acquaintances with an assortment of bulky junk and then declares the sale at an end, retaining all the ten-dollar bills.

Jamming paid well and yielded a certain artistic satisfaction, but it did not content Dufour. He felt that it was not creative and that it had only an oblique educational value. It was at the Louisiana State Fair at Shreveport, in 1927, that Lew found his real vocation. He recognized it instantly; Keats felt the same way when he opened Chapman's Homer. There was a medicine pitchman at the Fair who carried with him a few bottles of formaldehyde containing human embryos. The pitchman used the embryos only as a decoy to collect a "tip," which is what a pitchman calls an audience, but Dufour, who was at the Fair with his auction store, dropped in on the medicine show one evening and at once sensed there was money in the facts of life. He must have had an intimation of that vast, latent public interest in medicine which has since been capitalized upon by Dr. Heiser, Dr. Cronin, Dr. Hertzler, Dr. Menninger, and all the other authors of medical best sellers. "A scientist may know a lot about embryology and biology," Lew has since said, "but it don't mean anything at the ticket window because it's not presented right. I felt the strength of the thing right away." From the day when he decided to present biology effectively, Lew began to collect suitable exhibits.

The important thing in assembling a cast for a biology show is to get a graduated set of human embryos which may be used to illustrate the development of an unborn baby from the first month to the eighth. The series parallels, as the lecturers point out, the evolution of man through the fish, animal, and primate stages. As an extra bit of flash, a good show includes some life groups of prehistoric men and women huddled around a campfire. Sometimes it takes months to put together a complete set of specimens. While it is true, as Lew sometimes roguishly observes, that you cannot buy unborn babies in Macy's or Gimbel's, there are *sub-rosa* clearing houses for them in most large cities. It is now a small industry, though seldom mentioned by chambers of commerce. The embryo business even has its tycoon, to borrow a word from graver publications, a man in Chicago who used to be chief laboratory technician at a medical school. The specimens are smuggled out of hospitals by technicians or impecunious internes. Hospitals have a rule that such specimens should be destroyed, but it is seldom rigidly enforced; no crime is involved in selling one. Dufour can afford to keep companies standing by. The actors need no rehearsal and draw no salary. Early in his biological career, Lew thought of a terrific title for his show— "Life." He did not pay fifty thousand dollars for this title, as Henry R. Luce did when he had the same inspiration. He did pretty well with his "Life" exhibits, playing state and county fairs and amusement parks, but he didn't get to the big time until he teamed up with Joe Rogers.

During Dufour's years of orientation, Rogers had been acquiring a comfortable bank roll by merchandising unbreakable dolls and cotton blankets in western Canada. His merchandising apparatus consisted of a wheel with fifty numbers on it. The customers paid ten cents a chance, and after every whirl one customer or another collected a doll or a blanket. In order to keep their midways free of swindlers, the Canadian fairs make contracts awarding all the concessions at each fair to one firm of concessionaires. Rogers' wheels were honest but allowed a nice margin of profit, and he usually got the concessions. Joe had established his headquarters in Chicago, and he used to travel through Canada west of Toronto in the winter, signing contracts with fairs. He was always a heavy bettor on sporting events, and on his journeys acquired an expert knowledge of professional hockey, which, in those days, existed only in Canada. When big-league hockey was introduced to the United States; Rogers was the only betting man in Chicago who really knew what the odds on the teams should be. He won consistently for several seasons before his friends began to catch on. In addition to all this, he ran the Link cigar store and restaurant on Michigan Boulevard, a rendezvous for sporting men and politicians.

Lew and Joe joined forces for the first time before the Century of Progress in Chicago opened. Lew had his "Life" show, and Joe was able to finance a flashy building for it at the Fair. Showmen are incessantly forming one- or two-season partnerships for a particular promotion, and neither Lew nor Joe realized at once the significance of their merger. The firm began its history just with "Life," but within a week it opened a second exhibit—the two-headed baby. The baby, one of those medical anomalies that never live for more than a few gasps, was in a large bottle of formaldehyde. For years it had been the chief ornament of a country doctor's study, and the partners had picked it up for a couple of hundred dollars from a Chicago dealer in medical curiosa. They built a fine front for this exhibit, with a wooden stork carrying a two-headed baby prominently displayed over the entrance. They got a female talker for the show, a motherly woman who wore a trained-nurse's uniform and made her ballyhoo through a microphone.

"Wouldn't you like to see a *real* two-headed baby?" the nurse would ask sweetly. "He was *born* alive."

"Get that," Joe says. "We didn't say it was alive. We just said it was born alive." The partners had arranged the entrance so that people on the midway could see past the door to a woman in nurse's uniform who bent over some object they could not discern. If the people inferred that the object was a baby and the nurse was trying to keep it alive, that was their own business. No deception could be imputed to Dufour & Rogers. And anyway, a look at a two-headed baby, even in a bottle, is well worth fifteen cents.

"Did you ever see a *real* two-headed baby?" Rogers sometimes murmurs euphorically, apropos of nothing except a cheerful mood. "It was *born* alive." The partners grossed fifty thousand dollars with their pickled star. Thirty-five thousand was clear profit.

"It wasn't a fake," Dufour argues earnestly. "It was an illusion, like when Barnum advertised the 'cow with its head where its tail ought to be,' and when the people paid their money he just showed them a cow turned around in her stall. Just a new angle of presentation, you might say."

The new angle of presentation is the essential element of success on a midway. There are virtually no novel or unique attractions. Even the most extraordinary freaks seldom remain long without rivals. Thus, shortly after the appearance of Jo-Jo, the Dog-Faced Boy, the show world witnessed the debut of Lionel, the Lion-Faced Boy. The appearance of Frank Lentini, the Three-Legged Man, was closely followed by that of Myrtle Corbin, the Four-Legged Girl. Lalou, the Double-Bodied Man from Mexico, soon had a rival in Libera, the Double-Bodied Spaniard. This is because when one victim of a particular deformity begins to get publicity, other similar freaks see profit in making themselves known.

Dufour and Rogers have deep admiration for a young man named Jack Tavlin, who managed three midgets at the San Diego Fair and made money with them by calling them "leprahons." "A midget is not worth feeding," Mr. Tavlin, who was also working at the Flushing Fair, wisely observed. "Everybody knows what is a midget—a little man. But when I said, 'Come and see the leprahons,' the customers came. Afterward some of them would ask me, 'What is the difference between a leprahon and a midget?' I would say, 'Madam, it is a different species. A leprahon cannot reproduce theirself.' " Mr. Tavlin's midgets were very small, because they were only six or seven years old, and a child midget is naturally rather smaller than an adult one. He dressed the midget boy in a high hat and a dress suit and the two girls in evening gowns. He didn't say they were full-grown. The customers assumed they were. In time the juvenile midgets got into the hands of a less conscientious impresario, and the picture of the boy appeared in the magazine *Life* as a "life-size portrait of the world's smallest man—age 18 years, height 19 inches, weight 12 pounds." The boy was only nine years old then, but, as Mr. Tavlin says, "There is always some unscrupulous person that will take advantage of a reporter."

For the two summers of the Century of Progress, Lew and Joe prospered. "Life," the Two-Headed Baby, and Darkest Africa, the Ethiop village that they opened the first season, all made plenty of "paper money." The Hawaiian Village, their most ambitious promotion, earned no profit, but the partners broke even on it. A vista of paper money and excitement opened before Dufour & Rogers in the fall of 1934. The only requisite to continued success was a steady supply of world's fairs. Brussels and San Diego had announced expositions for 1935. The firm divided its forces. Rogers went to Brussels with "La Vie," a variation of "Life"; "Les Monstres Géants," a snake show featuring rattlesnakes, or *serpents à sonnettes*, a novelty in Belgium; and, as a feature attraction, a show like "Gang Busters," called for the Belgian trade "Le Crime Ne Paie Pas." Dufour took the same line of shows to San Diego, and in addition had the firm's mascot, the two-headed baby. "Le Crime Ne Paie Pas" had a collection of tommy guns and sawed-off shotguns reputedly taken from *les gangsters américains*, a rogues' gallery of photographs featuring postmortem views of Dillinger and an old Pierce-Arrow sedan billed as "*L'Auto Blindé des Bandits*." The old Pierce has especially thick plate-glass windows, and the doors and tonneau are indubitably lined with sheet metal. Its history is uncertain, but it must have belonged to somebody who was at least apprehensive of accidents. The car was like a box at the opera. In Brussels it passed on alternate Wednesdays as Dillinger's, on odd Fridays as Al Capone's, and at other times as Jack "Legs" Diamond's. Jack "Legs" Diamond was the most popular gangster in Belgium, Rogers says, because once he had tried to land at Antwerp from a freighter and had been turned back by the Belgian police. The Belgians felt they had had a personal contact with him. During the weeks before the Flushing Fair opened, Joe drove the armored car around the streets of New York, usually between the Fair grounds and the West Side Ruby Foo's, where he likes to eat.

The star of "Le Crime Ne Paie Pas" was a man named Floyd Woolsey, who sat in an electric chair and impersonated a murderer being executed. He had to give special performances for delegations of curious European police chiefs. Belgian journalists reported that "Le Crime Ne Paie Pas" gave them a fresh insight into American life. Dave Hennen Morris, at the time United States Ambassador to Belgium, found the show a fine antidote to nostalgia, but a few stodgy American residents of Brussels protested against giving Continentals such strange ideas of our culture. Therefore, acting on the Ambassador's suggestion, Rogers rechristened the show "Les Gangsters Internationaux." The inclusion of a few German gangsters in the rogues' gallery made everybody happy, and, as Joe says, "the heat was off." He thinks well of Europe except for the climate. "It is the wrong setup for snakes," he says. "Cold and rainy all the time." But the weather had no deterrent effect upon the crowds. The Belgians, Joe concluded, had given up hoping for fair weather.

During 1936 and 1937, Dufour & Rogers operated clusters of shows in the expositions at Dallas, Fort Worth, and Cleveland, but these were mere workouts: they had already begun to plan their layout for the World of Tomorrow. Throughout the Texas and Cleveland fairs, none of which was an unqualified success, Lew and Joe maintained a record of profit-making most unusual among concessionaires. Each time they emerged unscathed from another fair their prestige in the trade and the amount of paper money which they apparently had at their disposition increased.

The two men have divergent notions of pleasure. Rogers, noisy, pugnacious, and juvenile, likes to travel with sporting men. He will fly from a midway to an important prize fight a couple of thousand miles away and fly right back again when the fight is over. Dufour, despite his gauntness, is an epicure famous among carnival men. He has even invented two dishes—soft scrambled eggs with anchovies, and loose hamburger steak. He insists that his hamburger be made of a Delmonico steak cut into small pieces with a knife and that it be sautéed in a covered pan over a slow fire. Dufour's preoccupation with the finer things of life sometimes enrages Rogers. "I knew him when he had doughnut tumors," he says bitterly, "and now he has to have scrambled eggs with anchovies." Doughnut tumors are abdominal lumps which, carnies say, appear upon the bodies of show people who have subsisted for months at a time on nothing but coffee and doughnuts. "That Dr. Itch," Joe sputters at other times—it is his familiar name for his partner—"when trouble comes he lams and leaves me with the grief." But he values Dufour for his intellect. Both partners have been married for many years, and Mrs. Dufour and Mrs. Rogers hit it off well together.

The Dufour & Rogers reputation of always paying off stood them in particularly good stead when they bid for concessions at the New York Fair. Even an apparently flimsy building in the amusement area represented a big investment for the average outdoor showman. The buildings here had to be set on piles because of the low marshland; building specifications were strict; labor costs in New York were high. Would-be concessionaires had to furnish stiff guarantees of solvency. The "Nature's Mistakes" building, the least expensive of the Dufour & Rogers string, cost about $20,000. "Strange as It Seems," their most elaborate offering, cost nearly $100,000. Altogether, Lew Dufour says, their attractions at the Fair grounds represented an investment of $600,000. The partners usually incorporate each attraction separately and finance it by selling bonds. The corporation also issues common stock, of which around forty-nine per cent goes to the bondholders as a bonus, while the impresarios retain the rest. At the end of a fair, the corporation pays off the bondholders and the profits, if any, are divided among the holders of common stock. It is not a conservative form of investment, but the bank-roll men get action for their money.

Concessionaires paid a percentage of the gross receipts to the Fair, making a separate deal for each show. For "Strange as It Seems," for example, Dufour & Rogers agreed to pay around fifteen per cent on the first $500,000 of receipts. The show never reached that figure. The Fair administration provided either the ticket-taker or the cashier for each show—the option rested with the concessionaire. If the cashier was a Fair employee, the Fair collected the gate receipts at the end of the day and banked them, paying the concessionaires their share by check. Dufour & Rogers, with their usual acumen, prefer to have a Fair cashier and a Dufour & Rogers ticket-taker. "Then, if she takes any bad money, it is the Fair's hard luck and not ours," Mr. Rogers says.

"Strange as It Seems" is an example of an ancient American form of folk art, the freak show. Phineas T. Barnum was primarily an exploiter of freaks. He became a circus man late in life, and never got to be a good one. But after Barnum the freak show became a stale and devitalized art form. Syndicated cartoonists like Bob Ripley, who draws "Believe It or Not," and John Hix, Ripley's bustling young rival, who is author of the syndicated newspaper strip "Strange as It Seems," were instrumental in the revival, but the genius of the *risorgimento* was the late C. C. Pyle, a showman who realized that the American public loves to suffer. Pyle put on a large-scale freak show at the Century of Progress, calling it "Believe It or Not" and paying Ripley a royalty for the title. The selling point was that the highly peculiar principals in the show had been immortalized in the Ripley cartoons. The title had drawing power, but the unabashed appeal to the crowds' cruelty really put the show over. Women emerging from the exhibit advised friends not to go in. "You'll faint," they said. No stronger inducement to attendance could be offered—the friends went right in. Sally Rand topped the midway at Chicago during both summers of the Century of Progress, but the freak show finished a good second.

When Ripley's backers failed to come to terms with the World of Tomorrow, Lew and Joe moved in, using John Hix as a front man. Hix got five per cent of the gross for the use of his name and dutifully drew pictures of the freaks for his daily newspaper strip. Ripley, apparently peeved by the affront to his prestige, opened his own museum of curiosities on Broadway. Dufour & Rogers had exclusive freak-show rights at the World of Tomorrow, besides an excellent grasp of the neo-Frankenstein technique of breaking the audience down with horror. They had a man named Ellis Phillips in their show who drove a long nail into his nose, held up his socks with thumbtacks, sewed buttons onto his chest, and stuck hatpins through his cheeks. "It's a hell of an act," Joe Rogers said admiringly, "and we also have a very nice fellow who eats razor blades." The art of drawing up a bill for a modern freak show lies in alternating "strong" or "torture" acts in the layout, such as the tattooed girl, Betty Broadbent; the contortionist, Flexible Freddie, or the man who puts four golf balls in his mouth simultaneously. The customers move counterclockwise around three sides of the auditorium, and the strong acts are graduated in intensity, so that after passing the strongest of them the pleased patron will be within one bound of fresh air.

An ingenious gentleman named Nathan T. Eagle acted as manager. "The best ad for our show," Mr. Eagle said engagingly, "is the number of people who collapse or imagine they have delirium tremens after seeing it." The more important performers realize this and keep a painstaking record of how many people they cause to lose consciousness. Mr. Eagle's favorite performer was a Cuban Negro named Avelino Perez, who is always billed as the Cuban Pop-Eye because he can make his eyeballs pop far out of his head, either singly or in unison. Perez was a keen runner-up to the hatpin man in provoking comas. A gentleman who pulls weights on hooks passed through his eyelids was another close competitor.

Perez was in especially good form one evening, and on performing his first, or left-eye, pop, caused a patron who had just dined at a midway restaurant to turn green. Perez popped his right eye, and the man went down cold. "A couple of our boys got hold of this fellow and started rubbing his wrists and pushing smelling salts under his nose," Mr. Eagle says. "Just as he started to regain consciousness—he was lying there on the floor in front of the Cubano, you know—Perez looked down at him and popped both eyeballs. The fellow passed right out again. Great sense of humor, that Cubano."

• Sparring Partner •

Joe Louis' knockout of Max Schmeling in their second match was a triumph for the theory that fighters should have tough sparring partners. Each of his bouts since has been a triumph for the same theory. Louis trained for Schmeling with the best colored heavyweights his handlers could hire. They included a man named George Nicholson, who is considered the best sparring partner in the business. Writers covering Louis' camp frequently reported that the partners were outboxing the champion. Schmeling's camp was run on quite a different basis. His sparring partners were four virtually anonymous human punching bags, on whom he practiced his blows with impunity. They seldom hit back except by mistake, and when they did the German punished them. Louis paid twenty-five dollars a day apiece for his sparring partners; Schmeling paid ten. A Schmeling victory, therefore, would have meant economic catastrophe for the sparring-partner industry.

"It goes to show that you got to be in the best of condition no matter who you fighting," George Nicholson says of the German's defeat. And getting in the "best of condition" implies to Nicholson sparring partners at twenty-five dollars a day. "You can hire any kind of cheap help to get theirself hit," says Nicholson. "What you got to pay good money for is somebody that is not going to get hisself hit. By not getting hisself hit, a sparring partner does more good to a fighter, because it sets the fighter to studying why he ain't hitting him." Nicholson's heartfelt interest in the defensive aspect of boxing, critics think, makes him an ideal sparring partner. It is this same interest which prevents him from being a great fighter. He is one of the kindest and least aggressive men who ever pulled on a boxing glove. "My one ambition," George sometimes says, "is to make my parents happy."

One reason he prefers sparring to fighting is that it keeps him out in the country for weeks at a time. George loves nature, usually soaking up its beauties through the pores of his skin, with his eyes closed. He is never more content than when he can sprawl his five-foot-eleven-and-three-quarter-inch body in one of the deep lawn chairs at Dr. Joseph Bier's training camp at Pompton Lakes, New Jersey, where Louis has trained for eleven Eastern fights and prepared for his match with Tony Galento at the Yankee Stadium. It is pleasant to watch Nicholson in his chair, a straw sombrero cocked over his eyes, which are further protected by smoked glasses with octagonal lenses. His torso slopes backward at an extremely obtuse angle to his thighs. One leg, with a size-thirteen shoe at the end of it, is negligently crossed over the other knee. Sometimes he drops off to sleep.

At two o'clock in the afternoon a brisk, pink-cheeked Jewish trainer named Mannie Seamon appears on the lawn and says, "C'mon, George, time to get going." The big man arises and starts for the gymnasium at the back of the house to prepare for the few minutes of acute discomfort whereby he pays for his leisure. Louis in training usually boxes against three sparring partners in an afternoon, two three-minute rounds with each man.

Nicholson is at home at Pompton Lakes. He has been there to help Louis prepare for four fights. In 1936 he spent three weeks in the same camp with Jim Braddock, when Braddock was getting ready to fight Tommy Farr. Now and then, Nicholson gets a fight on his own account, but he doesn't earn much that way. A sparring partner must be a pretty good fighter to give a star a workout, but if he is a financially successful fighter he will not work for training-camp wages. Since there are not many bouts available for a run-of-the-mill Negro heavyweight unless he has a powerful white promoter building him up, the best sparring partners are apt to be Negroes. White boys of commensurate ability are usually in training for their own fights.

A partner's life is not arduous when he has a camp job. He may take some hard punches in a workout with a hitter like Louis, but boxers in training wear headguards and sixteen-ounce gloves, and Nicholson has seldom received a cut. Nor has he ever been knocked down in a sparring match. The trouble with the calling is that stars usually train only four weeks for a bout and fight at most two or three times each year. Sometimes a heavyweight champion skips a year without fighting at all. In the intervals a sparring partner has slim pickings. This sometimes discourages Nicholson, but not for long. His is a sanguine nature.

"When it's no business in the fall," he says, "I go home to my parents' place in Mantua, New Jersey, and hunts rabbits and squirrels with a gun. And when it's no work in the spring I go there and work in the garden. And then, also, I might get a fight in-between-times." He does not say this last with any conviction. He had just fourteen fights in his first four years as a professional, and his net income from them was less than fifteen hundred dollars. George won nine bouts and thinks he got bad decisions in a couple he lost. He was twenty-eight—a ripe middle age for a fighter.

Boxers never start out to be sparring partners, any more than actors start out to be understudies. Fighters take sparring jobs to bridge over gaps between engagements, and even after a boxer has earned his living for years by sparring, he is apt to think of it as a temporary expedient. When Nicholson began boxing he thought he might be a champion.

George was born in Mantua, where his father was a teamster. Later his family moved to Yonkers, and there he played tackle on the high-school football team. His parents have moved back to Mantua since George left school, but he has a brother who still lives in Yonkers, "a govament man," he says, "WPA." One of George's earliest ambitions was to be a prize fighter, because he was always reading about boxing in the newspapers. The beginning of his true career was delayed, though. At Yonkers High he got to thinking he might be a lawyer. He abandoned this project for a peculiar reason. "I got out of the habit of trying to study law," he says, "on account of I saw I couldn't talk fast enough." For a few years he was bemused. He had got to thinking of himself as a professional man and he couldn't seem to readjust. Even today most of his associates believe he is a college graduate. The misconception, based upon his polished manner, is strengthened by the fact that he played for three seasons on a colored professional football team called the All-Southern Collegians. The Collegians accepted him without a diploma, George explains now. He quit his books after the third year of high school and took a job as porter in a hospital, playing professional football on autumn Sundays. He got the boxing fever again when he was twenty-three, an unusually advanced age for a debut.

George then weighed 243 pounds, which was far too much for his height. "I was so fat that one time I missed and fell right down," he says. "But I always throwed a good right hand anyway." He won two amateur bouts at smokers, both on knockouts, and then lost a decision to a fellow named Moe Levine in a big amateur show in Madison Square Garden. "I bounced him around, but I didn't know enough to finish him," George says now with a hint of cultured regret. A strange accident removed him from the ranks of the amateurs. He entered the 1934 *Daily News* Golden Gloves Tournament and was rejected because of a heart murmur. Soon after, he went up to Stillman's Gymnasium, where he met a matchmaker and got himself a preliminary bout on a card at a small professional club. The State Athletic Commission doctor found his heart action normal. Once he had fought this professional bout, he was no longer an amateur and after the fight, for which he got twenty-five dollars, he hit a long spell of unemployment. "I was so broke I didn't have *no* money," he says.

It is much easier for an amateur boxer to make a living than it is for a professional. Almost every night of the week several amateur shows are held in the city. Like bingo games and raffles, they are a recognized means of raising money for fraternal organizations. In most shows there are four competitors in each class. They meet in three-round bouts, with the winners competing in a final match later in the evening. There is a standard scale of remuneration. The winner of the final receives a seventeen-jewel watch, which may be sold in the open market for fifteen dollars. The runner-up gets a seven-jewel model, for which he can obtain five or six dollars. The two losers in the first bouts receive cheap timepieces known in amateur-boxing circles as "consolations." They have a sale value of two dollars. A preliminary boy "in the professionals" gets forty dollars for a bout, but opportunities for employment are much more limited. Moreover, a State Athletic Commission rule restricts a professional to one bout every five days, whereas an amateur is free to compete every night.

Jim Howell, a Negro who is a frequent colleague of Nicholson as a sparring mate in the Louis camp, had a long career as an amateur. He remembers one week when he won four seventeen-jewel watches. "And it's funny," Howell says, "there's very few even the best amateurs that you can ask him the time and he got a watch. Or if it is, it's just a consolation." Now Howell is a professional and he hasn't had ten fights in the past year. But he still thinks he can break through into the big time.

Unemployment among professional boxers antedates the Hoover depression. There are about a thousand active prize fighters in Greater New York. At the height of the winter season seven boxing clubs operate, with from six to eight bouts on the average weekly card. Only about a hundred fighters out of the available thousand can possibly hope for weekly employment. When they do work most of them get from forty to seventy-five dollars, minus one third for their managers. The average boxer lives from one fight to the next on small loans. When he gets a match, he often owes his entire purse before he enters the ring. Colored boys have even bleaker prospects than their white competitors, but there is a high percentage of Negroes in any training gym. This is because their disadvantage, staggering as it is in the boxing world, is less than in ordinary industry. Even when they cannot get a match, they sometimes have a chance to spar with a white boy in the gymnasium, being paid from three to ten dollars for their trouble.

The plight of a starving boxer is particularly cruel because by his daily exertions he increases his appetite beyond ordinary human bounds. Worse than hunger is the fear of not being able to get up his dues, the dollar a week he must pay for the privilege of using the gymnasium and showers. There are other minuscular expenses which seem huge in the eyes of a boy with no match in sight: he uses ninety cents' worth of gauze and twenty-five cents' worth of tape a week to wrap his fists for sparring matches; he buys rubbing alcohol and Omega Oil, which he applies himself if he cannot afford a dollar for a professional rubdown. In order to avoid cuts he must buy a leather headguard.

Plunged into this athletic slum, Nicholson felt sad and lonely. He was about to go back to his job at the hospital when, in the fall of 1934, his solid frame and large white smile attracted the attention of Jim Braddock, at that time making his comeback, who also trained at Stillman's. Braddock had not yet got back to the point where he could pay experienced sparring partners. He noticed that the big colored boy "took a very good punch," a quality which Jim admired, and he offered to teach George some of the inner mysteries of the craft. Braddock got free workouts and Nicholson got free boxing lessons. Within six months Braddock was again in the big money, training for the fight in which he was to win the championship from Max Baer, and Nicholson had learned so fast that he qualified as one of Jim's paid sparring partners. Surprisingly enough, the heavy-set, oldish novice had innate style. He was a natural boxer with a willingness to take punishment when it was necessary. This is not the same as being a natural fighter, which calls for a certain streak of cruelty.

Nicholson still uses Stillman's as a business headquarters when he has no camp job and is running short of money. He loafs for three or four weeks after a training camp breaks up, then makes his appearance at the gymnasium, which is on Eighth Avenue between Fifty-fourth and Fifty-fifth. "More business transacts there than anyplace in the world," he explains. Trainers and managers are always glad to see him.

"George is a good boy," says Mannie Seamon, who is a sort of personnel director for training camps. "Some sparring partners will throw a head [butt] or throw an elbow and maybe give a man a cut so the fight will have to be postponed, but George don't cross nobody up. He boxes quick so the fighter can't stay lazy, and he keeps throwing punches so the fighter can't make lax. A good boy."

When there is no camp job in sight George will sometimes box with a heavyweight training for a minor bout, receiving five or ten dollars for his afternoon's work, according to the fighter's prosperity. He can usually pick up fifteen or twenty dollars a week, which covers living expenses, until he gets more regular employment. George is a bachelor. "I can't see my ways through to getting married the way things are," he says. When he is in the metropolitan region, he stays with the WPA brother and his family in Yonkers. He doesn't go to Harlem much, because, he says, he doesn't want to change his ways and run wild. George doesn't smoke or drink. At Stillman's he observes the other heavyweights in the training ring. He makes mental note of their styles so that he will be able to imitate them on request. A sparring partner must be versatile. For example, when Louis was training for Nathan Mann his sparring partners were urged to throw left hooks like Mann. But when he was training for Schmeling the script called for George to throw right hands to Louis' jaw. Louis never did learn to block them, but his trainers felt that he would develop a certain immunity through inoculation. In 1939 Nicholson was emphasizing left hooks again, like Tony Galento.

His greatest benefactor, George thinks, was Jim Braddock. "There is no discrimination with Jim," Nicholson says. "When I was training with him in 1936 for that Schmeling fight that never come off he put rocks in my bed just like anybody else." This is a reminiscence of the refined horseplay that always distinguishes Braddock's camps from those of less whimsical prize fighters. A Louis camp is more restful. "All we does is play catch with a baseball and sometimes talk jokes," Nicholson says. He first trained with Louis when the present champion was preparing for his fight with Braddock in Chicago. Having boxed so often with Braddock, Nicholson could illustrate all his moves beautifully. Boxers do not consider such a transfer of allegiance unethical. You hire a sparring partner, and he does his best for you while you pay him. He may be in the enemy's camp for your next fight. Braddock hired Nicholson again before the Tommy Farr fight.

The worst sparring partner in all history was a young giant named James J. Jeffries, who joined Jim Corbett's camp when Corbett was training for his bout with Bob Fitzsimmons in Carson City, Nevada, forty-one years ago. Jeffries knocked Corbett out the first time they put on the gloves, which had an evil effect on Corbett's morale. He lost to Fitzsimmons. Later the exsparring partner knocked Fitzsimmons out and became champion of the world. Nicholson has never come near knocking out Braddock or Louis or even Primo Carnera, whom he trained for one of his last fights, but sometimes he is engaged to box with young heavyweights whom he must treat tenderly. A beginner can learn much from a good sparring partner, but if the partner knocks his brains out, as the boys say, the novice loses his nerve. George's most delicate client was a former college football player with the face of a Hollywood star and the shoulders of a Hercules, who was being merchandised by a smart manager. The manager had interested three Wall Street men in his dazzling heavyweight "prospect," assuring them that he was potentially the greatest fighter since Dempsey. The Wall Streeters actually put the boxer and the manager on salary and bought the youngster an automobile. This was before the boy had had even one fight. The manager, in order to prevent his backers from hearing any skeptical reports, arranged to have the football player train in a private gymnasium frequented only by fat businessmen. He then hired Nicholson to spar with him, and each afternoon the Wall Streeters and their friends visited the gymnasium and watched their hopeful knock George about. George got five dollars a workout. They were much astonished subsequently when, after supporting their coming champion for a year and a half, he was knocked out in a four-round bout they got him with another novice.

George says there was nothing wrong about his conduct. "That manager hired me to box with that boy," he says. "He didn't hire me to hurt him."

There isn't much money in the sparring business, George concedes, but there doesn't seem to be much in anything else, either. The prospect of injury doesn't bother him, because he seldom takes a punch solidly. He "gets on it" before it develops power, or else he takes it on his forearms or shoulders, or at worst "rolls away" from it as it lands. "I like the old word for boxing," he once said. "The manly art of *de*fense. And I don't fear no man. Now, that Joe, he really can punch. He can really punch. What I mean, he can punch, really. Yet he ain't never no more'n shook me. And when I feel myself getting punch-drunk I'm going to quit. I'm going to look me up a profitable business somewhere that's a profit in it."

Nicholson was in his chair at Pompton Lakes when he made this declaration. The chairs at his left and right were occupied by Jim Howell and another large colored man named Elza Thompson. Each of the three had his left leg crossed over his right knee. After a long interval they recrossed their legs in unison, this time with the right on top. There was no spoken word to suggest the shift, just telepathy. Undisturbed by the musical sigh of Nicholson's voice, Howell and Thompson were apparently asleep. Yet the triple movement was perfectly synchronized, like something the Rockettes might do, but in slow time.

At the phrase "punch-drunk" Howell had opened one eye.

"How you going to know you punch-drunk, George?" he

inquired. "A man punch-drunk, he don't know he punch-drunk. That the sign he punch-drunk."

Nicholson thought this over in deep gloom for a while.

Then he said, "Sometime when I boxing with a fellow that hit me right on the button, and I know he ain't got no right to hit me on the button, and I boxing with him again and he hit me on the button again, then I going to quit."

After this the three sparring partners all fell asleep.

• The Jollity Building •

I—Indians, Heels, and Tenants

In the Jollity Building, which stands six stories high and covers half of a Broadway block in the high Forties, the term "promoter" means a man who mulcts another man of a dollar, or any fraction or multiple thereof. The verb "to promote" always takes a personal object, and the highest praise you can accord someone in the Jollity Building is to say, "He has promoted some very smart people." The Jollity Building—it actually has a somewhat different name, and the names of its inhabitants are not the ones which will appear below—is representative of perhaps a dozen or so buildings in the upper stories of which the small-scale amusement industry nests like a tramp pigeon. All of them draw a major part of their income from the rental of their stores at street level, and most of them contain on their lower floors a dance hall or a billiard parlor, or both. The Jollity Building has both. The dance hall, known as Jollity Danceland, occupies the second floor. The poolroom is in the basement. It is difficult in such a building to rent office space to any business house that wants to be taken very seriously, so the upper floors fill up with the petty nomads of Broadway—chiefly orchestra leaders, theatrical agents, bookmakers, and miscellaneous promoters.

Eight coin-box telephone booths in the lobby of the Jollity Building serve as offices for promoters and others who cannot raise the price of desk space on an upper floor. The phones are used mostly for incoming calls. It is a matter of perpetual regret to Morty, the renting agent of the building, that he cannot collect rent from the occupants of the booths. He always refers to them as the Telephone Booth Indians, because in their lives the telephone booth furnishes sustenance as well as shelter, as the buffalo did for the Arapahoe and Sioux. A Telephone Booth Indian on the hunt often tells a prospective investor to call him at a certain hour in the afternoon, giving the victim the number of the phone in one of the booths. The Indian implies, of course, that it is a private line. Then the Indian has to hang in the booth until the fellow calls. To hang, in Indian language, means to loiter. "I used to hang in Forty-sixth Street, front of *Variety*," a small bookmaker may say, referring to a previous business location. Seeing the Indians hanging in the telephone booths is painful to Morty, but there is nothing he can do about it. The regular occupants of the booths recognize one another's rights. It may be understood among them, for instance, that a certain orchestra leader receives calls in a particular booth between three and four in the afternoon and that a competitor has the same booth from four to five. In these circumstances, ethical Indians take telephone messages for each other. There are always fewer vacancies in the telephone booths than in any other part of the Jollity Building.

While awaiting a call, an Indian may occasionally emerge for air, unless the lobby is so crowded that there is a chance he might lose his place to a transient who does not understand the house rules. Usually, however, the Indian hangs in the booth with the door open, leaning against the wall and reading a scratch sheet in order to conserve time. Then, if somebody rings up and agrees to lend him two dollars, he will already have picked a horse on which to lose that amount. When an impatient stranger shows signs of wanting to use a telephone, the man in the booth closes the door, takes the receiver off the hook, and makes motions with his lips, as if talking. To add verisimilitude to a long performance, he occasionally hangs up, takes the receiver down again, drops a nickel in the slot, whirls the dial three or four times, and hangs up again, after which the nickel comes back. Eventually the stranger goes away, and the man in the booth returns to the study of his scratch sheet. At mealtimes, the Telephone Booth Indians sometimes descend singly to the Jollity Building's lunch counter, which is at one end of the poolroom in the basement. The busiest lunch periods are the most favorable for a stunt the boys have worked out to get free nourishment. An Indian seats himself at the counter and eats two or three *pastrami* sandwiches. As he is finishing his lunch, one of his comrades appears at the head of the stairs and shouts that he is wanted on the telephone. The Indian rushes upstairs, absentmindedly omitting to pay for his meal. Barney, the lunch-counter proprietor, is too busy to go after him when he fails to return after a reasonable time. An Indian can rarely fool Barney more than once or twice. The maneuver requires nice timing and unlimited faith in one's accomplice. Should the accomplice fail to make his entrance, the Indian at the counter might be compelled to eat *pastrami* sandwiches indefinitely, acquiring frightful indigestion and piling up an appalling debt.

Morty, the renting agent, is a thin, sallow man of forty whose expression has been compared, a little unfairly, to that of a dead robin. He is not, however, a man without feeling; he takes a personal interest in the people who spend much of their lives in the Jollity Building. It is about the same sort of interest that Curator

Raymond Ditmars takes in the Bronx Zoo's vampire bats. "I know more heels than any other man in the world," Morty sometimes says, not without pride. "Everywhere I go around Broadway, I get 'Hello, how are you?' Heels that haven't been with me for years, some of them." Morty usually reserves the appellation "heel" for the people who rent the forty-eight cubicles, each furnished with a desk and two chairs, on the third floor of the Jollity Building. These cubicles are formed by partitions of wood and frosted glass which do not quite reach the ceiling. Sufficient air to maintain human life is supposed to circulate over the partitions. The offices rent for $10 and $12.50 a month, payable in advance. "Twelve and a half dollars with air, ten dollars without air," Morty says facetiously. "Very often the heels who rent them take the air without telling me." Sometimes a Telephone Booth Indian acquires enough capital to rent a cubicle. He thus rises in the social scale and becomes a heel. A cubicle has three advantages over a telephone booth. One is that you cannot get a desk into a telephone booth. Another is that you can play pinochle in a cubicle. Another is that a heel gets his name on the directory in the lobby, and the white letters have a bold, legitimate look.

The vertical social structure of the Jollity Building is subject to continual shifts. Not only do Indians become heels, but a heel occasionally accumulates $40 or $50 with which to pay a month's rent on one of the larger offices, all of them unfurnished, on the fourth, fifth, or sixth floor. He then becomes a tenant. Morty always views such progress with suspicion, because it involves signing a lease, and once a heel has signed a lease, you cannot put him out without serving a dispossess notice and waiting ten days. A tenant, in Morty's opinion, is just a heel who is planning to get ten days' free rent. "Any time a heel acts prosperous enough to rent an office," Morty says, "you know he's getting ready to take you." A dispossessed tenant often reappears in the Jollity Building as an Indian. It is a life cycle. Morty has people in the building who have been Telephone Booth Indians, heels, and tenants several times each. He likes them best when they are in the heel stage. "You can't collect rent from a guy who hangs in the lobby," he says in explanation, "and with a regular tenant of an unfurnished office, you got too many headaches." He sometimes breaks off a conversation with a friendly heel by saying, "Excuse me, I got to go upstairs and insult a tenant."

As if to show his predilection for the heels, Morty has his own office on the third floor. It is a large corner room with windows on two sides. There is a flattering picture of the Jollity Building on one of the walls, and six framed plans, one of each floor, on another wall. Also in the office are an unattractive, respectable-looking secretary and, on Morty's desk, a rather depressing photograph of his wife. The conventionality of this *décor* makes Morty unhappy, and he spends as little time as possible in his office. Between nine o'clock in the morning, when he arrives and dejectedly looks through his mail for rent checks he does not expect to find, and six-thirty in the evening, when he goes home to Rockaway, he lives mostly amid the pulsating activity outside his office door.

The furnished cubicles on the third floor yield an income of about $500 a month, which, as Morty says, is not hay. Until a few years ago, the Jollity Building used to feel it should provide switchboard service for these offices. The outgoing telephone calls of the heels were supposed to be paid for at the end of every business day. This system necessitated the use of a cordon of elevator boys to prevent tenants from escaping. "Any heel who made several telephone calls toward the end of the month, you could kiss him good-by," Morty says. "As soon as he made up his mind to go out of business he started thinking of people to telephone. It was cheaper for him to go out of business than settle for the calls, anyhow. The only way you can tell if a heel is still in business, most of the time, anyway, is to look in his office for his hat. If his hat is gone, he is out of business." A minor annoyance of the switchboard system was the tendency of heels to call the operator and ask for the time. "None of them were going anywhere, but they all wanted to know the time," Morty says resentfully. "None of them had watches. Nobody would be in this building unless he had already hocked his watch." There are lady heels, too, but if they are young Morty calls them "heads." (Morty meticulously refers to all youngish women as "heads," which has the same meaning as "broads" or "dolls" but is newer; he does not want his conversation to sound archaic.) Heads also abused the switchboard system. "One head that used to claim to sell stockings," says Morty, "called the board one day, and when the operator said, 'Five o'clock,' this head said, 'My God, I didn't eat yet!' If there had been no switchboard, she would never have known she was hungry. She would have saved a lot of money."

As a consequence of these abuses, the switchboard was abolished, and practically all the heels now make their telephone calls from three open coin-box telephones against the wall in a corridor that bisects the third floor. The wall for several feet on each side of the telephones is covered with numbers the heels have jotted down. The Jollity Building pays a young man named Angelo to sit at a table in a small niche near the telephones and answer incoming calls. He screams "Who?" into the mouthpiece and then shuffles off to find whatever heel is wanted. On days when Angelo is particularly weary, he just says, "He ain't in," and hangs up. He also receives and distributes the mail for the heels. Angelo is a pallid chap who has been at various periods a chorus boy, a taxi driver, and a drummer in one of the bands which maintain headquarters in the Jollity Building. "Every time a heel comes in," Angelo says, "he wants to know 'Are you sure there isn't a letter for me that feels like it had a check in it? . . . That's funny, the fellow swore he mailed it last night.' Then he tries to borrow a nickel from me so he can telephone."

Not having a nickel is a universal trait of people who rent the cubicles, and they spend a considerable portion of the business day hanging by the third-floor telephones, waiting for the arrival of somebody to borrow a nickel from. While waiting, they talk to Angelo, who makes it a rule not to believe anything they say. There are no booths in the corridor because Morty does not want any Telephone Booth Indians to develop on the third floor.

Morty himself often goes to visit with Angelo and terrifies the heels with his bilious stare. "They all say they got something big for next week," he tells Angelo in a loud, carrying voice, "but the rent is 'I'll see you tomorrow.' " Morty's friends sometimes drop in there to visit him. He likes to sit on Angelo's table with them and tell about the current collection of furnished-office inhabitants. "Who is that phony-looking heel who just passed, you want to know?" he may say during such a recapitulation. "Hey, this is funny. He happens to be legitimate—autos to hire. The heel in the next office publishes a horse magazine. If he gets a winner, he eats. Then there's one of them heels that hires girls to sell permanent waves for fifty cents down, door to door. The girl takes the fifty cents and gives the dame a ticket, but when the dame goes to look for the beauty parlor it says on the ticket, there is no such beauty parlor at that address.

"We got two heels writing plays. They figure they got nothing to do, so they might as well write a play, and if it clicks, they might also eat. Then we got a lady heel who represents Brazilian music publishers and also does a bit of booking; also a head who is running a school for hat-check girls, as it seems the hat-check profession is very complicated for some of the type of minds they got in it. Those heads who walk through the hall are going no place. They just stick their potato in every office and say, 'Anything for me today?' They do not even look to see if it is a theatrical office. If they expected to find anything, they would not be over here. What would anybody here have to offer? Once in a while a sap from the suburbs walks into one of the offices on this floor thinking he can get some talent cheap. 'Sure,' some heel says, 'I got just the thing you want.' They run down in the lobby looking for somebody. They ask some head they meet in the lobby, 'Are you a performer?' They try the other little agents that they know. The whole date is worth probably four dollars, and the forty cents' commission they split sometimes four ways."

Morty's favorite heel of the current lot is a tall Chesterfieldian old man named Dr. Titus Heatherington, who is the president of the Anti-Hitlerian League of the Western Hemisphere. Dr. Heatherington for many years lectured in vacant stores on sex topics and sold a manual of facts every young man should know. "The line became, in a manner of speaking, exhausted," Dr. Heatherington says, "because of the increasing sophistication of the contemporary adolescent, so I interested myself in this great crusade, in which I distribute at a nominal price a very fascinating book by Cornelius Vanderbilt, Jr., and everything in it must be exactly as stated, because otherwise Hitler could have sued Mr. Vanderbilt for libel. Incidentally, I sell a lot more books than I have for years. I do particularly well at Coney Island."

Heels are often, paradoxically, more affluent than the official lessees of larger offices. Many fellows who rent the big units take in subtenants, and if there are enough of them, each man's share of the rent may be less than the $10 a month minimum rent a heel has to pay. One two-desk office on the fourth, fifth, or sixth floor may serve as headquarters for four theatrical agents, a band leader, a music arranger, a manager of prize fighters, and a dealer in pawn tickets. They agree on a schedule by which each man has the exclusive use of a desk for a few hours every day, to impress people who call by appointment, and the office is used collectively, when no outsiders are present, for games of rummy. All the fellows in the office receive their telephone calls on a single coin-box machine affixed to the wall. Subtenants often make bets among themselves, the amount of the wager corresponding to each bettor's share of the rent. The loser is supposed to pay double rent, the winner nothing. This causes difficulties for Morty when he comes to collect the rent. The official lessee always protests that he would like to pay on the dot but the other boys haven't paid him. Subtenants who have won bets consider themselves absolved of any responsibility, and the fellows who are supposed to pay double are invariably broke. Morty makes an average of fifteen calls to collect a month's rent on an office, and thus acquires a much greater intimacy with the tenants than the agents of a place like Rockefeller Center or River House.

Desk room in a large office has the advantage of being much more dignified than a cubicle on the third floor, but there is one drawback: Morty's rule that not more than two firm names may be listed on the directory in the lobby for any one office. Callers therefore have to ask the elevator boys where to find some of the subtenants. If the elevator boys do not like the subtenant in question, they say they never heard of him. Nor will the implacable Morty permit more than two names to be painted on any office door. Junior subtenants get around the rule by having a sign painter put their names on strips of cardboard which they insert between the glass and the wooden frame of the door or affix to the glass by strips of tape. "You cannot let a tenant creep on you," Morty says in justification of his severity. "You let them get away with eight names on the door, and the next thing they will be asking you for eight keys to the men's room."

Morty's parents were named Goldberg, and he was born in the Bensonhurst region of Brooklyn. He almost finished a commercial course in high school before he got his first job, being an order clerk for a chain of dairy-and-herring stores. In the morning he would drive to each of these stores and find out from the store managers what supplies they needed from the company's warehouse. Since he had little to do in the afternoons, he began after a while to deliver packages for a bootlegger who had been a high-school classmate and by chance had an office in the Jollity Building. The name on the door of the office was the Music Writers Mutual Publishing Company. About a quarter of the firms in the building at that time were fronts for bootleggers, Morty recalls. "Repeal was a terrible blow to property values in this district," he says. "Bootleggers were always the best pay." Seeing a greater future in bootlegging than in dairy goods and herring, Morty soon went to work for his old classmate on a full-time basis. The moment Morty decided that his future lay on Broadway, he translated his name from Goldberg into Ormont. " '*Or*' is French for gold," he sometimes explains, "and '*mont*' is the same as 'berg.' But the point is it's got more class than Goldberg."

By diligent application, Morty worked his way up to a partnership in the Music Writers Mutual Publishing Company. The partners made good use of their company's name. They advertised in pulp magazines, offering to write music for lyrics or lyrics for music, to guarantee publication, and to send back to the aspiring song writer a hundred free copies of his work, all for one hundred dollars. The Music Writers Mutual agreed to pay him the customary royalties on all copies sold. There never were

any royalties, because Morty and his partner had only the author's hundred copies printed. They kept a piano in their office
and hired a professional musician for thirty-five dollars a week
to set music to lyrics. Morty himself occasionally wrote lyrics to
the tunes clients sent in, and had a lot of fun doing it. At times
the music business went so well that the partners were tempted
to give up bootlegging. There were so many similar publishing
firms, however, that there was not a steady living in it. "But you
would be surprised," Morty says now, "how near it came to paying our overhead." The volume of mail made it look bona fide.
They built up a prosperous semi-wholesale liquor business, spe-
cializing in furnishing whisky to firms in the Garment Center,
which used it for presents to out-of-town buyers. "The idea on
that stuff was that it should be as reasonable as possible without
killing anybody," Morty says. "It was a good, legitimate dollar."
The depression in the garment industry ruined the Music Writers Mutual Publishing Company's business even before repeal
and left Morty broke.

The Jollity Building belongs to the estate of an old New York
family, and in the twenties the trustees had installed as manager
one of the least promising members of the family, a middle-aged,
alcoholic Harvard man whom they wanted to keep out of harm's
way. Morty had been such a good tenant and seemed so knowing
a fellow that the Harvard man offered him a job at twenty-five
dollars a week as his assistant. When the manager ran off with
eleven thousand dollars in rents and a head he had met in the
lobby, Morty took over his job. He has held it ever since. The
trustees feel, as one of them has expressed it, that "Mr. Ormont
understands the milieu." He now gets fifty dollars a week and
two per cent of the total rents, which adds about two thousand
a year to his income.

The nostalgia Morty often feels for the opportunities of prohibition days is shared by the senior tenant in the building, the proprietor of the Quick Art Theatrical Sign Painting Company, on the sixth floor. The sign painter, a Mr. Hy Sky—a name made up of the first syllable of his first name, Hyman, and the last syllable of a surname which no one can remember—is a bulky, red-faced man who has rented space in the Jollity Building for twenty-five years. With his brother, a lean, sardonic man known as Si Sky, he paints signs and lobby displays for burlesque and movie houses and does odd jobs of lettering for people in all sorts of trades. He is an extremely fast letterer and he handles a large volume of steady business, but it lacks the exhilaration of prohibition years. Then he was sometimes put to work at two o'clock in the morning redecorating a clip joint, so that it could not be identified by a man who had just been robbed of a bank roll and might return with cops the next day. "Was that fun!" Hy howls reminiscently. "And always cash in advance! If the joint had green walls, we would make them pink. We would move the bar opposite to where it was, and if there was booths in the place, we would paint them a different color and change them around. Then the next day, when the cops came in with the sap, they would say, 'Is this the place? Try to remember the side of the door the bar was on as you come in.' The sap would hesitate, and the cops would say, 'I guess he can't identify the premises,' and they would shove him along. It was a nice, comfortable dollar for me."

Hy has a clinical appreciation of meretricious types which he tries unsuccessfully to arouse in Morty. Sometimes, when Hy has a particularly preposterous liar in his place, he will telephone the renting agent's office and shout, "Morty, pop up and see the character I got here! He is the most phoniest character I seen in several years." The person referred to seldom resents such a description. People in the Jollity Building neighborhood like to be thought of as characters. "He is a real character," they say, with respect, of any fascinatingly repulsive acquaintance. Most promoters are characters. Hy Sky attributes the stability of his own business to the fact that he is willing to "earn a hard dollar." "The trouble with the characters," he says, "is they are always looking for a soft dollar. The result is they knock theirselves out trying too hard to have it easy. So what do they get after all? Only the miss-meal cramps." Nevertheless, it always gives Hy a genteel pleasure to collaborate, in a strictly legitimate way, with any of the promoters he knows. The promoter may engage him to paint a sign saying, "A new night club will open soon on these premises. Concessionaires interested telephone So-and-So at such-and-such a number." The name is the promoter's own, and the telephone given is, as Hy knows, in a booth in the Jollity lobby. The promoter, Hy also knows, will place this sign in front of a vacant night club with which he has absolutely no connection, in the hope that some small hat-check concessionaire with money to invest in a new club will read the sign before someone gets around to removing it and take it seriously. If the concessionaire telephones, the promoter will make an appointment to receive him in a Jollity cubicle borrowed from some other promoter for the occasion and will try to get a couple of hundred dollars as a deposit on the concession. If successful, he will lose the money on a horse in the sixth race at an obscure track in California. The chances of getting any money out of this promotional scheme are exceedingly slight, but the pleasure of the promoter when the device succeeds is comparable to that of a sportsman who catches a big fish on a light line. Contemplation of the ineffectual larceny in the promoter's heart causes Hy to laugh constantly while lettering such a sign. A contributory cause of his laughter is the knowledge that he will receive the only dollar that is likely to change hands in the transaction—the dollar he gets for painting the sign.

Musicians are not characters, in Hy's estimation, but merely a mild variety of phony. As such, they afford him a tempered amusement. When two impressive band leaders in large, fluffy overcoats call upon him for a communal cardboard door sign, toward the cost of which each contributes twenty-five cents, he innocently inquires, "How many of you are there in that office?" One of the band leaders will reply grandiosely, "Oh, we all have separate offices; the sign is for the door to quite a huge suite." Hy laughs so hard he bends double to relieve the strain on his diaphragm. His brother, Si, who lives in continual fear that Hy will die of apoplexy, abandons his work and slaps Hy's back until the crowing abates. "A suite," Hy repeats weakly at intervals for a half-hour afterward, "a huge suite they got, like on the subway at six o'clock you could get." Hy also paints, at an average price of twenty-five cents, cardboard backs for music racks. These pieces of cardboard, whose only function is to identify the band, bear in bright letters its name, which is usually something like Everett Winterbottom's Rhumba Raiders. When a Jollity Building band leader has acquired a sign for his door and a set of these lettered cardboards, he is equipped for business. If, by some unlikely chance, he gets an engagement, usually to play a week end in a cabaret in Queens or the Bronx, he hurries out to the curb on Seventh Avenue in front of Charlie's Bar & Grill, where there are always plenty of musicians, and picks up the number of fellows he requires, generally four. The men tapped go over to Eighth Avenue and get their instruments out of pawn. A musician who owns several instruments usually leaves them all in a pawnshop, ransoming one when he needs it to play a date and putting it back the next day. If, when he has a chance to work, he lacks the money to redeem an instrument, he borrows the money from a Jollity Building six-for-fiver, a fellow who will lend you five dollars if you promise to pay him six dollars within twenty-four hours. Meanwhile, the band leader looks up a fellow who rents out orchestra arrangements guaranteed to be exact, illegal copies of those one or another of the big bandsmen has exclusive use of. The band leader puts the arrangements and his cardboards under his arm and goes down to Charlie's to wait for the other musicians to come back from the hock shop. That night Everett Winterbottom's Rhumba Raiders ride again. The only worry in the world the Raiders have, at least for the moment, is that they will have to finish their engagement before a union delegate discovers them and takes away their cards. Each man is going to receive three dollars a night, which is seven dollars below union scale.

II—From Hunger

It is likely that when the six-story Jollity Building, so called, is pulled down, it will be replaced by a one- or two-story taxpayer, because buildings along Broadway now derive their chief incomes from the stores at street level, and taxpayers, which earn just as much from their stores, are cheaper to operate. When the Jollity Building comes down, the small theatrical agents, the sleazy costumers, the band leaders in worn camel's-hair overcoats, the aged professors of acrobatic dancing, and all the petty promoters who hang, as the phrase goes, in the Jollity Building's upper floors will spill out into the street and join the musicians who are waiting for jobs and the pitchmen who sell self-threading needles along the curb.

Meanwhile, day after day, small-time performers ride the elevators and wander through the grimy halls of the Jollity Building looking for work. Jack McGuire, who in the evening is a bouncer in Jollity Danceland, on the second floor, thoroughly understands the discouraged performers. "They're just like mice," he says, "they been pushed around so much." Jack is a heavyweight prize fighter who recently retired for the forty-eighth time in the last five years. He still looks impressively healthy, since few of his fights have lasted more than one round. "It was the greatest two-minute battle you ever seen," he said a while ago, describing his latest comeback, against a local boy in Plainfield, New Jersey. "For the first thirty seconds I was ahead on points." Jack's face is of a warm, soft pink induced by the prolonged application of hot towels in the Jollity Building barbershop, which is just off the lobby. Sprawled in the sixth barber chair from the door, he sleeps off hang-overs. His shoulders, naturally wide, are accentuated by the padding Broadway clothiers lavish on their customers. Among the putty-colored, sharp-nosed little men and the thin-legged women in the elevators, he looks like an animal of a different breed. His small eyes follow the performers constantly. During the day, Jack is a runner for a great number of agents. He learns from them where there are openings for various types of talent—ballroom-dancing teams, Irish tenors, singing hostesses, and so on—and then steers performers to the agents handling the jobs. He has strolled about the Jollity Building so long that he knows hundreds of them by sight. "Such-and-such an agent is looking for a ballroom team," he will tell a husband-and-wife pair he knows. "A week in a Chink joint in Yonkers." He gives them one of the agent's cards, on which he writes "Jack." If the team gets the week, at forty dollars, it must pay a commission of four dollars to the agent, and another of two dollars to Jack. The second commission is entirely extralegal, since Jack is not a licensed agent, but Jack often steers performers to a job they wouldn't have had otherwise, so they don't kick. Agents are glad to have Jack work with them, because buyers of talent want instantaneous service and few acts can be reached by telephone during the day. Sometimes, when an act is held over for a second week and fails to pay the agent his additional commission, Jack is engaged to put the muscle on the unethical performer. When Jack encounters him, usually in Charlie's Bar & Grill or at the I. & Y. cigar store, which are both near the Jollity Building, he says, "Say, I hear your agent is looking for you." The hint is enough ordinarily. When it is not, Jack uses the muscle.

The proprietor of Jollity Danceland is the most solvent tenant in the building and he pays by far the largest rent. The dance hall has an entrance of its own on the street and is reached by stairway and elevators reserved for customers. Jack receives five dollars a night for bouncing there. At one time the proprietor planned to put the bouncers on a piecework basis, but he changed his mind, to Jack's lasting regret. "I would of bounced all the customers," he says. "I would of made my fortune sure." Between the hours of six and eight every evening, at a small gymnasium west of Tenth Avenue, Jack trains a few amateur boxers he manages. There is not much money in managing amateurs, who never earn more than sixteen dollars in a night, but Jack thinks that someday one of his protégés might show promise, and then he could sell the boy's contract to an established manager. With all these sources of income, McGuire would live in affluence, by Jollity Building standards, if it were not for his thirst, which is perpetual. When he drinks, he sometimes threatens to put the muscle on strangers who refuse to pay for his liquor. This detracts from his popularity at the neighborhood bars, and the bartenders resort to chemical expedients to get rid of him. Jack is proud of the immunity he has developed. "I got so I like those Mickey Finns as good as beer," he often tells acquaintances.

Although Jack has never paid any office rent, he is on familiar terms with Morty Ormont, the lugubrious renting agent of the Jollity Building, whom he encounters in the barbershop and at the lunch counter in the basement. He sometimes borrows a dollar from Morty, always giving him a hundred-dollar check on a bank in Lynchburg, Virginia, as security. Morty, of course, knows that Jack has no account in the bank. In the Jollity Building, checks are considered not as literal drafts on existent funds but as a particularly solemn form of promise to repay a loan, since it is believed that the holder of a bad check has it in his power to throw the check writer into jail for twenty-five years. When Jack repays the dollar, usually in four installments, Morty gives the check back to him. Practically everybody in the Jollity Building carries a checkbook. Fellows who cannot borrow from Morty even by giving him checks sometimes ask him to vouch for them so they can borrow from six-for-fivers, the chaps who lend five dollars one day and collect six dollars the next. "Will you O.K. me with a Shylock, Morty?" one of these suppliants will ask. "You know I'm an honest man." "In what way?" Morty demands cynically if he does not know the man well. If the fellow says, "In every way," Morty refuses to O.K. him, because he is obviously a crook.

The prize-fight managers who hang in the Jollity Building are, as one might expect, of an inferior order. The boys they handle provide what sports writers like to call the "stiff opposition" against which incubating stars compile "sterling records." "When the Garden brings in some fellow that you never heard of from Cleveland or Baltimore or one of them other Western states, and it says in the paper he has had stiff opposition," says a Jollity Building manager known as Acid Test Ike, "that means the opposition has been stiffs. In other words, the class of boys I got." It is Acid Test who manages Jack in all of his comebacks. For each comeback, Ike and Jack go to some place like Lancaster, Pennsylvania, or Wheeling, West Virginia, where there happens to be a novice heavyweight, and Ike tells the sports editor of the local newspaper, "My man will give this kid the acid test." Then Jack gets knocked out. Naturally, Ike also has to manage smaller fighters who will get knocked out by middleweights and light-weights. "A fellow could make a pleasant dollar with a stable of bums," he sometimes says, "only the competition is so terrific. There is an element getting into the game that is willing to be knocked out very cheap." Acid Test Ike always wears a bottle-green suit, a brick-red topcoat, and an oyster-white hat. "It don't take brains to make money with a good fighter," he says rather bitterly when he feels an attack of the miss-meal cramps coming on. "Running into a thing like that is just luck."

Performers, when they arrive at the Jollity Building looking for work, usually take an elevator straight to the floor on which the agent who most often books them is located. After leaving this agent, they make a tour of the other agents' offices to see if anyone else has a job for them. Only when rendered desperate by hunger do they stray down to the third floor, where the people Morty calls the heels hold forth in furnished offices each about the size of a bathroom. Since the heels constitute the lowest cat-egory of tenant in the building, no proprietor of a first-class chop-suey joint or roadhouse would call on them for talent. "The best you can get there," performers say, "is a chance to work Saturday night at a ruptured saloon for *bubkis*." "*Bubkis*" is a Yiddish word which means "large beans."

One of the most substantial agents in the building is Jerry

Rex, a swarthy, discouraged man who used to be a ventriloquist. He has an unusually large one-room office, which was once the studio of a teacher of Cuban dancing. The walls are painted in orange-and-black stripes, and there are several full-length wall mirrors, in which the pupils used to watch themselves dance. Mr. Rex sits at a desk at the end of the office opposite the door, and performers waiting to speak to him sit on narrow benches along the walls. Rex has an assistant named Dave, who sits on a couch in one corner of the room. Rex always professes to be waiting for a call from a theater owner in, for example, Worcester, Massachusetts, who will want four or five acts and a line of eight girls. He urges all the entertainers who drop in at his place to sit down and wait with him. "Also, a fellow who owns the biggest night club in Scranton is going to pop up here any minute," he tells the performers confidentially. "You better wait around." The man from Worcester never calls up, but the performers don't mind killing a half-hour with Jerry. "It rests your feet," one woman singer has said, "and also you meet a lot of people you know." Jerry leaves Dave in charge of the office when he goes out. "If Georgie Hale pops up here looking for me," Jerry always says in a loud voice as he is leaving, "tell him that Billy Rose pulled me over to Lindy's for a bite." Then he goes downstairs to the lunch counter, where he may try to talk Barney, the proprietor, into letting him charge a cup of coffee. Rex, when he is not attempting to impress performers or rival agents, is a profoundly gloomy man. "You got only three classes of performers today," he sometimes says. "Class A, which means, for example, like Al Jolson and Eddie Cantor; Class B, like the Hartmans, for instance, or Henny Youngman, that can yet get a very nice dollar, and Class Z, which is all the little people. Small-time vaudeville is definitely out. All you got is floor shows, fraternal entertainments, and in the summer the borsch circuit. An entertainer who can average thirty dollars a week all year is Class Z tops. There ain't no such entertainer. A husband-and-wife team *might* make it."

Jerry does not consider his large office an extravagance, because he lives in it twenty-four hours a day, which is a violation of the building laws, and saves the price of a hotel room. He sleeps on the couch, while Dave, a blue-chinned young man with the mores of a tomcat, sleeps on one of the wall benches. Jerry occasionally buys a bottle of beer for the porter who cleans the offices. The grateful porter always does Jerry's first, so the agent can get a good night's rest. Every morning, Jerry washes and shaves in the men's room on his floor. Dave often contents himself with smearing face powder over his beard. Dave is of a happier temperament than his employer. He likes to think of himself as a heartbreaker and is full of stories about the girls who wander through the Jollity Building halls. He calls them heads and boskos. "Bosko" has a definitely roguish connotation. One may safely say to a friend, "That was a beautiful head I seen you with," even if one does not know who the head was. But if one says "bosko," and the woman turns out to be the friend's wife, one has committed a social error. Dave has a tried technique for forming acquaintanceships in the Jollity Building. "I know this head is a performer, or she would not be in the building," he says. "So I go up to her and say, 'What do you do?' If she says, 'I dance,' I say, 'Too bad, I was looking for a singer.' If she says 'sing,' I say, 'Too bad, I was looking for a dancer.' In that way we get acquainted, and if she looks promising, I pull her down to Barney's for a celery tonic."

Women performers have a better chance of getting cabaret jobs than men, because they mix with the customers. Jerry, who grew up in the sheltered respectability of vaudeville, resents this. "I booked a man with a trained dog into one trap in Astoria," he recently said, "and after one night they canceled him out because the dog couldn't mix. There never was such a tough market for talent. I book an acrobatic act in which, as a finish, one guy walks offstage playing a mandolin and balancing the other guy upside down on his head. The understander only plays a couple of bars, you see, for the effect. I booked them for an Elks' smoker in Jersey, and the chairman of the entertainment committee didn't want to pay me because he said the members don't like musical acts. To stand this business, you got to have a heart of steel." Most agents in the Jollity Building, when they supply talent for a whole show, book themselves as masters of ceremonies and collect an extra ten dollars for announcing the acts. Jerry has given up this practice.

"When I get out on the stage and think of what a small buck the performers are going to get, I feel like crying," he says, "so I send Dave instead."

A fair number of the performers who look for jobs in the Jollity Building have other occupations as well. Many of the women work as receptionists or stenographers in the daytime and make their rounds of agents' offices after five o'clock. Hockticket Charlie, an agent who is one of Jerry Rex's neighbors on the fourth floor, has a side line of his own. Hockticket Charlie is a tall, cross-eyed man with a clarion voice and a solemn manner. By arrangement with a number of pawnbrokers of his acquaintance, he sells pawn tickets. The chief reason anyone purchases a pawn ticket is that he holds the common belief that a watch accepted in pawn for ten dollars, for example, must in reality be worth around forty dollars. The fellow who buys a ticket for five dollars is therefore theoretically able to obtain a forty-dollar watch for a total outlay of fifteen dollars. Hockticket Charlie's pawnbroker friends, aware of this popular superstition, make out a lot of tickets to fictitious persons. Charlie sells the tickets for a few dollars each to performers in the Jollity Building. Each ticket entitles the purchaser to redeem a piece of secondhand jewelry—for not more than three times its value—which the broker has bought at an auction sale. Hockticket nearly always pays off colored performers with pawn tickets which will theoretically permit them to purchase diamonds at a large reduction. By paying ten dollars to a broker, the holder of one of these tickets can often acquire a ring easily worth three dollars. Sometimes Hockticket engages a number of performers to play a date in what he calls "a town near here," and tells them to meet him at the Jollity Building, so that they can all ride out to the date together. He loads them into a rickety bus which he has chartered for ten dollars, and the "town near here" turns out to be Philadelphia. If the acts traveled there singly, they would collect railroad fares for the round trip. Instead, Charlie collects all the railroad fares from the Philadelphia house manager who has booked the show. He often succeeds in paying the bus owner with hock tickets. Morty Ormont has a sincere admiration for Hockticket Charlie.

Another agent on the fourth floor, and the most sedate one in the building, is a woman named Maida Van Schuyler, who books stag shows for conventions and for the banquets large corporations give in honor of newly elected vice-presidents or retiring department heads. Mrs. Van Schuyler, a tall, flat-chested woman with fluffy white hair, was at one time a singer of arch numbers like "I Just Can't Make My Eyes Behave" and "Two Little Love Bees Buzzing in a Bower." As such, she recalls, she lent a touch of class to New England and Ohio vaudeville around 1912. The walls in an anteroom of her office are hung with numerous framed mottoes, such as "What Is More Precious Than a Friend?" and "Seek for Truth and Love Will Seek for You." A plain young woman sits in the anteroom and takes the names of visitors in to Mrs. Van Schuyler. When Mrs. Van Schuyler does not wish to see them, she sends out word that she is terribly sorry but one of her best-beloved friends has just passed away and she is too broken up about it to talk. If the visitor waits around a minute, he may hear a loud, strangling sob. Mrs. Van Schuyler, who is very much interested in spiritualism, often says that she would like to retire from the stag-show business and become a medium. "There isn't a dime left in this lousy business," she remarks. "The moving pictures have spoiled it, just like they did with vaudeville."

Every now and then, one of Mrs. Van Schuyler's shows is raided but the detectives give her advance notice because she provides the entertainments for a number of police banquets. "We have to make a pinch, Mrs. Van Schuyler," they say apologetically, "because the shooflies are working in our territory and we can't let a big brawl like this run without getting turned in." Shooflies, as all the world knows, are policemen in mufti assigned to make a secret check on the activities of other policemen. Within a week or two after the raid, which never results in a conviction, the friendly detectives return and say, "It's all right, Mrs. Van Schuyler, we got the shooflies taking now." With this assurance, Mrs. Van Schuyler can go ahead with her business. She seldom employs the ordinary entertainers who wander around the Jollity Building, but relies on specialists whom she lists in a large card file. "It is a highly specialized field of entertainment, darling," she tells gentlemen who are negotiating with her for their organizations. "Our girls must have poise, discretion, and *savoy faire*." To old friends like Morty Ormont, she sometimes says less elegantly, after an all-night party with a convention of textbook publishers or refrigerator salesmen, "You ought to seen those apes try to paw the girls."

Performers on their way to see one of the agents on the

fourth floor are sometimes frightened by wild fanfares from an office occupied by an Italian who repairs trumpets. A musician who brings a trumpet to the Italian always blows a few hot licks to demonstrate that the instrument is out of true. When he calls for the trumpet, he blows a few more to see whether it is all right again. Once a swing dilettante stood in the hall for half an hour listening to the noises and then walked in and said that it was the best band he had ever heard and he wanted it to play at a rent party he was giving for some other *cognoscenti*.

Not all the transients in the Jollity Building halls are entertainers making the rounds of the agents. There is a fellow known as Paddy the Booster, who sells neckties he steals from haberdashers, and another known as Mac the Phony Booster, who sells neckties which he pretends to have stolen but are really shoddy ties he has bought very cheaply. Naturally, Paddy looks down on Mac, whom he considers a racketeer. "It takes all kinds of people to make up a great city," Jack McGuire sometimes tells Paddy, trying to soothe him. Also, every floor of the building has at least one bookmaker, who hangs in the hall. "In winter, the bookmakers complain because we don't heat the halls better," the beleaguered Morty Ormont says. A dollar is the standard Jollity Building wager. The accepted method of assembling it is to drop in on an acquaintance and say, "I got a tip on a horse, but I'm short a quarter." One repeats this operation until one has accumulated four quarters. It sometimes takes a long time, but there is always an oversupply of that. This system reduces the risk of betting to a minimum. On the infrequent occasions when some momentarily prosperous tenant bets important money on a race—say, five dollars—two or three of the hall bookmakers get together and divide up the hazard.

A stranger would be puzzled by some of the greetings exchanged by performers wandering between agents' offices. "Why, Zasu Pitts!" a gaunt young man wearing suède shoes and an overcoat of mattress filling will shout at a girl younger, twenty pounds heavier, and obviously poorer than Miss Pitts, whom she doesn't even faintly resemble. "Clark Gable!" the girl will shout, throwing her arms around him. "I haven't seen you since I thumbed a ride from that crumb in Anniston, Alabama!" The man and woman are not talking this way for a gag; they are survivors of a Hollywood-double troupe, a form of theatrical enterprise that has replaced the *Uncle Tom* show in out-of-the-way areas of the United States. In a double troupe, which usually travels in a large, overcrowded old automobile, all the members are supposed to be able to imitate Hollywood stars. They play in moving-picture theaters or grange halls, usually for a percentage of the receipts. Members of these companies seldom know each other's real names, even when they have heard them. In recounting their wanderings, they are likely to say, "Mae West was driving, see, and she goes to sleep. And only Ray Bolger seen the truck coming and grabbed the wheel, we would of all landed in some broken-down hospital in Henderson, North Carolina." The Hollywood doubles earn less and eat worse than the barnstormers of fifty years ago, but they have the pleasure of identifying themselves with the extremely wealthy. Some players are able to impersonate two or even three Hollywood stars to the complete satisfaction of an audience in Carbondale, Illinois. Sleeping on dressing tables, the doubles dream that they are lolling at Palm Springs, like in the *Daily Mirror*. A boy who impersonates Ned Sparks and Jimmy Durante once told Jerry Rex that he was downhearted only once in his mimetic career. That was at a county fair in Pennsylvania where some doubles were performing on an open-air stage under a hot sun. "I give them everything I had," the boy said, "and them apple-knockers just sat there from sorrow. They never even heard of Jimmy Durante or Ned Sparks. They broke my heart."

Summer, which used to be the dead season for entertainers, is now the period during which they eat most frequently. There are several rehearsal rooms in the Jollity Building, and throughout June they are full of uproar as the performers prepare for their migration to the Catskill Mountains resorts. "Up there the kids work for pot cheese," Jerry Rex says. "Here they don't even make themselves a chive." In the Catskills, a personable young man who can act as master of ceremonies, tell funny stories, give lessons in the conga, perform card tricks, direct amateur theatricals, do a screamingly funny eccentric dance, and impersonate stars of screen and radio can earn twenty-five dollars a week and room and board for ten consecutive weeks, provided he has a sensational singing voice. Performers at various hotels add to their incomes by uniting for occasional benefit shows, the beneficiary always being the entertainer at the hotel where the show is staged. "If a guy does not shoot crap with the guests," Jerry Rex says, "he has a chance to save himself a buck." Returning from the mountains after Labor Day, bloated with pot cheese, the actor sometimes survives until October, Jerry says, before developing doughnut tumors, a gastric condition attributed by him to living on crullers and coffee and which is usually a forerunner of the miss-meal cramps. By November, the performer no longer feels the cramps, because he is accustomed to being from hunger and not having what to eat. Then he starts talking about a job that has been promised to him in Miami if he can get there, and he tries, unsuccessfully, to promote somebody for railroad fare. Meanwhile, he plays any date he can get. Sometimes he doesn't work for a week and then has a chance to play a couple of dates in a night, perhaps a smoker in the west Bronx and a church party in Brooklyn, the first of which will net him $4.50 and the second $2.70, after the deduction of Jerry Rex's commissions.

The Jollity Building has at least a dozen tenants who teach voice, dancing, and dramatic art, and a few who specialize in Latin-American dance routines and acrobatics. The financial condition of the professors, which is solvent in comparison to that of the performers, musicians, and theatrical agents in the building, is a perpetual source of amusement to Morty Ormont. "The singers are from hunger," he says; "the performers are from hunger, and every day we get saps in the building who pay for lessons so they can be from hunger, too." Parents who believe their children are talented are the staple prey of the professional teachers. Seldom does a Jollity Building elevator make a trip without at least one bosomy and belligerent suburban woman, holding fast to the hand of a little girl whose hair is frizzled into a semblance of Shirley Temple's. Often several of the Shirleys and their mothers find themselves in a car together. The mothers' upper lips curl as they survey the other mothers' patently moronic young. The Shirleys gaze at each other with vacuous hostility and wonder whether their mothers will slap them if they ask to go to the bathroom again. All the Shirleys have bony little knees and bitter mouths and, in Morty's opinion, will undoubtedly grow up to be ax murderesses.

III—A Soft Dollar

Barney, who owns the lunch counter in the basement of the so-called Jollity Building, never turns his head away from his customers for a second while working. Even when he is drawing coffee from the urn, he keeps looking over his shoulder, and this, in the course of his eighteen years in business, has given him a nervous neck twitch. "I know their nature," Barney says in explanation of this mannerism. "If I'll turn my head, they'll run away without paying." With all his vigilance, Barney cannot foresee when a client will eat two *pastrami* sandwiches and then say, after fumbling in a vest pocket, "Gee, Barney, I thought I had a quarter in my pocket, but it turned out to be an old Willkie button." Barney is a short, gray-faced man in his fifties who looks at his customers through thick, shell-rimmed spectacles that are usually clouded with steam from the coffee urn or with dabs of corned-beef grease. The customers see Barney against a background of cans of beans, arranged in pyramids. The cans, stacked on a shelf behind his counter, constitute a decorative scheme he never changes, except when he lays a fat, shiny stick of bologna across the can forming the apex of one of the pyramids.

Once, recently, Barney startled Hy Sky, the Jollity Building sign painter, and Morty Ormont, the renting agent, by announcing the return of prosperity. This was an event that neither of his listeners, confined for the most part in their associations to theatrical people, had suspected. "The taxi drivers who come in here are asking for sandwiches on thin bread, so they can taste the meat, and they are eating two sandwiches for lunch, usually," Barney said. "From 1929 until very lately, everybody was asking for sandwiches on thick bread, one sandwich should fill them up." The lunch counter is at one end of the Jollity Building's poolroom, and most of Barney's customers are either people who work in the building or pool players. The taximen are his only customers from the daylight world.

"The bookmakers in the building are also eating regular," Barney said, continuing his survey of business conditions, "and even a couple of prize-fight managers recently came in and paid cash. With musicians, of course, is still the depression. Also with performers." Barney takes it for granted that anyone connected with the stage is broke, and if he can detect a speck of theatrical make-up under a woman's chin or behind an ear, he will refuse to give her credit. He even declines to believe that any performers receive regular remuneration in Hollywood. "It is all publicity," he says. "George Raft still owes me thirty-five cents from when he used to hang here." Musicians, although imperceptibly less broke, on the average, than actors or dancers, are almost as irritating to Barney. They sit at his counter for hours, each with one cup of coffee, and discuss large sums of money. Since most of the year musicians wear big, shaggy coats made of a material resembling the mats under rugs, they fill twice as much space as bookmakers or taxi drivers. Their coats overflow onto adjoining stools. "Three hours is average for a musician to drink a cup of coffee," Barney says, "and then sometimes he says he hasn't got the nickel, he'll see me tomorrow. Tomorrow is never."

Regulars who hang at Barney's counter may be identified by the manner in which, before sitting down, they run their hands under the counter. They are reaching for a communal dope sheet, a ten-cent racing paper giving the entries at all tracks. The regulars at Barney's chip in and buy one copy every day. This economy permits each of them to lose to bookmakers every week several dimes that would otherwise have been spent at newsstands. Barney has little contact with the pool players, although he does a good deal of business with them. A number of mulatto girls who rack up the balls on the pool tables also act as waitresses for the players. The girls pay Barney cash for all the cups of coffee they carry away. Presumably they collect from the players. "It is a pleasure they can have," says Barney.

One of the more conspicuous fellows who eat at the lunch counter and spend a good deal of time there between meals drinking coffee is called Marty the Clutch. Marty gets his name from his humorous custom of mangling people's fingers when he shakes hands with them. Strangers to whom he is introduced usually sink to their knees screaming before he releases their right hand. Casual acquaintances consider Marty a big, overgrown boy brimming with animal spirits. Only old friends really appreciate him. They know that when Marty has numbed a stranger's hand, he can often get a ring off the fellow's finger unnoticed. "It is very cute when you think of it," says Acid Test Ike, who is a manager of punch-drunk prize fighters. "I once seen the Clutch get a rock off a ticket broker big enough to use for a doorstop. By the time the scalper noticed the ring was gone, he thought a bosko he knew had clipped him for it, so he busted her nose." The Clutch is a big, square-shouldered man with a forehead barely sufficient to keep his hair from meeting his eyebrows. He used to be a prize fighter, but, he says, he worked with a gang of hijackers several nights a week and this interfered with his training, because he was always getting shot. Acid Test Ike considers this an amiable prevarication. "The Clutch never was a hijacker," he says. "He just gives that as a social reference. Really, the Clutch is a gozzler." This term means a fellow who gozzles people—chokes them in order to rob them. The gozzling business cannot be very good, because Marty is customarily as broke as most other patrons of the lunch counter. Every time Barney looks at Marty the Clutch, he rubs his throat nervously.

To Barney, the most interesting people in the Jollity Building are the promoters, the fellows who are always trying to earn, in the local idiom, a soft dollar. This is a curiosity he shares with Hy Sky and Morty Ormont, and sometimes the three of them get together at the lunch counter and discuss, with happy chuckles, the outrageous swindles perpetrated by fellows they know. One mental giant of whom all three speak with awe is a chap known as Lotsandlots, or Lots for short, who is in the land-development business. Lots's stock in trade is a tract of real estate in the Jersey marshes and a large supply of stationery bearing the letterheads of non-existent land companies and the Jollity Building's address. Prospects are carefully selected; generally they are close-fisted men with a few thousand dollars saved up. Each receives a letter informing him that he has won a lot in a raffle conducted by one of the land companies to publicize a new development. The winner, according to the letter, is now the owner, free and clear, of one building lot in some out-of-the-way district. With the lot goes an option to buy the lots on either side of it for a couple of hundred dollars apiece. The man receiving such a letter is distrustful. He knows that one house lot is not much use, and he suspects that the whole thing is just a dodge to sell him more land, so he doesn't even go out to look at his prize. In a week or so, Lotsandlots calls on the skeptic and says he hears that the man is the lucky owner of three lots in a certain undeveloped neighborhood. Lotsandlots says he represents a company that is assembling a site for a large industrial plant. He offers to buy the man's three lots for a good price, but begs him to keep the offer confidential, as publicity would interfere with his firm's efforts to pick up land. The lucky man of property always lets Lotsandlots think that he owns all three plots outright. He says that Lotsandlots should give him time to think the matter over and come back in a couple of days. Then, as soon as Lotsandlots leaves, the fellow hurries down to the land company's office in the Jollity Building to exercise his option on the two adjoining lots, which he expects to sell at a whacking profit. He pays four hundred dollars or five hundred dollars to the "office manager," an assistant promoter in Lotsandlots' employ. The manager gives him clear deed and title to two lots in a salt marsh. The man goes away happily, and then waits the rest of his life for Lotsandlots to reappear and conclude the deal.

"The art in it," Hy Sky says admiringly, "is the sap never knows Lots is running the land company. A good boy, Lots." Lots is a humorist, too. When anyone asks him if he does much business, he says, "Lots and lots," which is how he got his name. When he says it, he rolls his eyes so knowingly that Hy Sky, if he is around, suffers an attack of laughter resembling whooping cough.

Another respected promoter is Judge Horumph, a bucolic figure of a man who wears a stand-up collar, a heavy gilt-iron watch chain with a seal ring on it, and high, laceless shoes with elastic sides. The Judge's face is tomato red marked by fine streaks of eggplant purple. Barney and his customers are disposed to believe Judge Horumph's story that he was once a justice of the peace in a Republican village upstate, a region in which about one man in every three enjoys that distinction. The Judge, when he is working, sits at a telephone all day, calling various business houses that like to keep on the good side of the law—particularly firms with large fleets of trucks, because such firms are constantly dealing with traffic and parking summonses, and they don't want to offend anybody. He says, "This is Judge H-r-r-umph." The name is indistinguishable, but no layman knows the names of a tenth of the judges in New York, and it would be impolite to ask a judge to repeat. "I am giving some of my time to a little charitable organization called Free Malted Milk for Unmarried Mothers," the Judge says. "I know that ordinarily it would be an imposition to bother you people, but the cause is so worthy . . ." Rather often, the owner or manager of the firm tells the Judge he will send five or ten dollars. "Oh, don't say 'send,'" Judge Horumph booms jovially. "I know how prone we all are to forget these little things. I'll send a telegraph boy right over to get your contribution." The Judge is a man of real culture, Morty Ormont says, but he has one failing, and that is strong drink. Judge Horumph's one serious run-in with the law resulted from his throwing a whisky bottle at a Jollity Building wag who offered to buy him a malted milk.

The hero of the best stories that Barney and Hy Sky and Morty Ormont sit around telling one another is a promoter named Maxwell C. Bimberg, who used to be known in the Jollity Building as the Count de Pennies because he wore a pointed, waxed, blond mustache just like a count and because he was rather stingy except about gambling and women. The Count was a tiny, fragile man with large, melting eyes and a retreating chin. "He was a little wizened man that didn't look like nothing at all," Hy says, "but Maxwell C. Bimberg had a brilliant mind."

Hy recalls how he helped the Count de Pennies conduct a crusade against pari-mutuel betting in New York State in which the Count fleeced a prominent bookmaker who felt that his business was menaced by the movement to legalize the betting machines. The Count induced the bookie to finance a campaign of street advertising against the proposition, which was to be voted on at the polls. The Count was to have twenty signs painted, large enough to cover the side of a wagon. The signs were to say, "Mayor LaGuardia says vote 'No'!" Then the Count was to hire ten wagons, put the signs on them, and have them driven around the center of town the day before the referendum. The bookie peeled several hundred-dollar bills off his bank roll to pay for the operation. The promoter went to Hy Sky and ordered just two signs, allowing the painter a generous profit on them. He had the signs placed on a wagon that he hired for one hour. The wagon then drove a couple of times through the Duffy Square region, where the bookmaker hung, and returned to the stable. There the signs were shifted to another wagon, which made the same circuit, and so on. The bookie saw several wagons during the day and was happy. Count de Pennies saved the price of eighteen signs and reduced wagon hire by ninety per cent. "Maxwell C. Bimberg had a brilliant mind!" Hy Sky repeats when he tells of this successful promotion.

Morty Ormont's reminiscences about the Count are not all tender. "He was always borrowing a nickel for a telephone call, but one day he asked me for a loan of three dollars so he could get his teeth out of hock to con a sucker," Morty says. "I loaned it to him, and the next day I saw him looking very happy, with his teeth in. As soon as he spotted me he started with a small mouth. 'I am sorry, Morty,' he says, 'but the sucker didn't show, so I haven't got the three bucks.' So I turned him upside down—you know how little he was—and six hundred dollars fell out of his left breech."

The Count's admirers in the Jollity Building generally speak of him in the past tense, although it is improbable that he is dead. Some detectives employed by a railroad are looking for the wizened man as a result of one of his promotions, and consequently he has not been seen for some time around the Jollity Building. The project which irritated the railroad was known as the Dixie Melody Tours. The Count sold bargain-rate tour tickets to Florida which included train fare, hotel rooms, and meals. At the end of every month, the Count settled with the railroad and the hotels for the accommodations the tourists had bought through him. The tours were actually bringing the Count a fair income when, at the end of the third or fourth month, he decided to pay the railroad with a bad check. "It must have been a terrible temptation to him to stay honest," Morty says, "but he resisted it." "He always thought very big," Barney recalls affectionately. "I said to him lots of times, 'Be careful, Count. Nobody can promote a railroad.' He would say, 'What do you mean? This is strictly legitimate.' But I could see in his eyes he was thinking of larceny. 'Already I promoted some of the smartest people on

Broadway,' he was thinking. 'Why not a railroad?' He always thought too big."

The Count made his first appearance in the Jollity Building a dozen years ago, when he was the manager of the widow of a famous gunman. He rented a furnished office, about six feet square, on the third floor and pasted on the outer side of the door a card saying, "Maxwell C. Bimberg, Presentation of Publicized Personalities." He booked the gunman's widow as an added attraction in burlesque theaters, and since that seemed to work out pretty well, he tried to sign up several acquitted female defendants in recent and prominent murder cases. The women were eager to sign contracts, but the Count found it difficult to make money with them. One reason, he said, was that "It is hard to write a routine for an acquitted murderess. If she reenacts the crime, then the public gets the impression that she should not have been acquitted."

One Wisconsin woman who had been acquitted of killing her husband with ground glass came to New York and rented an apartment to live in during her stage career under his management. She used to invite the Count to dinner every evening, and he had a hard time thinking of excuses which would not offend her. "Every time she says 'Home cooking,' " the Count would tell Barney, "I feel like I bit into a broken bottle." At last the life of the gunman's widow was violently terminated by one of her husband's business associates. An astute detective sat down next to the telephone in the murdered woman's flat and waited for the murderer to call up, which to a layman would have seemed an unlikely eventuality. The first person to call was the Count. He was phoning to inform his star that he had booked her for a week's engagement at a theater in Union City, New Jersey. The detective had the call traced. A couple of other detectives arrested the Count in the Jollity Building and pulled out his mustache one hair at a time to make him tell why he had killed his meal ticket. This experience cured the Count of his desire to make other people's crimes pay. After his mustache grew again, he decided to marry an elderly Brooklyn woman whom he had met through an advertisement in a matrimonial journal. The bride was to settle three thousand dollars on him, but the match fell through when she declined to give the Count the money in advance. "If you have so little confidence in me, darling," he said, "we would never be happy." "And also," he told Morty Ormont subsequently, "I didn't want to lay myself open for a bigamy rap."

The Count next organized a troupe of girl boxers, whom he proposed to offer as an added attraction to the dance marathons then popular. "It was not that the idea was any good," Morty Ormont says when he tells about the Count, "but it was the way he milked it. After all, what is there smart about selling a guy a piece of something that might make money? Smart is to sell a guy for a good price a piece of a sure loser. The Count went out and promoted Johnny Attorney, one of the toughest guys on Broadway, for a grand to pay the girls' training expenses and buy them boxing trunks and bathrobes. The Count trembled every time Johnny looked at him, but with him, larceny was stronger than fear. So he gives all the girls bus fare to Spring Valley, New York, and tells them he will meet them there and show them the training camp he has engaged. Then he takes the rest of the grand and goes to Florida." When Morty reaches this point in the story, Hy Sky can seldom restrain himself from saying, reverentially, "Maxwell C. Bimberg had a brilliant mind!"

"By the time the Count came back from Florida," Morty says, "Johnny Attorney was running a night club on Fifty-second Street. The Count walks into Johnny's joint as if nothing had happened, and in fifteen minutes he cons Johnny into making him a banquet manager. He booked a couple of nice banquets into there, but when Johnny would send the bill to the chairman of whatever club it was that held the banquet, the chairman would write back and say, 'I see no mention on your bill of the deposit I paid your Mr. Bimberg.' The Count had glommed the deposits. So after that he had to play the duck for Johnny for a couple of years. Whenever Johnny would get shoved in the can for assault or manslaughter, the Count would come back to town. That gave him quite a lot of time in town, at that."

Morty and Hy agree that the Count had a rare gift of making women feel sorry for him because he looked so small and fragile. "He made many a beautiful head," Morty concedes with envy. "If I had met a refined, educated girl like you when I was still young, my whole life would have been different," the Count would tell a head who might be a minor burlesque stripper. He would invite her to his tiny office in the Jollity Building to plan her Hollywood career. This office, he would assure her, was just a hide-out where he could get away from the crowds of people who besieged him for bookings at his regular place of business. The Count always made a point of stopping at the switchboard which then served the furnished-office tenants, collectively known to Morty Ormont as the heels. "Did that girl from the Paradise Restaurant call me this afternoon?" he would ask the operator. "You know, the one I got a job for last week? And by the way, if Monte Proser calls up in the next half-hour, tell him I'm out. I'm going to be busy." The mainsprings of feminine character, the Count used to tell his friends, were avarice and mother love. He would make extravagant promises of contracts in shows or moving pictures which he would tell every girl he was on the point of closing for her. Then he would say sadly, "Your success is assured, but I will never be happy. I am a Broadway roué, and no decent girl would look at me." "Oh, don't say that, Mr. Bimberg," a girl might beg, remembering she had not yet signed the contract. (The Count used to say, "You would be surprised how sorry a girl can feel for a man that is going to make a lot of money for her.") "Oh yes, I cannot fool myself," the Count would sob to the girl, and tears would flow from his large, protruding eyes as he grabbed for his protégé's hand. If the girl put an arm around his narrow shoulders to steady him, he would work into a clinch. If she pulled away from the lead, the Count would sometimes fall to his knees and sniffle. "Why should I live another day?" he would wail. "Tomorrow your contract is coming through. If I lived through tonight, I could collect my ten-per-cent commission, which would amount to perhaps a couple of thousand bucks. Is that a reason to live?" Usually the girl would think it was a pretty good reason. The Count did not always succeed. "When a bosko wouldn't have nothing to do with him," Hy Sky says, "Maxwell C. Bimberg became very emotional." He once offered a female boxer forty dollars to let him hold her hand. The boxer declined, saying, "I would rather wake up in a hole with a snake than in a room with Count de Pennies." The Count was very discouraged by her remark and hated to hear it quoted.

An enterprise which the Count's admirers remember with considerable pleasure was the Public Ballyhoo Corporation, Ltd. To launch this concern, the Count spent a couple of weeks promoting a bookmaker known as Boatrace Harry. The Count kept on telling Boatrace Harry about the great incomes that he said were earned by publicity men like Steve Hannagan, Benjamin Sonnenberg, and Richard Maney. Then he allowed Harry to invest a couple of thousand dollars in Public Ballyhoo, Ltd. He had letterheads printed saying that Public Ballyhoo, Ltd., would supply "anything from an actress to an alligator" for publicity stunts. The Count became so interested in his idea that he forgot to duck with Boatrace Harry's money. The manager of a theater showing the first run of a picture called *Eskimo* asked the Count to secure a genuine Eskimo to pose on top of the marquee with a team of huskies. The Count made a good try. He found in the telephone directory some kind of society for the preservation of the American Indian and obtained from it the addresses of two alleged Eskimos. One turned out to be a Jewish tailor in Greenpoint; this was obviously a wrong listing. The other, who lived in Bay Ridge, was a real Eskimo who had a job in a foundry. He turned down the job, however, and begged the Count not to give his secret away, because his girl would make fun of him.

The Count had a number of other disappointments. He saw a classified advertisement inserted in a newspaper by a man who said he wanted to buy cockroaches in quantity. The Count knew where he could buy some large tropical roaches which had been a feature of a recently raided speakeasy called La Cucaracha, where the customers could race roaches along the bar, instead of rolling dice, to see who would pay for their drinks. In his enthusiasm, the Count bought five hundred *cucarachas*, at a nickel apiece, from the prohibition agents who had raided the place. The Count knew some newspaper reporters from the days when he had exploited murderesses and boxing girls, so he called several of them up and told them of the big deal he had on the fire. They thought it was funny, and the story was published in the early editions of a couple of afternoon papers. The advertiser, however, did not want racing cockroaches. He wanted to feed the roaches to tropical birds, and the Count's acquisitions could have eaten the birds. Ordinary household roaches, obtainable from small boys in tenement neighborhoods at low cost, were better for the aviarist's purpose. The Count was stuck with five hundred hungry bugs. He turned them loose on the third floor of the Jollity Building and left for Florida with what remained of Boatrace Harry's money. Barney attributes the unusual size of the bugs in the Jollity Building today to the thoroughbred out-cross.

Morty was naturally quite angry with the Count at first, but after a few weeks began to miss him. "You have to hand it to him. He had a good idea all the same," Morty says now. "The story about the roaches was in all the papers, and with that kind of publicity he could have gone far. A week after he left, a guy called up and asked for Mr. Bimberg. I asked him what did he want, and he said he had read about Public Ballyhoo, Ltd., and he was in the market for some moths. So I told him, 'I haven't any moths, but if you'll come up here, I'll cut holes in your pants for nothing.' "

The Count de Pennies must have convinced himself that he was a publicity man. When he reappeared in the Jollity Building after he had lost Boatrace Harry's money at Tropical Park, he got a job with a new night club as press agent. The place had one of those stages which roll out from under the bandstand before the floor show starts. The Count decided he could get a story in the newspapers by sending for the police emergency squad on the pretext that one of the show girls had been caught under the sliding stage. The policemen arrived, axes in hand, and refused to be deterred by the Count's statement that there was no longer any need of them because he had personally rescued the girl. "You know very well that poor little girl is still under there!" the sergeant in charge roared reproachfully, and the coppers hilari-ously chopped the stage to bits. The Count lost his job.

What was perhaps the zenith of the Count's prosperity was reached during the brief life of the Lithaqua Mineral Water Company. Lithaqua was formed to exploit a spring on the land of a Lithuanian tobacco farmer in Connecticut. The water of the spring had a ghastly taste, and this induced the farmer to think it had therapeutic qualities. A druggist who was related to a murderess the Count had formerly managed organized a company to market the water. He gave the Count ten per cent of the common stock to act as director of publicity. The Count "sent out the wire," as fellows in the Jollity Building sometimes say when they mean that a promoter has had a third party act as go-between, to Johnny Attorney and Boatrace Harry. "Why be thick all your life?" he had his intermediary ask Johnny. "The Count has something big this time. If you will call it square for the few hundred he owes you, he will sell you ten per cent of the mineral-water company for exactly one grand." The Count had the same offer made to Boatrace Harry, and he sold his ten per cent of the stock to each of them for one thousand dollars. He sold his share in the enterprise to five other men, too, and was just beginning to think he had better go to Florida again when a chemist for a consumers' research group discovered that seepage from the vats of a near-by dye works accounted for the bilious flavor of the tobacco farmer's water. This got the Count out of a difficult situation. Even Johnny and Boatrace could understand that ten per cent of a worthless business was not worth quarreling about.

During this period of affluence, the Count lived in a hotel on West Forty-eighth Street. "There was even a private shower," intimates recall solemnly when they evoke the glories of that era. The Count took to wearing cinnamon-colored suits with pointed lapels that flared from his waistline to an inch above his shoulders and trousers that began just below his breastbone. Every day he bet on every race at every track in the United States and Canada, and he invariably lost. Almost four weeks elapsed, Morty Ormont recalls with astonishment now, before the Count again had to borrow nickels to make telephone calls.

The Dixie Melody Tours followed several promotions of an increasingly prosaic nature. "The tours was too legitimate for his character," Hy Sky says sadly. "There was nobody left for him to promote, only the railroad. So he went ahead and promoted it. Maxwell C. Bimberg was too brilliant!" Morty Ormont is more realistic. "In every class of business there has got to be a champion," he says. "The Count de Pennies was never no good to nobody, but he was the champion heel of the Jollity Building."

• Mrs. Braune's Prize Fighters •

In times like these, the lodging-house conducted by Mrs. Rosa Braune on West Ninety-second Street, near Central Park, is a peaceful and comforting place. It is almost entirely inhabited by prize fighters, who are the most tranquil of athletes. Unlike baseball players and jockeys, fighters seldom have noisy arguments. Not fighting is their avocation. Mrs. Braune's house gives a city dweller the same soothing sense of continuity that the round of seasons is said to impart to peasants. There are always new fighters coming up, old ones going down, and recurrent technical problems to discuss. I hadn't been to see Mrs. Braune and her lodgers since midsummer of 1939, and, as the world had gone through a lot in the interim, I visited the house a few days ago with certain misgivings. Happily, I found everything serenely unchanged.

Most of Mrs. Braune's lodgers are under the direction of Al Weill, a bulbous man who is the thriftiest and most industrious fight manager of the day. The two windows of his office—an indication that he is at least twice as opulent as any competitor—overlook the land of the Telephone Booth Indians, but he is too wise to stable his prize fighters in the vicinity. Fighters not in his charge occasionally stop at Mrs. Braune's house, but Mrs.

Braune doesn't encourage them. Prize fighters are drawn inevitably to parks, and the Central Park reservoir, around which they can take their morning runs, makes the neighborhood especially popular with them. Weill has a family and a home of his own on the upper West Side; his viceroy at Mrs. Braune's is Charles Goldman, a trainer and an old friend of mine. Goldman is a brisk little man with a flattened nose and a thickened right ear. These add authority to his comments on professional subjects. He used to be a smart bantamweight and never lets any of his pupils forget it. Charlie opened the door and greeted me as soon as I had rung Mrs. Braune's bell. This was not strange, because he lives in the front parlor of the old-fashioned brownstone house. His wide windows are a strategic point from which he can see any fighter who comes home late at night or tries to bring a girl in with him. From them he can also check on the boys as they leave for their morning runs in the park.

We shook hands, then Goldman yelled up the stairs for Mrs. Braune and took me into his room to wait for her. It is a big room, and there are three beds in it. A French-Canadian fighter named Dave, who is not under Weill's management but lives in the neighborhood, was sitting on one of them talking in French to a Weill featherweight named Spider. Goldman introduced me, and then Spider said, raptly, "Go on, Dave, talk more French." "Spider don't understand him," Goldman said seriously, "but he thinks it sounds pretty." When Mrs. Braune came in a couple of minutes later, Dave stopped talking, because Mrs. Braune, a German Swiss, understands French and would not have liked what he was calling Spider. "It's better than double talk," Dave said to me with a grin. The two boys went out, and as they were leaving, Goldman said, "Don't get into no crap games." The house stands in a tree-shaded block of almost identical brownstones, all with high stoops, and usually there is a crap game in progress on at least one of them. Goldman disapproves of crap games because they take a fighter's mind off business. Whenever one of the boys is arrested and fined two dollars for shooting crap, Goldman gloats over his misfortune.

Mrs. Braune is about sixty years old and built like a large, soft cylinder with a diameter not greatly inferior to its axis. She has a pink face, sparse gray hair parted in the middle, and calm blue eyes. She is so much like the conventional idea of American motherhood that no fighter in his right mind would think of talking back to her. Mrs. Braune once ran a rooming house at 19 West Fifty-second Street—an address which disappeared some years ago when the next-door neighbors, Jack and Charlie, bought the building and added it to their restaurant at No. 21. Her clients in that house included a Fifth Avenue jeweler who had a lot of girl friends and suffered from a complaint that Mrs. Braune calls "the gouch," theatrical people, who were noisy and kept late hours, and a number of White Russian countesses, whom she calls in retrospect "the Countesses of Having-Nothing." The countesses were much the worst pay. Mrs. Braune prefers her present lodgers, who are in bed by ten o'clock except when they are professionally engaged. She is sure of getting the room rent from Weill's fighters, at least, because Al pays it and takes the money out of their earnings. He is always urging his boys to live frugally and put their money in the bank. They have a hard time obtaining a couple of dollars a week from him for spending money. He telephones at ten every evening to ask Mrs. Braune if the boys are all in their rooms. Sometimes she covers up for a fighter she thinks must be staying on at the movies for the end of a double feature, but she doesn't condone any really serious slip. Weill has five-year contracts with his boys, and if one of them won't behave, even for Mrs. Braune, Weill simply declines to make any matches for him. This means that the fighter must get some other kind of work, a prospect so displeasing that discipline at Mrs. Braune's is usually perfect.

The one detail of Mrs. Braune's appearance that sets her apart from other landladies is a pair of miniature leather boxing gloves pinned high on her vast bosom. She likes to show them to visitors, for they have been autographed by Lou Ambers, twice lightweight champion of the world. Ambers, she explains, was her star lodger for years and was responsible for her entrance into the prize-fight business. In 1935, before he became illustrious, Ambers asked her for a room. He was training for a fight and had no money in the meanwhile. Mrs. Braune let him run up a bill of seventy or eighty dollars, a proceeding so extraordinary that after the fight Ambers induced his manager, Weill, to put all his fighters in her house. Ambers knew it was a lucky house, because he had won the fight. The boys living at Mrs. Braune's won a long series of bouts, and Weill began to call it, grandiloquently, the House of Destiny. It is impossible to tell how much Mrs. Braune's motherly discipline contributed to the winning streak, but the manager was sure it had some effect. Besides, the house is clean, and Mrs. Braune's rentals have always been reasonable. Now, after six years of it, she says, she feels like an old-timer in the fight game, and Goldman reports that once he even heard her telling a tall heavyweight how to "scrunch himself over so he wouldn't get hurted."

Weill practices a kind of pugilistic crop rotation. He has under his management fighters who are valuable properties now and others he thinks will be profitable in from one to four years. Fight people speak of a boy as being one or two or three years "away." Weill even has one towering youngster who hasn't yet had a professional bout but is living at Mrs. Braune's while he learns his trade. A manager gets from thirty-three and a third to fifty per cent of a fighter's purses, which, in the case of Ambers or Arturo Godoy, another Weill property, runs into considerable money. Often, however, a fighter on the way up doesn't earn his keep, and then Weill has to carry him. Weill pays Mrs. Braune the fighter's room rent and gives him a weekly five-dollar meal ticket. The ticket is good for five dollars and fifty cents in trade at a Greek lunchroom on Columbus Avenue. This arrangement keeps the boy from overeating, Weill explains. He makes his bookings in an office in the Strand Building, on Duffy Square. Usually he keeps a fighter working in towns like New Haven, Utica, and Bridgeport until he seems ripe for a metropolitan career. The boys come back to the house on Ninety-second Street after each bout.

"I prefer fighters than any other kind of lodgers," Mrs. Braune said to me. "They got such interesting careers, like opera singers, but they are not so mean."

"She is just like a mother to them boys," Goldman said admiringly. "She presses their trunks for them, so they will look nice going into the ring, and sometimes when I tell a boy he is getting too fine, she fixes him a chicken dinner. They don't board here regularly, but she likes to cook for them now and then. A fighter can't stay down to weight all the time or he will work himself into t.b. Now and then he has got to slop in. Mrs. Braune is a restraining influence on them kids. They got too much energy."

A boy walked down the hall past the open door, and Goldman called him in to show me a sample of the student body. "This is Carl Dell, a welterweight," Goldman said. "He spends all his time writing long letters to dolls." "Charlie is always worrying about maybe I would have a good time," Dell said before acknowledging the introduction. "He is always beefing." Dell has a strong, rectangular head with the small eyes and close-set ears of a faun. Goldman, perhaps affected by some remote sculptural association, said, "Look at him. He has a head like an old Roman." He said Dell had been a good amateur and had won thirty-seven straight fights after turning professional. He had lost a couple of decisions in recent months, but that was natural, as he had begun to meet good men. "It is a lot in how you match a fellow," Goldman said, "but anyway, he is a great prospect." "I beat a fellow out on the coast that they said was the champion of Mexico," Dell said, "and when I was down in Cuba, I beat the champion of Cuba. That is two countries I am champion of already." Dell is twenty-three years old and is at least a year "away." He told me he came from Oneonta, New York, and had spent three years in the CCC, a government enterprise which develops fine arms and shoulders. Then he had won a lot of prizes in amateur tournaments and finally turned professional. He said he had never had any kind of job except boxing.

Goldman began talking to me about the importance of concentration in shadowboxing. Dell looked embarrassed, seeming to know that the little trainer was talking at him. Mrs. Braune just sat quietly, as if used to such seminars.

"One of the most important things in training is shadowboxing," Goldman said, getting into the middle of the floor and assuming a guard. "Most boys, now, when they are shadowboxing they are just going through the motions and thinking of some broad, maybe. Shadowboxing is like when the teacher gives you a word to take home and write out ten times, so you will know it. In the examination you only get one chance to spell the word. The best two moves I ever had come to me when I was shadowboxing, but I was not just going through the motions with a swelled head, thinking of some broad. I always used to have a move where I feinted a jab and stepped to the left to get away, and one day it come to me, 'Why not really jab when I step that way? If I hit, I am in position to throw a right, and if I miss, I got my right hand up anyway.' " Goldman went to his left, jabbed, and threw a right. "Then the thought come to me," he said, " 'Why not throw a left hook for the body instead, and that will bring me in position for a right uppercut?' Now, when I straighten up with that uppercut the guy is going to cross me with a right, ain't he? Sure! He can't stop himself. So then, as I throw the uppercut, I duck to the left in one motion, see?" The little man moved his feet and swayed to his left. "And I come up under his right!" he exclaimed.

Dell had been watching with the detached interest of a boy who has no talent for mathematics but must pass a required course in trigonometry. "Do you get it?" Goldman asked him, abandoning his pretense of talking to me. "Sure," Dell said without enthusiasm, "but I guess I would rather just wear the guys down." He went away, saying he had to write a letter to his girl.

In addition to listening to Goldman's expositions of theory, routine for the prize fighters at Mrs. Braune's includes a long run around the reservoir early every morning and laboratory exercises at Stillman's Gymnasium on Eighth Avenue from noon until about three o'clock. At Stillman's, the fighters box against boys from other managers' strings, to avert possible upheavals in the Braune home. A boy who has had a hard workout is content to do nothing for the rest of the day, which is exactly what a trainer wants him to do.

Mrs. Braune, who used to take a normal matronly pleasure in promoting marriages between young people, has come to feel differently about marriage now that she is interested in prize fighters. Most managers don't like fighters to get married. "One manager is enough," they often say. Mrs. Braune concurs in this prejudice, because when the boys get married they stop living in rooming houses. Also, she takes a proprietary attitude toward any fighter who has lived in her house and she thinks that no young woman can give a pugilist proper care. Lou Ambers got married last year. He had lived in the rear parlor of Mrs. Braune's house for four years, remaining there even after he had become lightweight champion of the world and a great drawing card. The rear parlor has cooking arrangements, and a fellow named Skids Enright, an old short-order cook from Herkimer, New York, Lou's home town, used to live with him and do the cooking. The fighter was never extravagant. After his marriage Ambers went to live in Herkimer. A few months later he was knocked out by a lightweight named Lew Jenkins, who was also married but had been in that condition long enough to develop a tolerance for it. Another Weill fighter, Joey Archibald, won the featherweight championship, got married, and then lost a decision to a bachelor from Baltimore. Archibald is not acutely missed at Mrs. Braune's, however. Because of his unbearable erudition, her other lodgers never felt close to him. "Do you know what Archibald said to me?" Ambers once asked Goldman. "He said 'equilibrium.' " Goldman and Whitey Bimstein, Ambers' trainer, had a hard time restoring friendly relations. Arturo Godoy is also married, but Mrs. Braune feels that, being a South American, he can stand it.

I gathered that because of all the marriages and the absence of a couple of fighters who were on expeditions to the provinces, there are not as many boys as usual stopping at Mrs. Braune's. Goldman mentioned, besides Spider and Dell, a clever welterweight named Al Nettlow, Marty Serve, a coming lightweight, and Tony, the twenty-year-old heavyweight who hasn't fought yet. Tony came in while we were talking, and, after Goldman had introduced him to me as "possibly a future heavyweight champion if he's got the stuff in him," just sat there listening to us. He was bashful, I guessed, because he had not had a fight and so had nothing to talk about. "He is pretty big for a baby, only six feet five inches," Mrs. Braune said, "but he don't make no trouble at all. I was going to get him a special long bed, but he says no, he would just as soon sleep slanting." Some fighters are difficult about beds, Mrs. Braune said, and keep asking for new ones until they have tried every bed in the house. They sleep reasonably well in any of them, apparently, but there seem to be gradations in the profundity of a fighter's unconsciousness, caused by differences in bed springs and not explainable to other persons. Mrs. Braune's hands, while she talked to Goldman and me, were busy with a darning egg and a pair of socks undoubtedly belonging to a prize fighter.

There is a Mr. Braune, but, like most rooming-house husbands, he stays in the background. Until about twenty years ago, he and Mrs. Braune ran a stationery store. Then, she told me, she leased the Fifty-second Street rooming house which disappeared into Jack and Charlie's. The new business was somewhat in the family tradition, she felt, because one of her maternal uncles in Switzerland had kept a big hotel near Lake Geneva. "I would like to see again the Genfersee," she said parenthetically. "The Lake of Geneva, you know. But conditions must be pretty hard over there now. I got confidential postcards from the old country that every mountain is full of cannons. Still, what can they do now they got Hitler all around them?" She went on to say that the fighters are always offering her tickets to bouts but she never goes. She's afraid she couldn't stand the sight of blood. She does listen to fights on the radio, though, whenever she has a chance. When Ambers was fighting Henry Armstrong, the great colored boxer, Mrs. Braune prayed between rounds that her lodger would grow stronger. "And he did get stronger in the last," she said. "He won."

"Why don't you go upstairs and see Marty?" Goldman suggested. "I got to make some phone calls, but just say who you are, and he will be glad to see you. Marty is the baby of the house. He's only nineteen. He went up to Van Cortlandt Park Sunday and wanted to show the other boys how good he could play football. So he is laid up with a skinned nose and a sprained ankle." I climbed to the third floor to see Marty. Over the bed in which the boy lay hung a picture of the late Pius XI and, under the picture, a crucifix. Marty wore a large silver religious medal around his neck. His small, impish face made him look younger than nineteen, but his biceps and forearms were big and brown. He was restless, lying in bed with nobody to talk to, and was glad to see me. He said he had just been looking through an old scrapbook of newspaper clippings about his amateur fights. "I had ninety-three of them," he said. "I only got three or four dollars a fight. I was the highest-paid amateur in the Hudson Valley." Marty said his real name was Mario Severino and that he came from Schenectady. (Weill, since he got Ambers, has picked up several fighters from upstate.) "I didn't know anything before I turned professional," the boy said. "I thought I did, but I didn't. Amateur fighters aren't smart like my roommate, Al Nettlow. Al is a real cutie." Nettlow, he explained, is seldom around the house until the weather gets very cold because he is a "fishing nut." He leaves before dawn every morning he can get off training and takes the long subway ride out to Sheepshead Bay, where he boards one of the deep-sea boats that take fishermen out all day for two dollars. When he gets back, he tries to make the other fighters eat the fish he has caught, but only Tony, the heavyweight, who almost always uses up his weekly meal ticket in five days, displays any enthusiasm. Nettlow is a very clever fighter and is now of near-championship class. I gathered from Goldman that if he wins a title, he will probably want to pose in his publicity pictures with a dead swordfish.

Marty said that he had had thirty-nine professional fights

and had won them all. "Mr. Weill gets me guys that I figure to lick," he said modestly. "He is a great manager. But he gave me hell for playing football. I don't like a sprained ankle. I got to fight once a week or I don't feel good."

I went downstairs and said good-by to Mrs. Braune and to Charlie Goldman, who by that time was clipping a newspaper account of the death of a preliminary boy in a Brooklyn prize ring. The boy had died of heart failure. Goldman collects newspaper stories he thinks will be instructive to his wards. "He was a nice kid," Goldman said to me, "but he never trained right. He relied on his ticker to get him by. He had plenty of moxie, but it is just like I am always saying to my kids. If the flesh is weak, the spirit don't mean a thing."

• Turf and Gridiron •

One of the pleasantest clubs in town, prior to 1940, was the Turf and Gridiron, which occupied the third and fourth floors of a narrow building at 20 West Forty-sixth Street. It cost thirty-three dollars a year to belong to the Turf and Gridiron, and it was not to be confused with the Turf and Field, which has headquarters at Belmont Park and annual dues of a hundred dollars. The Turf and Gridiron was the social club of the New York bookmakers. It was exclusive in only one sense. In the hall on the ground floor—the club being the only tenant of the upper floors—there was an iron gate, such as used to protect speak-easies in the twenties. A colored elevator boy looked at visitors through the bars before admitting them. This precaution was taken because certain persons believed that the clubmen carried large sums of money. Most of the members were held up once or twice, and some of them so often that they became connoisseurs of criminal technique. It was all the result of a misconception. The bookmakers sent their funds direct from the race track to a bank every night in an armored car, and drew their working cash from another car at the track the next day.

The club came into being in 1934, when the state legislature rescinded criminal penalties for accepting bets at race tracks. Like the repeal of prohibition, a few months earlier, this action of the legislature restored an older order of things. Prior to 1909, when, at the urging of Charles Evans Hughes, then governor, the legislators made the practice of the bookmaking trade a misdemeanor, the bookies of New York formed an honorable and highly respected guild. Moreover, between 1909 and 1934, most of the present Turf and Gridiron clubmen took bets anyway. Their position, like that of bootleggers during the last years of prohibition, was delicate, although not exactly dangerous. The Restoration period was brief, for in 1940 the legislature legalized pari-mutuel machines and by that act outlawed the bookmakers again.

Turf and Gridiron members were for the most part substantial, conservative-looking gentlemen of at least middle age. Younger men, it seems, lacked the equanimity the profession requires. The wallpaper in the club lounge on the third floor was a fawn-and-brown plaid, like an old-time bookmaker's vest. There was a big American flag by the fireplace, and over the entrance to the bar a framed picture of a celebrated horse named Master Charlie, which was owned a dozen years ago by Tom Shaw, a prominent member. On a first visit, a casual observer might have thought the Turf and Gridiron a reform organization, for the club bulletin board was perpetually covered with newspaper clippings denouncing racetrack betting. It was always the pari-mutuel form of betting that was attacked in these clippings, however, under headlines like "MACHINES TAKE WPA WORKERS' PAY" or "MUTUELS GUTTING TEXAS, SAYS GOVERNOR."

The guiding spirit of the club was its founder, Timothy James Mara, a large man with baby-pink cheeks and a square, massive jaw. Mara is a half inch over six feet tall, weighs two hundred and five pounds, and was fifty-four years old last August at Saratoga, when he gave himself his usual gargantuan, impromptu birthday party by inviting everybody he met during the evening to join his table. One summer, at the Arrowhead Inn there, he started out with his wife and wound up with a hundred and fifty guests. Mara lives in an eight-room apartment at 975 Park Avenue during most of the year, and he and Mrs. Mara also have a summer home in Luzerne, New York. He is one of eight honorary life members of Lodge No. 1, Benevolent & Protective Order of Elks. (The other seven include Nicholas Murray Butler, Governor Lehman, and former governors Charles S. Whitman and Alfred E. Smith.) In 1925, Mara established the New York Football Giants, the professional eleven which plays at the Polo Grounds. Later he presented the franchise to his two sons, Jack and Wellington, both Fordham alumni. It was because of the Giants that the club on Forty-sixth Street was called the Turf and Gridiron, rather than something like the Turf Association or the Odds Club. At various times in the past he has taken flyers in the liquor-importing business, the promotion of prize fights, and stockbrokerage.

The first dollar Mara bet on a horse started him on his way to all these glories. He was a twelve-year-old newsboy on Union Square at the time, and he lost the dollar. He forgets the name of the horse involved, but he remembers that it was ridden by an ex-newsboy named Micky Clemens. The experience taught him the irrelevancy of sentiment in horse racing. It also taught him that the bookmakers usually win. From that day on, his ambition was formed. The bookmakers to whom he delivered papers on his news route seemed to him singularly blessed among the people of the East Side. They dressed the best and worked the least.

His newspaper route ran along Broadway from Wanamaker's store to Seventeenth Street, and included several popular hotels, like the St. Denis and the Union Square. Sometimes hotel guests would ask him where they could place a bet, and he would take their money to the bookmakers he knew. If the bettors lost, the bookies would pay Tim a five-per-cent commission. If the bettors won, Tim would deliver the winnings, and often receive a tip. During that period Tim was a pupil in Public School 14, on Twenty-seventh Street near Third Avenue. He sold newspapers in the late afternoon, and in the evenings worked as an usher at the Third Avenue Theatre, a temple of melodrama. Tim's father died before Tim was born. In his neighborhood, therefore, he enjoyed the good will that falls to a bright, cheerful Irish boy who is at the same time the son of a poor widow. Among the early friends he made was Mike Cruise, the leader of the Tammany Central Association on East Thirty-second Street. Tim has been a good Tammany man ever since, and is frequently credited with great political influence, an impression he does nothing to discourage.

When Tim left public school he was thirteen. His first real job was with a lawbook firm on Nassau Street, delivering rebound volumes to attorneys. This gave him an opportunity to extend his betting business, for some of the lawyers played the races, and on days when they were busy in court they left betting commissions for him to execute. After working for several years for the lawbook dealers, he opened a place of his own, the New York Law Bindery, at 99 Nassau Street. More bookmaking than bookbinding went on there. By then he had established a regular following among bettors, and they telephoned their wagers to him.

His greatest patron was Thomas W. O'Brien, immortal in reminiscence as one of the few bettors who beat the races. Chicago O'Brien was this phenomenon's nom de course, and he was a retired bricklayer. At the appearance of O'Brien money in the betting ring, odds dropped like a barometer before a typhoon. Chicago therefore bet through agents, who placed thousands of dollars by telephone with poolrooms out of town. The agents were men who had established their credit in the gambling world. Young Tim was already in this class. Sometimes he placed $50,000 on a single race for the O'Brien account.

Knowing that O'Brien was generally right, he would put $1000 of his own money on the same horse. If the horse lost, he had a five-per-cent commission, $2500, coming to him from the books, so he was certain of a $1500 profit anyway.

As his clientele grew, Tim began to cover the smaller bets himself, instead of passing them on to the bookmakers. The mathematical background he had gained at P.S. 14, although simple, was adequate for his needs. Bookmaking is based on a kind of arithmetical shorthand called "percentage." An even-money horse is said to be 50 per cent; a 2-to-1 horse, 33 per cent; a 3-to-1 horse, 25, and a 4-to-1 horse, 20. If there should be two horses in a race, both at even money, the book would be 100 per cent: if the bookmaker bet $1000 against each, he would break exactly even. If there should be three horses, and he laid $1000 at even money against each, he would stand to win $1000 no matter what happened. This would be a 150-per-cent book. Generally, the makers of the books aim at an arrangement of odds that will work out to about 115 per cent. A typical book on an eight-horse race might be arranged in this manner, if the bookmaker planned to lay $1000 against each entry:

ENTRY	ODDS	PERCENTAGE	RISK
Favorite	2–1	33	$1000 to win $500
Second choice	5–2	28	$1000 to win $400
Third choice	4–1	20	$1000 to win $250
Fourth choice	6–1	14	$1000 to win $167
Long shot A	10–1	9	$1000 to win $100
Long shot B	10–1	9	$1000 to win $100
Outsider A	30–1	3	$1000 to win $33
Outsider B	50–1	2	$1000 to win $20

118

If the favorite should win, the book would have to pay out $1000 of the $1070 it took in from the bettors on the other horses. If the second choice should win, the profit would be $100 greater. A victory for the extreme outsider would mean a profit of $550 for the book.

The bookmaker's troubles come in filling the book. His customers always insist on betting more than he wants to cover on certain horses and on ignoring others, so his system of checks and balances is shattered. The bookmaker lowers the odds against the horses most in demand, but often this expedient does not suffice. He cannot afford to turn away trade, so he tries to place some of the money with other bookmakers. This form of hedging, also prevalent among insurance underwriters, is called laying off. Concomitantly, other bookmakers lay off with him. Bookmakers bet against bookmakers, like the people of the Hebrides who lived by taking in one another's washing. Odds sometimes change so radically in response to the market that by post time the book's percentage has been erased, and the bookmaker has become a bettor on a rather large scale.

From the beginning, Mara displayed an exceptional flair for this form of mathematical catch-as-catch-can. In 1921, he made up his mind to abandon city betting and go out to the track. It was like the decision of a stock-company actor to invade the big time. Tim didn't begin at the bottom, by accepting the two- and five-dollar bets of the ordinary grandstand patrons. Optimistically, he set up business in the enclosure at Belmont, ground usually restricted to bookmakers of long experience. A ticket to the enclosure costs twice as much as one to the grandstand; it is assumed that enclosure patrons bet more heavily.

A bookmaker's success in the long run depends on the size of his clientele. If a man has a following, bookmakers believe he will eventually cash in on what is called the hidden percentage.

Hidden percentage is a thing distinct from ordinary percentage. It is the tendency of bettors to be content with modest gains when they are winning but, when losing, to insist on betting more than they can afford in an effort to recoup. After a day of beaten favorites, Tim has great faith in this psychological ace in the hole.

A bookmaker on a New York track needed a considerable sum for overhead expenses, as well as his capital for betting. For the privilege of operating, he had to pay a daily fee averaging ninety dollars to the racing association that owns the track. He also paid a few dollars a day to John Cavanagh, a gentleman known as a "racing stationer," who provided him daily with a few pencils, blank sheets of paper, and cardboard slips bearing the names of all the entries, which were usually tacked up at one side of the bookmaker's slate. Besides selling cardboard, Cavanagh acted as arbiter of the betting ring. All sorts of disputes arise about bets. Cavanagh's decision was final. A bookmaker needed a crew of from five to eight assistants, each of whom drew from ten to twenty-five dollars a day. With him constantly were a sheet writer, who recorded all his bets; a cashier, to handle the money, and a ticket writer, who kept track of transactions with credit customers. Most bookmakers also employ a bet caller, who receives the money of cash bettors. The caller bawls out the bet and the badge number of the customer, such as "Aneroid, sixty to fifteen, badge 1347." Tim did not employ a caller, preferring to call the bets himself. He enjoyed the feel of the bills in his palm, and was not opposed to the sound of his own voice. In addition to these employees on fixed post, every bookmaker had two "outside men." One outside man scouted around the betting ring, noticing what odds other books were laying, and particularly whether the professional betting men were placing large amounts on any of the entries. He reported to his boss at brief intervals. The other outside man bet for the book; his job was laying off. On an average weekday, Mara handled bets amounting to between ten and fifteen thousand dollars; on a Saturday or holiday, as much as thirty thousand dollars.

In Mara's quality of surface good humor he excelled all his confreres. Unlike most of the Turf and Gridiron members, he managed to look like the popular conception of a sporting man, even without wearing a fancy vest. His big, pink, happy face, with its frame of wavy, ginger-colored hair, is that of a man who would give anyone a break. Perched on his high stool in the enclosure betting ring, he met all comers joyfully, with a robust voice and feeble jokes. "Where did you dig that one up?" he would ask a client who bet a long shot. "I'll give you my watch if it wins." If the bettor was a steady customer, he sometimes gave him an extra point. Ignoring the odds of 17 to 5 marked on his slate, he would magnanimously make it 18. This was usually a sign he was sure the horse would lose. Win or lose, however, Tim maintains his smile. It did not come off even after a filly called Sally's Alley won the Futurity Stakes in 1922. Tim, who had been contemptuous of the filly, dropped sixty thousand dollars on the race. "I been shot at by sharpshooters," he said afterward. Wise bettors have found him a more difficult target since.

Because of his apparently excellent connections, Tim in 1926 became a figure in national politics as manifested in the professional prize ring. James A. Farley was then Chairman of the New York State Athletic Commission. Farley, who had always dreamed of luring the colored voters away from the Republican party, had recognized Harry Wills as the leading contender for the world's heavyweight championship, then held by Jack Dempsey, who was in notoriously poor shape. Gene Tunney, an Irish-American heavyweight born in Greenwich Village, also was challenging Dempsey. Tex Rickard, the promoter, preferred this match. But since the New York Irish always voted Democratic anyway, there were no votes to gain by aiding Tunney. Tunney's manager, Billy Gibson, was a bookmaker of the common grandstand variety. Scrambling for political support, Gibson thought that Mara could induce Governor Smith to overrule the Athletic Commission. In return for Tim's influence, Gibson and Tunney promised him twenty-five per cent of the fighter's earnings as champion if Tunney beat Dempsey. The influence didn't work. Eventually, however, Rickard put the match on in Philadelphia, where it drew more than a million dollars, and Tunney won the title. When Mara asked for his share of the earnings, Tunney said that since Mara had not done anything for him, he owed nothing to Mara. After Tunney retired as champion, in 1928, the bookmaker brought action against him for $405,000. The Mara-Tunney suit came to trial in the New York Supreme Court in the fall of 1930. The jury found for Tunney. Mara's attorneys appealed for a new trial. Tunney in 1932 paid Mara $30,000 to settle the case, and since then both men have claimed a victory.

Before the autumn of 1925, Mara had never seen a football game. In that season he became the owner of New York's first big-league professional football team. Bookmakers, like clergymen and physicians, are famous for their susceptibility to new forms of investment. So when promoters of the National League of Professional Football Clubs, which had begun in the Middle West, decided to invade New York, they offered the franchise to Mara. He bought it because it cost only $2500. He hired Bob Folwell, former coach at the Naval Academy, to assemble a team.

The first edition of the Giants included a glittering set of names, but wasn't a particularly good team by professional standards. Mara's publicity man distributed vast numbers of complimentary tickets. He even supplied a band and a cheering section of small boys to simulate college atmosphere. But the Giants lost money until the postseason game against Red Grange and the Chicago Bears. In 1925, Grange was America's leading hero. When, at the end of the 1925 intercollegiate season, he turned professional and his New York debut was announced, the ticket line began to form at Mara's office in the Knickerbocker Building. Thousands of enthusiasts were turned away from the Polo Grounds on the Sunday of the game. The contest drew $56,000 and gave Tim such a millennial vision of what professional football might eventually be that he became an irrepressible football fan. On one occasion, when his Giants beat the Bears in Chicago, 3–0, he rushed out on the field like a freshman to grab the ball from the referee. "The winning team gets the ball!" he yelled, a stickler for campus tradition. The referee didn't know him and waved him away. Tim grappled with him; some Chicago players joined the scuffle, and when Tim broke away, there were cleat marks on his habitual spats. But he had the ball under his arm.

The president of Mara University, as those whimsical fellows, the sports writers, sometimes term the football Giants, usually watches the games from a window of the baseball Giants' clubhouse behind center field. He gets enough fresh air at the race track in summer, he says. Ever since Tim started the team, his immediate family has gone football-mad. Mrs. Mara, an attractive, young-looking woman whom Tim married in 1907, made an important suggestion at the first game she saw. She noticed that the Giants' bench was on the south side of the field, and as twilight came on was in shadow. She said the Giants ought to move to the warm side and let the visiting postgraduates suffer. Tim's sons, although neither played football at Fordham, have developed into subtle theorists from attending Giant practice.

Mara's most startling peculiarity does not at once meet the

eye. It takes time to explain, and most people are incredulous even after he explains it. Mara is destitute. His only assets are about one hundred dollars in pocket cash and two watches. This poverty, in which he takes a good deal of honest, jovial pride, stems from another law suit, which closely followed his wrangle with Tunney. In 1928, after Al Smith had been nominated for President on the Democratic ticket, out-of-town Democrats showed a marked reluctance to contribute to the Smith campaign fund. John J. Raskob, National Chairman of the party, turned for aid to the County Trust Company of New York, a bank friendly to Tammany. A state law forbids banks to lend funds to political parties. The County Trust officers, however, said they saw no objection to lending money to responsible Democrats on their own notes, endorsed by Raskob. In spite of Smith's having disappointed him in the Tunney affair, Mara signed a note for $50,000, and the bank turned the cash over to the Democratic National Committee. Other Tammany men of substance signed similar notes. After the election, the bank moved to collect on the notes. Mara and several of the other signees were at first astonished, then indignant. They protested that the notes had been dummies, made so that the bank might have collateral to show for its loans to the party. They admitted an agreement that, if the National Committee failed to raise $4,000,000 for its campaign, it might use the notes. But, Mara said, the records of the committee showed it had raised $4,006,000 in cash. The bank sued Mara and Patrick Kenny, a Yonkers contractor, in a test case. Smith administered the *coup de grâce* to his beautiful friendship with Mara by appearing on the stand for the County Trust.

"The jury didn't believe him," Tim recalls with relish. "They believed me." But although the jury absolved Mara and Kenny, the bank wouldn't. For two years the case dragged through the higher courts, and the County Trust won its appeal. When it tried to collect, the bank found that Mara was legally destitute, although he appeared the picture of prosperity. He had founded a large and flourishing coal firm, the Mara Fuel Company; his wife and his brother owned all the stock in it. His sons owned the football team, now consistently profitable. As for the book-making business conducted under his name, Tim said he had no financial interest in it; he was just a manager. Tim's credit customers of the track received weekly statements and settled by check, but he had no bank account. When the customers won, they got checks signed by Walter Kenny, Tim's cashier, who is a son of his codefendant.

Tim's destitution does not interfere with his enjoyment of life. Daily he visits the various business enterprises in which he has no financial interest. During the racing season, he still spends all his afternoons at the track, nowadays in the character of a simple bettor. Periodically he makes trips to Washington, from which he returns with casual anecdotes of what he said to important politicians and what they said to him. Occasionally he plays golf. Last fall, shortly before the Elks made him an honorary life member, he presented them with an organ. Jimmy Walker accepted the gift in the name of the lodge.

Tim has his sentimental side. He enjoys singing ballads like "The Rose of Tralee." He even has his softer moments at the track. During one spring meeting at Jamaica, he was touched to the core by the fine spirit of a man who insisted on paying him fifty dollars which the man said he had borrowed from Tim fifteen years before. Tim accepted the money under protest. In the next race, the mysterious stranger bet him two hundred dollars on a horse named Galloping, 2 to 1 to show, and won four hundred dollars from him. "Maybe," Tim says, "it would have been better if I'd never seen the bum."

• Your Hat, Sir? •

In the year 1904 a man named Harry Susskind, then in his early twenties, looked through a window of Captain Jim Churchill's crowded restaurant at Forty-sixth Street and Broadway. He noticed that the male patrons laid their overcoats and hats on chairs and balanced their walking sticks precariously against tables. This represented a loss of income to Captain Churchill, a retired police officer, since obviously if every third or fourth chair was occupied by an overcoat, the space available for customers was reduced by a third or a quarter. To Susskind, the overcoats represented a financial future. He went in and proposed that Captain Churchill set aside a corner of the vestibule for coat racks. He offered to provide a couple of girls to help customers off with their coats, to check them, and return them as the customers went out. This would, incidentally, relieve Captain Churchill of responsibility for hats that customers sometimes exchanged by mistake and for canes that bibulous owners insisted they had brought into Churchill's when as a matter of fact the sticks were safe in the umbrella stand at home. Susskind promised to wear a uniform and personally supervise the checking. Over and above all the services he proposed to render, he offered Captain Churchill three thousand dollars a year. Churchill had considered hiring a couple of wardrobe attendants himself, but had boggled at the extra expense. He accepted Susskind's offer on the spot, and the young man became the first lessee of a hat-check concession in New York. Susskind made a profit of about twenty-five thousand dollars in his first year at Churchill's.

Susskind had a good idea of the true value of such a concession because he had worked as a hat-check boy, in pea jacket and tight pants, at the Café Martin on Fifth Avenue, and later at the brand-new Astor. At these smart resorts and a few others, hat-checking had existed for a long time, but the managements had never thought of renting out the concession. In some places, attendants were allowed to retain their tips in lieu of salaries. In others, hat-check rights were granted to a headwaiter or doorman as a perquisite of office. The owners of these gratuitous concessions paid the salaries of the hat-check boys and received from them what proportion of their tips the boys thought it prudent to yield. Only an ex-hat-check boy could understand the vastness of the possibilities.

The titular *vestiaire* at Martin's was an old retainer named Louis, who paid nothing for the concession. Louis' boys used to palm alternate tips and drop the coins inside their uniforms. They wore long underdrawers in those days, and coins would remain safe between the legs of the drawers and the skin of the wearer. Despite the leakage of silver, the concessionaire grew wealthy. Susskind had had opportunity to study the Broadway mentality at the Astor and decided that pretty girls would draw heavier tips than boys. He had also learned that it was extremely flattering to regular patrons to memorize their faces and say, "No check," when they gave him their wraps. Recognition enhanced their self-esteem, and they tipped generously. He taught this mnemonic method of boosting tips to his employees at Churchill's, where he paid his girls twenty-five dollars a week.

When the concessionaire, wise to the ways of checkers, was

in personal charge of his business, he could exercise a vigilance impossible to a hotel functionary with other duties. If he thought a girl was stealing an unreasonable amount, he could discharge her. By trial and error he could build up a fairly reliable personnel. Susskind bought more concessions with his profits from Churchill's. When George Rector seceded from his father's restaurant and opened his own place on Forty-eighth Street, Susskind paid him three thousand dollars for his coatroom concession before he opened. Shortly before the United States entered the World War, Susskind, in partnership with his brother Joe, ran the cloakrooms of sixty restaurants and employed six hundred men and women. Harry continued to wear his uniform at Churchill's, which had moved to larger quarters twice since he opened shop there. Joe wore the livery of the Hotel Knickerbocker, where the brothers had an extremely profitable concession. The Susskinds put managers in their concessions in other restaurants, paying them a small percentage of the profits. Complete honesty is not expected in the hat-check business, and most of the managers stayed within reason.

The public was more ingenuous then than now, and most restaurant patrons believed that the Susskinds' girls retained their tips. The girls wore a kind of musical-comedy French-maid costume and put their tips in their apron pockets as they received them. The Susskinds were wise enough not to install the locked boxes into which many present-day hat-check operatives drop their tips as soon as they get them. But the arrangement could not be kept a secret indefinitely. S. Jay Kaufman of the old *Globe* and Karl K. Kitchen of the *Evening World*, who were the Broadway columnists of circa 1917, gave the true state of affairs considerable publicity. Harry Susskind began to sense an undertone of antagonism. People kidded him about driving to work in a special-body Cadillac and then donning a hat-check attendant's uniform. Susskind lived in style in those days. He had an apartment on Riverside Drive, then fashionable, a house in Pelham, and a camp in the Adirondacks. His two children attended the Edgewood School in Greenwich, where, he likes to recall, they were classmates of a Rockefeller child.

Hat-checking was no longer a dignified business, the Susskind brothers decided when the criticism increased. Even worse than the effect of the publicity on tipping, which fell off sharply, was the invasion of the hat-check field by cloak-and-suiters with money to invest. Bids for concessions rose and the margin of potential profit decreased. By that time the brothers had accumulated about one million dollars and they retired. Joe Susskind died in 1930. Harry opened several large restaurants, invested in real estate, played the stock market heavily, and lost virtually everything he had. Then, a small, gnomish, gray-haired man, slightly cynical about everything, he was back in the hat-check business. He leased the concession at a minor night club on West Fifty-second Street, until it closed.

There is practically no illusion about the hat-check business now. A well-founded skepticism governs most patrons' reactions. Resentful customers often say to girls, "Here's ten cents for you and ten cents for the greaseball you work for"—a remark as unsound as it is wounding, for the girl has to surrender the twenty cents anyway. A few out-of-town visitors may retain their naïveté, but there is little consolation for the concessionaire in them. Some are so naïve that they do not tip at all. Hat-checking has evolved into a cold, calculating, highly competitive industry.

The girls have a union—Wardrobe and Checkroom Attendants' Union, Local No. 135—with a scale of minimum wages. Its office is at 1650 Broadway. If a member is caught by her employer "knocking down" a tip, her union card is suspended. Mr. Benny Jacobs, business secretary of the local, acts as a casting director for night-club proprietors. Some like blond girls, some brunettes, to match the color schemes of their places. Jacobs gets requests for pert girls or cultured types to fit places with swing or class atmosphere. John Perona of El Morocco, for example, insists on tall, cultured brunettes, although the local argued him into taking a young woman with dark chestnut hair as an experiment. Concessionaires usually let proprietors specify the type of comeliness they require. The union has seven hundred members, and there are seldom more than four hundred employed simultaneously, so a considerable range of types is always available. Many of the girls are members of Chorus Equity too.

Girls earn twenty-five dollars a week in what Local No. 135 calls Class A clubs. In this group it includes El Morocco, the Stork Club, Fefe's Monte Carlo and like places. In the smaller Class B clubs, girls get twenty dollars. Not only cloakroom girls but cigarette and flower vendors and washroom matrons belong to the union, which is affiliated with the Building Service Employees' International of the American Federation of Labor. Checkroom workers in the hotels are not organized and earn less than the night-club girls, a condition for which various excuses are offered. Union girls in night clubs work approximately nine hours a night for six nights a week. They are entitled to one week's vacation with pay for every nine months they work, if the club lasts nine months.

All night-club concessions now include the doorman, the washroom attendants, the cigarette girls, the girls who sell stuffed dogs, limp dolls, and gardenias, programs in places vast enough to have them, and any other little item the concessionaire chooses to peddle.

"For every girl up front taking clothes from the customers and giving them back, you got to have two people behind the counter putting coats on racks and seeing they don't get mixed," one entrepreneur says. "If the front girl kept the tips, who would pay the hangers? And then how about the washroom attendants? In the average night club, they don't take in as much as you pay them." This is a routine defense among concessionaires.

Reputedly the most successful concessionaire is a vehement, youngish man named A. (for Abraham) Ellis, who does business under the name of Planetary Recreations, Inc., from an office on an upper floor of the Manhattan Opera House, which he now owns. He bought the old theater with profits from the hat-check business. He operates the ballrooms and banquet halls at the Opera House, and his customers check a lot of coats. Ellis leases the concessions at half a score of other restaurants. He became involved in theatricals in 1935 when he paid $15,000 for concessions at *The Eternal Road*, the big Reinhardt production that was delayed for a year by money troubles. Before the show could open, Ellis had to contribute $4000 toward the Equity bond to cover actors' salaries. He lost $10,000 on the deal. If the show had had a long run, he says, he would have made "a fortune of money." For the three years of the French Casino's success, Ellis had the concession there. He paid a flat sum of $31,000 a year, with a percentage arrangement that brought the total up to $50,000 annually. When Billy Rose took over the place during the winter he raised Ellis' rent to $40,000 in advance and a percentage. Ellis paid about $20,000 for the Cotton Club.

The Stork Club concession was rented for $15,000 to a syndicate of employees. The proprietors of "21" long ago presented their concession to Jimmy, a doorman who is said to have saved them from infinite grief during the prohibition period. Renée Carroll, the red-haired girl at Sardi's, pays nothing for her concession, because the management values her gift for remembering the names of moving-picture publicity men and making them feel like celebrities.

The most conservative concessionaires operate in hotels. A painfully sedate and now defunct graduate doorman named J. Bates Keating had the concessions at the Astor, the Pierre, and the Edison for many years. He liked to talk about the unobtrusiveness of his service—no vulgar, obstreperous flower or cigarette girls pushing sales. Cigarette girls in hotels work for the lessee of the stand in the lobby. The Waldorf retains its own checkrooms, but pays ten per cent of the gross receipts to the manager, an experienced concessionaire.

The strangest feature of the hat-checking business is the complete absence of tangible merchandise or a fixed charge. The stock in trade consists of cardboard checks, worth two dollars a thousand wholesale, and the customer is not allowed to retain even the check when he leaves. A patron who takes his hat and walks out, paying nothing to the check girl, is liable to no pursuit, physical or legal. In reputable resorts, the contract between concessionaire and proprietor specifies that no patron is to be caused embarrassment. Yet less than one per cent of the people who use checkrooms omit the tip.

Shortly before the war, there was a national crusade against tipping. The shocking discovery that many tippees turned over their take to a third party spurred the crusaders. Governor Charles S. Whitman of New York was a leading anti-tipper, and the city had a Society for the Prevention of Useless Giving. A man named William Rufus Scott, of Paducah, Kentucky, wrote a book called *The Itching Palm* which urged the human race to give up tipping. Scott said that the psychological basis of tipping was one part misguided generosity, two parts pride, and one part fear of being unfavorably noticed. The last motive is unquestionably important. During the hours when checking is desultory, the patron walking up to the counter feels that he has the undivided attention of the cloakroom staff. He probably tips a quarter. When patrons are leaving in a hurry at the close of a floor show, men sneak in dimes. The more efficient concessionaires keep hour-by-hour graphs that prove this.

"A tip is what one American is willing to pay to induce another American to acknowledge inferiority" was another of Scott's dicta. Largesse exalts the ego of the tipper in almost exact ratio to the inconsequence of the service. Heralds in the Middle Ages had a nice living in gratuities from feudal landlords who would hang a peasant for holding out a ducat of rent. The state of Washington once passed a law against tipping, but repealed it after a couple of years because people tipped anyway and juries wouldn't convict.

The most plausible hypothesis of modern tip motivation was promulgated by Louis Reverdy, a French lawyer, in his thesis, "Le Pourboire," for the Doctor of Laws degree of the Sorbonne in 1930. Reverdy says that men first tipped for display. Now, he thinks, they tip from a sense of duty, since they realize that the tips constitute the tippee's means of livelihood. This is true even when the customer knows that the cloakroom girl works for a concessionaire and when he feels that it is the duty of the restaurant to check his coat free. For he knows that the individual girl will lose her job if nobody tips her. By withholding his tip, he would sacrifice an amiable individual to a cold principle. The chances are that he is inspired to even greater sympathy if the girl happens to be comely. Concessionaires, of course, are aware of this and pick their girls accordingly, but they place no premium on actually beautiful girls. "A girl who's a real knockout gets herself a guy in a couple of weeks," Abe Ellis once explained, "and then you got to break in another girl."

The contemporary tipper gets little positive pleasure from

tipping. Less than one per cent of the patrons at the French Casino tipped fifty cents, and there was no significant correlation between the amount patrons spent in the restaurant and the size of the tips they gave in the lobby. Most men oscillate between the dime and quarter levels, the average tip at a large Broadway place being sixteen cents. Girls report that at East Side clubs like El Morocco there may be a slightly higher ratio of quarter tippers to dime tippers. But fifty-cent-plus tippers are as rare on the East Side as on Broadway. Perhaps twice a week, in any club doing a large volume of business, eccentric patrons tip girls five dollars or more. The recipient is allowed to keep half of any tip in this class, turning the rest in to the concessionaire.

Men in the hat-check business admit that the customers don't enjoy tipping. But, they say, nobody ever went to an unpopular place merely because of free hat-checking. And conversely, when people want to attend a certain club, they don't stay home because of the cost of checking their hats. They are fond of telling how the Café Savarin on lower Broadway once abolished tipping, only to have the patrons force the money on the girls, and how the Hotel Algonquin had the same experience.

At private banquets in the Astor, hosts sometimes stipulate there shall be no tipping of cloakroom attendants. Keating, the concessionaire, used to cite one such affair attended by the late Nathan Straus, the free-milk man. Mr. Straus gave the girl a dollar. She handed it back to him. The thwarted philanthropist threw the dollar behind the counter and walked out. The experience of the Hotel Pennsylvania conflicts with these happy reminiscences of concessionaires. The Pennsylvania and all the other Statler hotels abolished hat-check concessions and hat-check tipping in 1933. Far from resenting this change, the Statler people say, patrons now check thirty-three and a third more articles per capita than they ever did before. At the restaurants Longchamps, where the hat-check tip is included in the ten-per-cent service charge, most patrons seem content to let it go at that.

The most skilled operatives of the concession business are not the young women of the cloakroom or the hangers who work behind the counter but the cigarette and novelty girls. They need salesmanship to maintain their level of sales and tips, and tact to avoid arguments with customers. If a girl is the subject of a complaint to the management, she generally loses her job. The worst sin a girl can commit is to recognize a man accompanied by a woman and remind him of a previous visit. The woman may be his wife and his previous companion may not have been. Standard brands of cigarettes sell for twenty-five cents in night clubs, and a girl's tips are expected to equal her gross sales. In the large Broadway clubs, the girls are sometimes demure, but at East Side places, the girls say, "A girl has got to talk very direct." "If you want to sell cigarettes to those guys," one girl reported, "you got to say things that would shock a medium-class man." The business of being a cigarette girl is so complex and requires so much ingenuity that a star can sometimes command thirty dollars a week.

"A good cigarette girl," Abe Ellis has said, "is far and in between. She has got to know just when to lay off and when to knock the customer down. And selling stuffed dogs to grown-up women is an art in itself."

The chief technical problem of the hat-check industry since its inception has been the safe conveyance of the customer's quarter to the pocket of the concessionaire. The girl receiving a tip can seldom conquer the atavistic notion that it was meant for her personally. Even hiring a watcher for each girl would not preclude collusion. Since there are no fixed rates of tipping, it is impossible to tell from the receipts on any given evening whether the girls have held out anything.

When the Susskind brothers ran virtually all the concessions in town, they used a common-sense personal-confidence sort of system which kept their help from robbing them too flagrantly. But since they obtained their leases cheaply, they could afford a good deal of tip leakage. Competitors, bidding against the brothers, reduced the margin of profit. Consequently they worked harder to protect their receipts, putting the girls in tight, pocketless uniforms and making them drop their tips through a slot in the counter as soon as they got them. Under the counter was a locked box.

Modern concessionaires, more efficient, use a variation of the Bedaux System. They keep charts from which they establish a norm of production for each girl and location. The concessionaire knows, when he goes into a new restaurant, approximately what to expect. If there is a minimum charge of $1.50, for example, the tipping should compare with that at the old Paradise. He will then expect, from each hundred tippers, a return of about thirteen dollars. The first crew of girls he puts in his new concession are reasonably safe if they approach that standard. The girls do not know exactly what their boss expects, so the assumption is they will try hard to make a good showing. After a few weeks, the concessionaire switches the girls to another place and brings in a new set. If the receipts fall off noticeably, he suspects the replacements. If receipts rise, he suspects the first group. He shifts individual girls in the same way. If a hypothetical Billie, checking hats at a certain club for a month, turns in an average of eleven cents a customer, while an equally hypothetical Mamie over a similar period averages sixteen cents, he bounces Billie. By continued shifts, he establishes an average for the place. This may not turn out the same as the average at the Paradise, however. The new club may get a high ratio of Southern patronage, which brings the average tip down, or of "collegiates," notoriously poor tippers, or of race-track men, notoriously good ones.

After each tour of the house, a cigarette girl turns in all the cash she has received. In this way she has no chance to hoard her tips for the evening. She might decide, if they were unusually good, that she could safely knock down a dollar for herself. Even at that, most cigarette girls manage to keep some part of their tips. Concessionaires never know exactly how much, but if the girl is a "producer," they don't care.

"Better a kid who takes ten in tips and knocks a buck," a pillar of the industry once said, "than a dummy who gets half the tips and turns in all she gets. But please don't use my name, because on such a question I hate to quote myself."

• The Boys from Syracuse •

Commonly, when a family achieves such fame that it has a street named in its honor, it moves to a better part of town. There are no Roosevelts on Roosevelt Street, no Astors within blocks of Astor Place, and no Vanderbilts on Vanderbilt Avenue except when Brigadier General Cornelius Vanderbilt pays an occasional visit to the Yale Club. Lee and J.J. Shubert, however, live almost entirely in, above, and around Shubert Alley, which runs from Forty-fourth to Forty-fifth Streets between Broadway and Eighth Avenue. The Alley, although it has a sidewalk and a roadway for automobiles, is a private street, part of the property rented to the Shuberts by the Astor Estate in 1912 on a lease which still has sixty-nine years to run. The rest of the leased area is covered by the Shubert, Booth, Plymouth, and Broadhurst theaters. Lee Shubert's private office is in the turret at the southeast corner of the Shubert Theatre building. His desk is directly above the "u" in the theater's sign. J.J., who long ago conceived a seignoral disdain for his given name of Jacob, lives just across Forty-fourth Street, on the tenth floor of the Sardi Building, which the Shuberts own; the sixth floor is given over to his offices. J.J. often says that he likes to live upstairs from his business. Lee has an apartment adjoining his offices on the fifth floor of the Shubert, but he seldom uses this suite except for shaves and sun-ray treatments, both endured in a barber chair which he has had installed there. He prefers to sleep in the Century Apartments, on the site of the old Century Theatre on Central Park West. Even there he is not outside the Shubert sphere, for the brothers hold a second mortgage on the apartment building.

The Messrs. Shubert have been the largest operators in the New York theater for so long that only a few persons remember that they were once boy wonders in Syracuse, where both of them were running theaters before they had reached their twenties. City records in Syracuse show that Lee was born there sixty-six years ago and J.J. five years later, but the brothers still have the brisk and querulous quality of two combative small boys who feel the teacher is down on them. A few years ago they addressed a manifesto to New York dramatic editors, insisting that they be referred to by the collective designation of "the Messrs. Shubert." "Lee and Jake," they felt, sounded much too flippant. Lee takes a quiet pride in being known as the fastest walker on Broadway. He walks fast even when he doesn't know where he is going. J.J. is distinguished for his bitter vehemence at rehearsals. "There is only one captain on this ship," he once shouted while rehearsing a musical, "the director and me!"

When Lee, in his office in the Shubert Theatre, wishes to communicate with J.J., in the Sardi Building, he summons Jack Morris, his secretary, and says, "Take a letter to Mr. J.J." When J.J. wishes to communicate with Lee, he says to his secretary, "Take a letter to Mr. Lee." This custom has given rise to a theater-district legend that the brothers are mortal enemies and do not speak at all. The legend is not founded on fact. When either of the Shuberts is really in a hurry to discuss something with the other, he walks across the street to do so. An even more fanciful theory has it that the story of animosity between the two has been fostered for business reasons by the Shuberts themselves. The exponents of this theory contend that when Lee wants to get out of a deal, he says that J.J. will not allow him to go through with it, and that when J.J. wants to get out of a deal, he blames Lee. Actually there is no overt hostility between the brothers. Mr. J.J. says that it was the intention of the Messrs., when they collaborated in the construction of the Sardi Building in 1926, to move all their executive offices there from the somewhat constricted quarters on the upper floors of the Shubert Theatre. That summer, Mr. J.J., who sometimes explains a predilection for foreign musical shows by saying, "I am more dynamic and Continental than Mr. Lee," made his annual trip to Europe to inspect the new vintage of operettas. When he returned, he found that his office furniture had been moved into the new building, but that Mr. Lee had treacherously remained in the Shubert Theatre. The Shubert enterprises have been a two-headed organism ever since, with Mr. Lee's casting department and executive staff on the north side of Forty-fourth Street and Mr. J.J.'s on the south side. The publicity and auditing departments are on Mr. J.J.'s side of the street; the real-estate, theater-booking, and financial departments are on Mr. Lee's. The balance of power is worked out to the last milligram: Mrs. Lillian Duffy, the plump, white-haired receptionist in Mr. Lee's office, has the authority to hire all girl ushers for Shubert theaters; Mrs. Loretta Gorman, Mrs. Duffy's practically identical sister, is Mr. J.J.'s receptionist and hires all the theater charwomen. But the brothers, like most two-headed creatures, have a single life line. All their real estate is held in common, and they have a joint checking account. The separate-office arrangement resembles one of those dual households advocated by married female novelists. The Shuberts retain community of interests, but avoid friction; each produces shows without interference from the other. Failure of one of Mr. J.J.'s shows is made easier for Mr. Lee to bear by the knowledge that it was Mr. J.J.'s idea.

Success is sweetened for Mr. Lee by the reflection that he will share in the profits. Things work out the same way on the other side of the street.

The brothers' chauffeurs amicably share the parking facilities of the Alley, which are also made available to producers and stars of companies playing the Shubert Theatre if the shows are hits. Katharine Hepburn, for instance, parked her car there regularly during the many months *The Philadelphia Story* filled the theater. Mr. Lee has three automobiles, all of them foreign—a Rolls-Royce, a Hispano-Suiza, and an Isotta-Fraschini. Mr. J.J. favors American cars. Mr. Lee explains that he has never owned any but European automobiles because when he is in this country he is too busy to go shopping. He finds his only moments of relaxation during cruises and trips abroad, when he sometimes has half an hour to spare. It was during one such trip that he signed up Carmen Miranda in Rio de Janeiro and brought her to New York to star in *The Streets of Paris*.

Mr. Lee comes to work every day shortly before noon. He leaves his desk to go home to the Century Apartments at three or four o'clock in the morning. When people ask him why he works such long hours, he says, "I am not a loafing kind of boy." The habit goes back to the days of the great commercial rivalry which existed for fifteen years between the Shuberts and the firm of Klaw & Erlanger. Abe Erlanger was an early riser. Once he told a friend, "I am up and at my desk while the Shuberts still are sleeping." Mr. Lee decided that the only way to beat Erlanger was to stay up all night. Erlanger and Marc Klaw, his partner, are now dead, but Mr. Lee still can't sleep nights. J.J. attributes his brother's outrageous workday to the fact that Lee has always been a bachelor. Although J.J. himself has not had a wife since he was divorced in 1918, he says that the experience of marriage, no matter how far in the past, so changes a man's metabolism that he never again wants to work more than twelve hours at a stretch. Shubert employees—house and company managers, play readers, and publicity men—have the sympathy of their professional colleagues, because they must remain virtually on call until Mr. Lee decides to go home. The Shubert play-reading department gets about fifty manuscripts a month throughout the year and filters the best ones through to Mr. Lee's office. Authors of these promising works are sometimes summoned at a grisly hour shortly before dawn to read their scripts aloud. Mr. Lee never reads a play himself; he merely looks at synopses drawn up by his readers. During an author's reading, Mr. Lee sometimes appears to fall asleep. This is a frightful experience for the playwright, who is afraid to offend the producer by awakening him and, in desperation, continues reading. Mr. Lee always maintains that he has heard every word. The concentration of the Shuberts on their business is looked upon by most theatrical people as unsporting. If the brothers were going to work so hard, these critics think, they should have taken up a trade instead of the theater. Mr. Lee's incessant activity, even though some of it is undoubtedly superfluous, has served him well during his forty-two years on Broadway. He has simply outworn most of his opponents.

Mr. Lee is a short man whose appearance is so ostentatiously youthful that he is usually suspected of being very old. His face is a deep copper red all year round, a result of the sun-ray treatments and sun baths which he takes whenever he gets a chance. A musical-comedy director, strolling near the Mazzini statue in Central Park one morning, saw Mr. Lee asleep in the open tonneau of one of his automobiles with his face turned toward the sun. Mr. Lee's chauffeur, also asleep, lolled in the front seat. Before the invention of the sun-ray lamp, it was customary for writers to mention Lee's "midnight pallor." Because of his high cheekbones, narrow eyes, and lank black hair, it was also customary to say that he looked Oriental. Now that he can take sun-ray treatments, his upturned eyebrows and the deep wrinkles at the corners of his eyes make him look something like a good-natured Indian—Willie Howard, perhaps, in war-chief make-up. Mr. Lee always wears conservative, well-fitted suits made for him by Gray & Lampel, on East Fifty-third Street, at $225 each, and he has a liking for thick-soled, handmade English shoes and pleated shirts, which he wears with stiff collars. He admires his extremely small feet. There is a sedulous avoidance of flashiness in his dressing, but nothing pleases him better than a compliment on his clothes. Joe Peters, Mr. Lee's valet, shaves him at eleven in the morning and at seven in the evening. When Mr. Lee needs a new valet, he goes to the Hotel Astor barbershop and hires a barber. It was there he got Peters and Peters' predecessor. He has had only three valets in thirty-two years. Mr. Lee takes good care of his figure. He often lunches on half a cantaloupe and an order of sliced tomatoes.

In contrast to his older brother, Mr. J.J. seems dumpy and rumpled. While Lee's hair is preternaturally black and lank, J.J.'s is gray and wavy. Although he is a small man, there is something taurine about the set of his neck and head, and there is a permanent suggestion of a pout on his lips. Mr. Lee's voice has an indefinable foreign intonation; he is always polite, tentatively friendly, and on guard. Mr. J.J., who has no trace of accent, can be an unabashed huckster, choleric and loud, but he can be warmer and more ingratiating than his brother when he wants to.

It is pretty nearly impossible to make a living in the American theater without encountering the Shuberts because they own, lease, or manage twenty of the forty-odd legitimate theaters in New York and control about fifteen theaters in other cities, a very high percentage of the total theaters, considering the low estate to which the road has declined. As theatrical landlords, the Shuberts have practically no real competitor in New York City, although Sam Grisman occasionally gets his hands on two or three theaters at a time. Theaters not owned or controlled by the brothers are for the most part in the hands of independent producers. Since the producer of a play usually turns over at least thirty-five per cent of the gross receipts as theater rent, the Shuberts, even if at any given time they had no show of their own running, could still conceivably be sharing in the profits of twenty attractions. This would give them by far the largest single take in the success of any theatrical season. In point of fact, however, they do produce shows. Like the movie-makers, they have to schedule their product with an eye to the number of theaters they must keep busy. If they have six theaters empty and only one manuscript of promise, they must go ahead and produce six shows anyway.

To make tenants for Shubert theaters, Lee, who is more active in theater management and real estate than his brother, will often finance another producer by lending him Shubert money on condition he brings his show into a Shubert house. The Shuberts have backed such disparate enterprises as the Group Theatre production of *Success Story* and a *jai-alai* tournament at the late Hippodrome. They supplied most of the money for *The Children's Hour* and *Shadow and Substance*, both earnest plays that the public would consider out of the Shubert line. Several years ago Mr. Lee backed Olsen and Johnson, a pair of vaudeville comedians, in expanding their seventy-minute unit show into a knockabout entertainment called *Hellz a Poppin*, which is still keeping the Shuberts' Winter Garden comfortably filled. When the Messrs. were sounded out on the production of a musical comedy for the World's Fair, Mr. Lee's reply—"Why should I make competition for my own houses?"—was typical. His creative instincts are weighed down by several thousand tons of concrete and twenty long-term leases. Inevitably the Shuberts make more bad bets than good ones. This does not mean that they lose money. "If we could hit one out of three," Mr. J.J. says very reasonably, "we would be doing fine."

When the Shuberts produce shows on their own account, they are likely to fall back on formulas that have served them well in the past. *The Student Prince* is typical of the Shubert tradition—the darling of the firm in retrospect and its present ideal. It made more money than any other show the Shuberts ever produced. When, in the season of 1925–26, there were nearly a dozen road companies of *The Student Prince* out, covering North America and Australia, the production sometimes grossed as much as $250,000 a week. Yet *The Student Prince* was only a musical adaptation of a German play that had already served the Shuberts well. On the first occasion, in 1903, they produced the play done into English and called *Old Heidelberg*, at the Princess Theatre. It was not conspicuously successful. Then they changed the name of the show to *Prince Karl*, got Richard Mansfield to play the title role, and put it into the Lyric, where it became a very remunerative hit. After the war a musical version of the original play appeared in Germany. The Shuberts commissioned Sigmund Romberg to write another score for the American edition. The late Dorothy Donnelly did the American book. Even today *The Student Prince* is not dead; he merely slumbers. The costumes for ten complete *Prince* companies hang in the Shubert storerooms at 3 West Sixty-first Street. In the Shuberts' opinion, *The Student Prince* is still a great show. Lee thinks it is not yet quite the time for a revival. He says that the time has to be right for any kind of show and that if the time is right for it, any kind of show is likely to catch on. "The trouble with a lot of producers," he has been known to explain, "is they have a couple of hits because the time is ripe for that sort of a show, and then they think they are geniuses, so they do the same sort of a show right over again, and it flops." A piece like *Hellz a Poppin*, for example, is not so much an innovation as a type of fast, unsubtle comedy which had been absent from Broadway so long that by 1938 it was new to a whole generation of playgoers. The Shuberts, true to form, followed through by having Olsen and Johnson more or less repeat themselves by working out gags for *The Streets of Paris*. If the brothers accept Mr. Lee's own advice, however, they won't attempt the same thing again—at least not right away.

The Shubert clichés are like an assortment of dry flies on which they try the public periodically. They don't expect a strike every time. J.J. is strongly committed to operettas, even though, as a concession to modernity, he will accept Cole Porter lyrics and an interpolated dance by the Hartmans now and then. Lee is more susceptible than his brother to current influences, because he gets around more. He takes advice from Harry Kaufman, a blocky, Broadway sort of chap with a wide, shining face, who began in the cloak-and-suit business and progressed into ticket brokerage. Kaufman, now in his middle forties, is active in the Tyson and Sullivan theater-ticket agencies, but he has a desk conveniently across the hall from Mr. Lee's in the Shubert Theatre. He divides his time between the agencies and Mr. Lee. Kaufman, through his ticket-selling connections, keeps his patron informed of box-office trends. "Mr. Shubert is the greatest affection of my life," says Kaufman. "He built the entire midsection of town, which is a weighty accomplishment. There is a bond of affection between us, and we have certain mutual ideas which we believe to be mutually sound, and in the long run we hope it will win." Kaufman serves as a scout for new talent. He saw some young people giving an impromptu Sunday-night revue in a camp at Bushkill, Pennsylvania, one summer and suggested to the Shuberts that it would be an inexpensive way of filling one of their theaters. Mr. Lee agreed, brought the show to New York as *The Straw Hat Revue*, and made a reasonably successful production of it. Kaufman also acts as a buffer between the Shuberts and stars already under contract to them. Kaufman has been known to send flowers to a sulking comedienne at his own expense. He is always the first to suggest that the star or the director of a Shubert company accept a cut in pay because the business is falling off. In one busy evening, Kaufman will go to dinner at a Broadway night club, where he hears a singer do a single number; to a play, to catch the big scene, and to a prize fight, timing his arrival to coincide with the round that promises the most action. In the intervals between these high spots he will stop in backstage at a couple of Shubert shows to see how things are running.

After such an eclectic three hours, Kaufman will return to Mr. Lee's office to play pinochle with him. Toward midnight, Mr. Lee's conferences with press agents and company managers begin. He often sandwiches hands of pinochle between conferences. When he has seen the last of his visitors, he and Kaufman sometimes make excursions to new night clubs to watch performers. Mr. Lee drinks very little—perhaps one brandy in the course of an evening—but he gets a certain stimulation from seeing lots of people around him. He returns to his office at three, to look at telegrams giving the receipts at theaters on the Pacific coast, where the time is three hours behind ours. Mr. Lee and Kaufman sometimes wander about the streets even after that, with a Shubert limousine trailing a short distance behind them. They wind up at Reuben's, on Fifty-eighth Street, where Mr. Lee usually drinks three cups of black coffee before heading for bed. These nocturnal walks have long been a habit of Mr. Lee's, and Kaufman is not the first of his walking companions. In former years, it is said, Mr. Lee on these walks paced off the dimensions of sites he intended to assemble for theaters. Now, at any rate, he walks just for exercise.

It was Kaufman who introduced Vincente Minnelli, the young designer and director, to Mr. Lee. Some of Minnelli's revues at the Winter Garden, like *At Home Abroad*, in 1935, and *The Show Is On*, in 1936, called for an investment entirely alien to the conservative Shubert tradition and shocked Mr. J.J.'s sensibilities. Mr. J.J. persists in preserving costumes and props, as well as ideas, from old productions. He sometimes escorts parties of contemporary chorus girls to the Sixty-first Street storerooms to try on the high headdresses and sequined pseudo-Orientalia of the 1913 Winter Garden show.

The Messrs. have entirely different styles of behavior at rehearsals. Mr. Lee is undemonstrative but insistent. Upon seeing a rehearsal of a play, he often commands the author to make the second act the first, the first act the last, and put the third act in the middle. This sometimes improves a play immeasurably. In theatrical matters, Mr. Lee has a tender heart. The late Sam Shipman once wrote a play about a boy brought up by his mother, whom the boy supposed to be a widow. In reality the mother was a divorcée. The brutal father returned and won the boy's sympathy. The boy deserted the mother at the end of the second act, before discovering what sort of cad the father had been. In the third act, of course, son came back to mother. Mr. Lee wouldn't stand for the boy's being away from the mother during the intermission. He made Shipman arrange to have the reunion before the second act ended. "What will I do for a third act?" Shipman asked him. "That's your business," Mr. Lee said. "I have a lot of other things to think of."

Mr. Lee often acts out bits in backstage corners for the benefit of his directors. "Look," he once told one of them, "anybody can play Cyrano. See?" He turned a chair around and straddled it, arms folded on the back, legs thrust out stiffly, as if in jack boots. Then he leaped lightly to his feet, flung an imaginary cape over his left shoulder, took two or three long strides, and jumped to *en garde*, an imaginary rapier in his right hand. "Da dill de-da," he said, thrusting briskly at an imaginary opponent. "Deedle dee dum! That's the way Mansfield used to do it. An actor like Everett Marshall can't miss!" When Mr. Lee feels that something is lacking in a musical show, he often says, "What we need here is a song that goes like this: 'Da, dum, de-dum-dum—dada, dada, de-dum, de-dum-dum.' " The tune always turns out to be "Sing Something Simple," but he never says so. Mr. Lee admires good actors, although he has spent the better part of his life trying to conceal that fact, because he does not want to pay them more than is necessary. Once, discussing actors, he said, "They are not an everyday-going class of people. They are very conceited, but the intelligence is still above the conceit." His respect for actors is tied up with his inability to picture himself as one. "Myself," he says, "I can't make an after-dinner talk even to half a dozen people. I must have some kind of complex."

Mr. J.J. screams at the chorus people in the shows he produces; to principals he is often polite. He has always admired tall women, and his shows are the last stronghold of the statuesque type of showgirl. No matter how engrossed he may become in the difficulties of putting on a show, he never forgets that he is first of all the owner of the theater. At the dress rehearsal just before the opening of *You Never Know* at the Winter Garden a couple of seasons ago, he was violently excited over the jerkiness of the production. "Such a stupid people," he repeated mournfully as he wandered, an incongruous little figure, among the ranks of showgirls, most of them six feet tall in their high heels. The chorus people were in costume; Mr. J.J., in his wrinkled gray suit, looked like a comedian about to liven up the scene. "Walk around some more!" he shouted. "Don't I get any use out of these dresses?" All at once he stopped the rehearsal and pointed in horror to a seat in the third row on which a Shubert underling had left a wet overcoat. Then he scrambled down off the stage, grabbed the coat, and held it aloft for the assembled cast to see. "Ruining my beautiful theater!" he howled. Shows come and go, their fate a matter of almost pure chance, but theater seats are the foundation of the Shuberts' fortune.

II

Before the Shuberts rose to eminence, the American theater was governed in totalitarian fashion by an organization known as the Syndicate, headed by Marc Klaw and Abe Erlanger. In 1905, when the Shubert brothers—Lee and J.J.—first defied the Syndicate, there were 5000 legitimate theaters in 3500 American cities. The Syndicate controlled the bookings of 1250 of these theaters; its list included almost every house that a first-class attraction could play with profit. The theaters were variously owned, but the Klaw & Erlanger booking office was the clearinghouse for shows, so Klaw & Erlanger could put any owner out of business by refusing to send him productions. They could put a producing manager out of business by denying him a route. The Shuberts fought this "malign octopus" (as the Shubert press agents usually referred to the Syndicate) until they had built up a benign octopus of their own, including nine hundred theaters that got shows through the Shubert office. Naturally, Mr. Lee and Mr. J.J. feel that the theater owes them a debt of gratitude for thus destroying a monopoly, but since few of the younger men in the trade remember the Syndicate, they are likely to consider the Shuberts themselves rather tentacular. This makes for what the Shuberts consider misunderstandings. During the jihad, or holy war, between the Shuberts and Klaw & Erlanger, the moving pictures gradually destroyed the legitimate theater in the provinces. Then the depression put a terrific crimp in it in New York. The theater in recent years has become a minor form of enterprise localized on Manhattan. But even though their army has shrunk to a squad, the Shuberts comport themselves like field marshals of industry. They have never taken to moving pictures. Mr. Lee says that the cinema is "a kind of make-believe."

The Shubert preoccupation with the theater dates back to 1885, when Sam, the eldest brother, now dead, made the only recorded appearances of a Shubert on the American stage. He was eleven years old, and his part was a walk-on in the first act of a Belasco production called *May Blossoms*, which at the time happened to be playing the Wieting Opera House at Syracuse. *May Blossoms*, a treacly thing, called for the engagement of four child actors in every town the company visited; this was much cheaper and less troublesome than taking children on the road. The company manager had picked Sam Shubert out of his classroom in the public school nearest the theater. The boy received a dollar a performance for a whole week, and the entire Shubert family, including ten-year-old Lee and five-year-old Jake, attended every night, on passes. The boys were entranced by this factitious world, so unlike the Seventh Ward, where the Shuberts and most other poor

Jews in Syracuse lived. David Shubert, the boys' father, peddled notions, underwear, and sundries among upstate farmers, riding out to the country on a train from Syracuse and then trudging from door to door with his wares on his back. *May Blossoms* gave Sam, Lee, and Jake their first intimation that there might be a pleasanter way of making a living. It was such a milestone in the Shuberts' lives that they later devised two operetta titles from that of the Belasco show. The operettas were *Maytime* and *Blossom Time*, both illustrious money-makers.

Sam was a precocious, imaginative boy. Since his death in 1905, the surviving brothers have agreed to consider him the family genius, and a portrait of him hangs in the lobby or lounge of every theater they operate. Soon after his dramatic debut, Sam became program boy at the Grand Opera House, the second-best theater in Syracuse, at $1.50 a week. Immediately his younger brothers' ambitions switched from the artistic to the commercial side of the theater, where they have been ever since. Sam was still wearing short pants when the manager of the Grand promoted him to assistant treasurer, which meant relief ticket seller. He had to stand on a box to reach the ticket window. When Sam moved over to the more elegant Wieting Opera House, at a higher salary, Lee succeeded him at the Grand. Lee, in his early teens, already had been an apprentice cigar maker and shirt cutter, and a haberdasher's clerk. The haberdasher was named Jesse Oberdorfer, and he, too, had theatrical inclinations. He was destined to be the first in a line of Shubert bank-roll men which since then has included George B. Cox, a Cincinnati millionaire; Andrew Freedman, Samuel Untermyer, and Jefferson Seligman. Syracuse had four legitimate theaters in the nineties. A job in a good provincial theater was the best possible introduction to the profession, for stars spent most of their time and earned most of their money on the road. Sam and Lee Shubert met actors like Richard Mansfield, Nat Goodwin, and Joe Jefferson in Syracuse. Before Sam and Lee were twenty, they rented road companies of *A Texas Steer* and *A Black Sheep* from Charles H. Hoyt, the author-manager, guaranteeing him a fixed return for the use of the productions which he had assembled and trained. The boys managed the companies, sent them wherever they could get a profitable booking, paid the actors' salaries, and made money on the deal. The formative years of the Shuberts resembled a piece by Horatio Alger or the editors of *Fortune*. They ran a stock company in Syracuse, cornered all four theaters there, and added houses in near-by Buffalo, Rochester, Albany, Troy, and Utica, and in Portland, Maine. Of these cities, only Buffalo and Rochester have so much as one legitimate theater now.

Sam and Lee drafted Brother Jake into the business when he was fourteen. Sam was not content with prosperity upstate; he wanted to produce plays, and a producer had to have a theater in New York City as a show window. Then, as now, an attraction could obtain few bookings on the road unless it had had a New York run. So, in 1900, Sam Shubert went down to New York, accompanied by the faithful haberdasher Oberdorfer, who had a bank roll of some thirty thousand dollars. Sam leased the Herald Square Theatre, a small, unpretentious house just across Thirty-fifth Street from the present site of Macy's. Lee followed Sam from Syracuse, leaving Jake in charge of the theaters upstate. Sam and Lee cajoled Mansfield into opening their theater for them with his production of *Julius Caesar*, an event which left little profit for the brothers because Mansfield took virtually all the receipts, but which immediately gave their theater prestige. The brothers followed up by leasing two more theaters and producing *Arizona*, *A Chinese Honeymoon*, and *Fantana*, all highly profitable shows. *Old Heidelberg*, a Shubert enterprise that looked like a failure at first, became a great success when, after the show had been renamed *Prince Karl*, Mansfield took over the leading role. The Shuberts, like everybody else in the industry, booked through Klaw & Erlanger.

All the Shubert hits up to this point, as Sam and Lee well understood, had been achieved by sufferance of the Syndicate. Klaw & Erlanger had established their dominion over the theater industry by performing a real service. Before their advent in the late eighties, the business had been in an impossibly confused state. It was then the custom of every house manager in America to come to New York and bargain for attractions with producers, usually in saloons around Union Square. Producers often booked their shows into two theaters for the same week, so that they would be sure to find one theater available when the playing date arrived. Managers just as often booked two shows for the same week, so that they would be sure of having some sort of production in their houses. If both attractions arrived on schedule, the manager would pick the better of the two. If a show had booked two towns for the same week and both theaters were available, the producer would pick the one promising the greater profit. It was practically impossible to enforce a contract. The owner of the Opera House in Red Wing, Minnesota, for example, could not very well abandon his theater and chase out to California to sue a defaulting road company even if the troupe had any assets worth attaching. Nor could the manager of a traveling company abandon his show while he waited upon the slow processes of the law in some Iowa town where the theater owner refused to honor a contract.

The Syndicate changed all this. It offered a steady supply of shows to member theaters and a full season's booking to producers in good standing, and it was in a position to enforce its rulings in case of dispute. By the time the Shuberts arrived upon the scene, however, Klaw & Erlanger had turned their control of the industry into a tyranny. Ordinarily, producers paid the Syndicate seven and a half per cent of their gross receipts in return for bookings, but when Erlanger "asked" the producer for a higher percentage, the producer had to comply or fold up. In the same way, a theater owner who wanted a particularly strong attraction had to pay a high premium to the Klaw & Erlanger office to get it.

The Syndicate, in order to protect its supremacy, had only to see to it that no one built up a chain of theaters powerful enough to support a rival booking office. When it began to look as if the Shuberts might do just that, Erlanger tried to curb them by refusing to route their musical comedy called *The Girl from Dixie* unless the brothers would agree to lease no more theaters.

The youthful Shuberts interpreted the refusal as a challenge. They announced the opening of an independent circuit of theaters that would play any man's show. The public had not yet forgotten the Boxer Campaign, and the Shubert press agent, J. Frank Wilstach, revived a slogan that John Hay had made popular in those days, "The Open Door." As a nucleus for their enterprise, the Shuberts had leases on three theaters in Manhattan and eight more upstate, and they had found a few other theater owners who were angry enough to pull out of the Syndicate with them. The brothers filled their circuit by renting vaudeville and burlesque houses in a number of towns and using them for legitimate shows. They had two principal allies among the producers in their campaign. One was Harrison Grey Fiske, the husband of Minnie Maddern Fiske. He had already offended the Syndicate, and for years his wife had been refused road bookings, although she was so great a star that she had been able to play steadily in New York. The other Shubert ally was David Belasco, who accused Abe Erlanger of muscling in for half the profits of his success *The Auctioneer*. The new combination wasn't much competition for the Syndicate at first, but after the Shuberts had confounded predictions by staggering through one season, they began to get more support. Any theater man could see the advantage of maintaining a competitive market.

At the beginning of each theatrical season during the great war for the theatrical Open Door, newspapers in every city in the land carried reports that the local playhouse was "going Shubert" or "staying Syndicate." It was a question of enormous import in one-theater towns. If the house went Shubert, the town might see David Warfield, Mrs. Leslie Carter, and Mrs. Fiske. If it stayed Syndicate, the matinee girls would be permitted to ogle William Faversham and the young men would have a chance to gape at Anna Held. Within a very brief time the boys from Syracuse became national figures. As underdogs, anti-monopolists, and employers of a succession of good publicity men, they had public sentiment with them. Editorial cartoonists usually drew them as three very small Semitic Davids (Jake, twenty-three, was by now almost an equal partner) squaring off to a corpulent Goliath labeled "Syndicate." To offset the Shubert good will, the Syndicate had most of the material advantages. Klaw & Erlanger had seldom built theaters, for they had been able to control enough of the houses already existing. The Shuberts had to build theaters in cities where they could not otherwise get a foothold, and they had to find financial backing for these theaters. Cox, the moneyed gentleman from Cincinnati, was one of their principal stand-bys in this phase of the fight. Lee Shubert has always had phenomenal success in raising money when he really needed it.

Sam Shubert was killed while trying to add a link to the chain of "open-door" theaters. The Shuberts wanted the Duquesne, in Pittsburgh, to break the jump between Philadelphia and

Chicago, in which cities they already had good houses. Sam was on his way to Pittsburgh with William Klein, who is still the Shubert lawyer, when the train they were on collided with a car full of dynamite outside Harrisburg. It was one of the worst wrecks in railroad history. Sam Shubert was so badly burned that he died two days later. For a time after this, Mr. Lee and Mr. J.J. called every theater they built the Sam S. Shubert Memorial Theatre. That was the official title of the Shubert here, too, until the brothers found that the funereal connotation was bad for business. Mr. Lee and Mr. J.J. have never traveled together since Sam's death. They take no chances on the extinction of the firm. If they have to go up to Boston to watch a show break in, Mr. Lee leaves New York on one train and Mr. J.J. follows him on another. After the show they return by separate trains. Each has made one or two trips by plane, but the same rule applies to air travel. They have never flown together.

Sam Shubert left such an impress on Mr. Lee that the latter has even taken over some of his brother's idiosyncrasies. One of these is his fast walk, with head thrown forward. Another is a custom of giving alms to every panhandler who accosts him. It was more than a custom with Sam; it was a compulsion. If he had no change in his pocket when approached by a beggar, he would hurry into a store to break a bill and then return to look for the man. Lee feels this compulsion too. He was walking up Broadway with a subordinate one day a year or so ago when a down-and-outer asked the underling for the price of a cup of coffee. "You asked the wrong man!" Mr. Lee shouted indignantly, almost pushing his employee off the sidewalk in his eagerness to get to the tramp. The Shuberts are always being approached by theatrical veterans hoping to make a touch. They are the only managers still active on Broadway whom the troupers of the period from 1900 to 1910 know personally, and both brothers are rated as generous. Their loyalty to aging chorus girls, who appear in Shubert shows year after year, has occasionally furnished first-nighters with material for humorous comment, but it has been a lifesaver for the girls.

The biliousness with which Mr. Lee and Mr. J.J. regarded the world during their struggle with the Syndicate was not assuaged by the newspapers. True, the Shubert press department hornswoggled a great many favorable editorials out of provincial journalists, but it was harder going here. *The Morning Telegraph*, at that time the great theatrical trade paper in New York, once ran a headline asking, "WHY IS LEE SHUBERT AND WHEREFORE?" The Syndicate, in the beginning of the controversy, had a much larger volume of theatrical advertising to place than the Shuberts, and that, in those days, determined the *Telegraph*'s news policy. When Sam Shubert first came to town, he had hired one of the *Telegraph*'s critics as his *sub-rosa* publicity man. This unscrupulous fellow took Sam's money and puffed his shows. The *Telegraph*'s subsequent reversal of policy left the Shuberts with a Continental slant on newspaper ethics. Mr. Lee ordered all Shubert advertising out of the *Telegraph* and kept it out for almost thirty years, although the newspaper changed hands several times in the interim. The *Telegraph* of that era referred to A. Toxen Worm, who had succeeded Wilstach as the Shubert press agent, as "Lee Shubert's vermiform appendix." As a medium for rebuttal, the Shuberts founded their own weekly trade paper, the *New York Review*, in 1910 and kept it up until 1931. "That newspaper which is bounded on the north by a saloon, on the south by a saloon, and facing a carbarn" was one of the *Review*'s more flattering references to the *Telegraph*. "The Shuberts, who evidently are trying to pile up a world's record of theatrical disaster, have added one more attraction to the long list of companies which have brought their tour to an end for lack of patronage" was a *Telegraph* comment on the demise of a Shubert show, and again, "This paper will never libel the Shuberts. It would be as cruel as unnecessary."

The *Telegraph* took particular pleasure during the hostilities in calling Shubert shows salacious, and hinting that they should be raided. Mr. Lee was particularly sensitive on this point; he felt black despair one November night in 1911 when he heard that the patrol wagons were being backed up to the curb in front of the Maxine Elliott Theatre, a Shubert house that had been rented to George C. Tyler and the Abbey Players of Dublin. The American première of Synge's *Playboy of the Western World* was taking place there, and Mr. Lee must have suspected that the show included something like a Dance of the Seven Veils. What the trouble really was, as any historian of the theater knows, was an old-fashioned Irish riot. Irishmen here resented Synge's "slander" on an ancient race and had gone to the opening to egg the actors. Mr. Lee, who had been attending another opening, rushed down the street to the Maxine Elliott and arrived in a dead heat with a man whom he recognized as a reporter for the *Times*. "If I had known there was one thing off-color about this show," Mr. Lee shouted to the reporter, "I wouldn't have let Tyler have the house!"

Mr. Lee concedes grudgingly that newspapermen today are probably honest, but he cannot for the life of him see why a hundred-dollar-a-week employee of a publisher should be allowed to impair a Shubert investment of fifty thousand dollars in a show. This does not prevent him from exploiting to the full any favorable reviews that accrue in the course of a season. He feels newspaper reviewers are naturally perverse, and admiration is wrung from them only by the supreme artistry of a particularly great production.

The Shuberts' feeling against the critics came to a head in

1915, when the brothers ordered the doormen of their theaters to bar Alexander Woollcott, the reviewer for the *Times*. Woollcott, then twenty-eight, had said about a farce called *Taking Chances*, "It is not vastly amusing." To the Shuberts the remark was evidence of violent animosity. They ordered the *Times* to send another reviewer to their attractions. The *Times* replied by throwing out all Shubert ads and Woollcott, backed by his bosses, applied to the United States District Court for an injunction restraining the Shuberts. He said he was being prevented from earning his livelihood as a critic. It was a glorious day for William Klein, the Shubert lawyer, who filed a brief listing all Woollcott's unfavorable criticisms of Shubert shows, with dissenting reviews by Woollcott's colleagues. Woollcott filed an equally long brief with concurrent opinions by the colleagues. The court ruled, to the astonishment of everybody, that the critic's fairness had nothing to do with the case; if the Shuberts wished to bar a man from their property, they had a right to do so. Admission to a place of amusement, the court found, is not a civic right but a license granted by the owner and revocable upon refund of the admission price. On the basis of this decision, the one sort of critic a theater may not bar is a Negro, because when a Negro is refused admittance there is a presumption that he has been so treated on account of race or color and he can sue the management for damages. Woollcott was white. Always realistic, the Shuberts soon made friends with Woollcott and the *Times*, which they had found the best medium for theatrical advertising.

A dozen years later, the Messrs. Lee and J.J. barred Walter Winchell, then dramatic reviewer for the *Graphic*, for writing "flip reviews." Presently Winchell began to write a Broadway column. Mr. Lee feels that Winchell's promotion was the result of their row and often reminds him that he should feel grateful.

Three years ago, Winchell, by his ecstatic plugging of *Hellz a Poppin*, a Shubert enterprise, counteracted the almost unanimous scolding which the other daily reviewers gave the show and had a good deal to do with turning it into the hit it is. Mr. Lee refused to be inordinately thankful. "Winchell has roasted some very good shows," he said.

The Shubert relations with actors, as with reporters, have been subject to frequent emotional disturbance. "The actor is a person so naturally conceited as to become unconsciously ungrateful," Lee once pronounced officially. "In most cases what passes for art is unmitigated self-assurance. It is a difficult thing to explain briefly how much the actor owes to the manager." It is hard to reconcile this low estimate of the actors' art with what the Shuberts said for the record about Joe Smith and Charles Dale of the Avon Comedy Four, who tried to break a contract with them. Attorney Klein's brief stated, "Defendants are novel, unique, and extraordinary. At every appearance they are received with long, loud, and practically continuous applause." The court ruled that Smith and Dale were irreplaceable. The Shuberts won a case on similar grounds against Gallagher and Shean. The comedians argued forlornly that they were terrible and that the Shuberts could hire any sort of turn to take their place. For a while after that, Shubert actors' contracts used to carry the clause, "I now admit I am unique and extraordinary." Mr. Klein says proudly that these cases, like the one against Woollcott, created legal precedent. He thinks that the Shuberts have had a considerable part in the development of American jurisprudence. Mr. Klein has been the Shubert lawyer for thirty-seven years and he says, in endorsement of his clients, "Nobody can show me a single case in which the Shuberts have failed to pay a judgment against them."

Consistency has never hampered the Shuberts. They have had

many wrangles with actors, but they were among the first managers to sign a closed-shop agreement with Equity in 1924. Approximately four times a year, during the busiest period of his life, Mr. Lee used to issue a statement that the time was ripe for the emergence of American dramatists; four times a year, just as regularly, he would announce that the theater was doomed unless the playwrights agreed to reduce royalties. Whenever the owner of a string of one-night stands quit the Shuberts during the Syndicate war, either Mr. Lee or Mr. J.J. would declare that first-class attractions could not play one-night stands profitably. When the same man returned to the Shuberts, one of the brothers would tell the press that the one-night stands made all the difference between a profitable tour and an unprofitable one. Once, when Chicago newspapers complained about the quality of the shows sent there, the Shuberts' *Review* announced, "Chicago does not realize she is in the position of a beggar who ought to be happy for every penny dropped in her tin cup." A couple of years after that, Mr. J.J. said that Chicago was the best theater town in the country and that he was going to make it the dramatic center of America. Self-consciousness is not a Shubert trait either.

III

By the mid-twenties, a quarter of a century after the first of the Shubert brothers came to New York from his home in Syracuse to do battle with the forces that were monopolizing the theater, the enemy, personified by the Klaw & Erlanger Syndicate, was groggy. The Shuberts owned or had long leases on about 150 theaters, and they controlled the booking of 750 more. They didn't have enough dramatic attractions to go around, even though two thirds of the important producing managers were now booking their shows into Shubert houses. A weakness of drama on the road is that provincial audiences demand the original Broadway casts. Operettas, on the other hand, are not so dependent on individual talent and get along all right on the road without first-string stars. The operetta, therefore, became the favored art form of the Shubert Theatre Corporation. Those were the days and nights when the Shuberts' publicity office never closed. Claude Greneker, their press agent, employed a lobster shift of assistants who went to work after midnight and pounded their typewriters until the day men began to come in. Time was beginning to help the Shuberts in their fight. Marc Klaw and Abe Erlanger, the Syndicate leaders, had been mature men in 1903, when the struggle started, while the Shuberts had been prodigies in their twenties. Now, as their rivals aged, the Shuberts were just hitting their stride. Klaw retired in 1926, and Erlanger died in 1930. Erlanger at his death was regarded as a wealthy man, but his estate, as it developed, consisted of two million dollars in assets and three million dollars in liabilities.

The operetta industry reached an all-time high in the winter of 1925–26. During that lush season, the Messrs. Shubert had ten companies of *The Student Prince* on tour in North America and one in Australia. The paths of the *Prince* companies often crossed those of five companies of *Blossom Time*, another Shubert operetta, which had been produced in 1921 and was hard to kill. By 1927 there weren't so many companies of *The Student Prince* and *Blossom Time* as there once had been, but five road companies of *My Maryland* had joined the survivors and the nation was still filled with song. The coffers of the Shubert Theatre Corporation were filled with cash, and in 1928 its stock, listed on the Exchange, reached a high of 85¼.

The manufacture of operetta companies for the road became a mechanical process with the Shuberts, like making new prints from the negative of a moving picture. Operettas had the advantage of sound effects, which the movies of 1925 hadn't. A man named Jack C. Huffman, who, before he retired in 1929, was the Shuberts' favorite director, staged the No. 1 productions. Two subordinate directors rehearsed the road companies, retaining all Huffman's stage business. The road units went out at intervals of about two weeks. It was customary to give each *Student Prince* cast a single break-in performance at the Jolson Theatre, where the No. 1 company played. No audience ever objected to the substitution, if any even noticed it. This gave the road companies self-assurance and permitted them to be billed as coming "direct from Broadway." Each *Student Prince* unit required forty male and twenty-four female choristers. *Blossom Time* and *My Maryland* called for less choral singing but increased the strain on the supply of prima donnas, ingénues, and presentable male singing leads. The Shuberts' musical-casting director, a motherly little man named Romayne Simmons, combed the chorus of the Metropolitan and the glee clubs of every police department in the land for recruits. Fortunately, Simmons says, the costumes worn by ladies in the early-nineteenth-century and Civil War eras, with which the operettas were respectively concerned, covered the figure from neck to ankle, so that the Shuberts did not have to worry much about the figures of the singing women they drafted. Friends at the Met sent Simmons young people who had tried out there but whose voices were not quite good enough for grand opera. There were even sinister rumors of singers waking up on the train to Toronto with a No. 5 company when the last thing they remembered was taking a drink with a Shubert representative at Hughie McLaughlin's bar on Forty-fifth Street.

It was during the time when Lee and his brother Jake, who now prefers to be known as J.J., were the most important men in the American theater that a type of humor classified as the "Shubert story" attained its vogue in the way that similar anecdotes have since automatically become part of the life and works of Samuel Goldwyn. There are three possibilities about the origin of any Shubert story. The incident may have involved a Shubert; it may have involved a less widely known producer and been credited to the Shuberts to make it sound funnier; and it may have been invented out of whole cloth at the bar of the Players Club or some less exclusive loitering place of actors.

One of the favorites is the story of the actor walking up Broadway, shaking his head and repeating aloud, "The rat!" Another actor stopped him and said, "So is his brother Jake!" A subtler variant concerns the actor at the Players who was hanging over the bar and ranting about the Shuberts when a confrere interrupted him. "They're not so bad," the second actor said. "No?" said the first actor. "Then why do they call them Shuberts?" A bit of counterpoint to this is the true anecdote about the Shubert press agent who warned Mr. Lee that a certain interviewer was inclined to be tart. "What can he possibly think of bad to say about me?" Mr. Lee asked earnestly.

Concerning the Shubert appreciation of the arts, there is the story of how Mr. J.J. attended a rehearsal of a musical show and thought the orchestra played too loudly. "Very softly!" he told the violins. "Play only on one string!" The quotation is accurate, but the attribution is wrong. It was Erlanger who said it at one of his rehearsals. On the same pattern is the tale of an actor in a Shubert drama who read a line beginning, "I am Omar Khayyam." "You don't know anything," Mr. Lee is supposed to have told him. "You should say, 'I am Omar *of* Khayyam.'" " 'I am Omar *of* Khayyam,'" the submissive actor intoned. Later one of the more literate Shubert subordinates apprised Mr. Lee of his error.

Next time the actor said, " 'I am Omar *of* Khayyam,' " Mr. Lee stopped him. "Let's cut out the 'of,' " he said. "The act's a little too long already." This story might have been told of any producer at any period in history and in a related form was probably familiar to the boys who hung out with Menander in the Athenian equivalent of Lindy's.

Such stories have never bothered the Shuberts. They have never pretended to any rich cultural background and they know that their shrewdness in affairs of the theater is often underestimated because of their lack of polish. They see business as a form of combat. Mr. Lee recently said, "I like to take a play and bet my money *against* it." Money, Mr. Lee thinks, is the best measure of success in the theater. There is no doubt that the brothers, beginning at the bottom, have made more money out of the legitimate stage than any other two men who ever lived. Mr. Lee acknowledges, however, that they have lost a great deal of it in bad real-estate investments and in the stock market.

When there was a European theater of consequence, the Shuberts liked to buy shows that had already succeeded abroad. They would sometimes buy by cable without having seen the script. Afterward they would Americanize their purchases by introducing James Barton into the second scene as an American sailor who had lost his way in the grand duke's palace. "The advantage of a play that you bought in Paris," Mr. Lee says now, "was that it was usually a German play that had been translated into French, so that by the time you had it translated into English, you got the services of three great authors on one script." He is sorry that because of the collapse of the Central European theater it is now usually necessary to start from scratch. Even Czecho-Slovakia, he reminds friends, was occasionally the source of a play. "Bill Brady got one there," he recalls, "the bug play." By this Mr. Lee means *The Insect Play*, which was produced here as *The World We Live In*.

The Shuberts, to quote Mr. Lee again, have never been loafing boys. The brothers, as nearly as he can remember, built the Forty-fourth Street, the Lyric, the Shubert, the Booth, the Broadhurst, the Plymouth, the Morosco, the Bijou, the Ritz, the Forty-ninth Street, the Nora Bayes, the Ambassador, the Forrest, the Jolson, and the Maxine Elliott theaters. They converted a horse exchange, where New Yorkers used to buy carriage horses, into the Winter Garden. The Empire is the only theater now showing legitimate plays in New York which was in business before the first Shubert came here. Shubert competitors built the rest of the local theaters, so Mr. Lee in a way feels responsible for them too. Once, riding on Forty-sixth Street in his Isotta-Fraschini, he said, "If I hadn't built all these theaters, they would be dark today."

The brothers made two invasions of England—the first in 1904, when they built the Waldorf Theatre in London, which they had to abandon two years later, and the second in the early twenties. They acquired six London houses on their second try, but again they lost out. London was the only city in the world that rejected *The Student Prince*. British critics said it was pro-German. The Messrs. Shubert also made two attempts to break into vaudeville, in 1906 and in 1921, and both were expensive failures. A kind of recurrent stubbornness is a Shubert trait. They retreat, but they come back for more. In the early thirties they tried a show called *A Trip to Pressburg* three times with different stars. It never got further than Pittsburgh, but the Shuberts still own it, and someday it will reappear.

The resilience of Mr. Lee and Mr. J.J. is magnificently illustrated by the tangled affairs of the old Shubert Theatre Corporation, which vanished as a result of receivership proceedings in

1931. The Shuberts might have been spared this financial embarrassment if a prediction made by Mr. Lee in 1910 had come true. In that year he said he did not believe the shares of any theater corporation would ever be listed on the Stock Exchange. Times and the Shuberts' minds changed, and in 1924 the brothers organized the Shubert Theatre Corporation, with 210,000 shares of common stock. This was duly listed on the Exchange, and during the first five years the corporation consistently reported earnings of over one million dollars. In organizing this enterprise, the Shuberts turned over to it many of their theaters but withheld certain valuable properties, which included the Winter Garden, Shubert, Broadhurst, Booth, Plymouth, Cort, and Daly theaters as well as the Sardi Building and considerable other nontheatrical real estate. They explained that they had partners in these holdings who were opposed to entering the corporation. The brothers still own or have long leases on these personally held properties, which never became involved in the ups and downs of the corporation.

In 1933, two years after the receivership, Mr. Lee, with his brother as partner, bought in all the assets of the defunct corporation for four hundred thousand dollars, a price which barely covered the costs of the receivership. The creditors were glad to receive even that small amount, however. They had discovered that the leasehold on a theater is practically worthless in the eyes of bankers, who know neither how to produce a play nor how to put such a property to any other profitable use. The Shuberts lumped together all that could be salvaged from the Shubert Theatre Corporation in a new company called the Select Theatres Corporation. They kept fifty per cent of the stock of the new organization for themselves and distributed the rest among those who had held stock in the old corporation. The Select stock never has paid dividends, either to the Shuberts or to anybody else.

Through Select, the brothers maintain their control over a large number of theaters, and this protects their strategic position in the industry. Among the theaters now owned by Select are the Barrymore, Ambassador, Hudson, Maxine Elliott, Forty-sixth Street, Golden, Longacre, Imperial, Morosco, and Majestic. Lee is president of Select, and J.J. is general manager. The overhead costs of all Shubert enterprises, including the salaries of Lee and J.J., are charged to Select and the Shubert personal holdings; each Shubert production is a new corporation in which Mr. Lee and Mr. J.J. usually own all the stock. The precise financial status of the Messrs. is one of the thousand and one topics of idle speculation in Broadway taverns. Recently, from Mr. William Klein, who has been their attorney for thirty-seven years, came the nearest thing to an official statement yet heard on the subject. "Neither of the Messrs. Shubert," he said, rubbing his hands together vigorously, "will ever be buried in potter's field."

The brothers have great confidence in each other's integrity; one never questions the other's drafts on the joint Shubert cash account. On the other hand, they are seldom in agreement about business policies and twice a year they meet in Mr. J.J.'s apartment atop the Sardi Building for a formal dinner and argument. They are attended by attorneys on these occasions. During the rest of the year they lead separate social existences. Mr. J.J. lives in his apartment alone except for a cook and maid, and he seldom goes out at night. The living room, which runs the whole width of the building, is adorned with lighting fixtures from the old Hotel Knickerbocker and with a great deal of Louis XIV furniture. All of the furniture, he likes to assure visitors, was bought especially for the apartment—none of the pieces are leftovers from shows. At the west end of the room there is a wrought-iron door from a Venetian palace, on which the most noticeable adornment is a female figure with six breasts. The door weighs three and a half tons. The space behind one of the dining-room walls is hollow and filled with a large supply of liquor which Mr. J.J. acquired at reduced prices during prohibition and which he has as yet barely sampled. He isn't much of a drinker, but he never could resist a bargain. The dining room has Syrian furniture inlaid with mother-of-pearl and ivory, and on a terrace in front of the living room there is a fountain from the Knickerbocker lobby. Despite these and other attractions of his apartment, Mr. J.J., when he's at home in the winter, spends most of his time in the bathroom, reading in an armchair which he has installed there. This is because the bathroom is the only comfortably warm room in the place. The heat in the Sardi Building, above the first floor, is turned off at seven o'clock in the evening and all day on Sunday. Since it is impossible to warm the apartment on the top floor without heating the whole building, Mr. J.J. retires to the bathroom, which he has fitted up with an elaborate battery of electric heaters. He does all his play-reading there. When he occasionally goes out, it is usually to Lindy's for a cup of coffee at about midnight. He also likes to sit through double features at fourth-run movie houses. Mr. J.J. prefers to lunch in his apartment, but when he has to talk business with someone at noon, he eats with the person at Sardi's, on the first floor of his residence. Vincent Sardi, the proprietor, used to be a captain of waiters at the Little Club, a night place that the Shuberts owned many years ago. He is a good tenant now, and the Shuberts always believe in patronizing people who do business with them.

Mr. Lee almost invariably lunches at Sardi's. Actors who want him to notice them eat there too. Lee often convinces people who work for him that they also should live in the Century Apartments, where he lives and in which the brothers have an interest. *Hellz a Poppin* had hardly become a hit when Mr. Lee induced Chic Johnson, one of its stars, to take an apartment in the Century. Both the Messrs. Shubert like to say that they "never learned to play—never had time," but Mr. Lee at least gets about a good deal. He says he does so to maintain contacts. "Maybe I would like to play," he says plaintively, "but there is no one around I care to play with."

Mr. Lee's office in the Shubert Theatre Building is in a turret and therefore circular—not more than twelve feet in diameter. Into it is squeezed the desk he has used ever since he came to New York, a chair, a sofa, a gilt statue of a nymph and faun, and an autographed photograph of Colonel Lindbergh. A short passageway leads from Mr. Lee's office to that of his secretary, Jack Morris, which in turn opens into the waiting room, a bleak place with French-gray furniture grouped around a snake plant, and two unchanging, disregarded signs—"No Smoking" and "No Casting until August." The gray chairs usually are occupied by a queue of petitioners waiting to see Mr. Lee. It is a point of pride with him that he never refuses to see anybody who is willing to wait a few hours. The passageway between Mr. Lee's office and his secretary's has an extra door leading directly into the waiting room, but only the experienced understand this door's significance. When Mr. Lee is ready to grant an audience, he pops out at the Morris end of the passageway and beckons to the man who has advanced to the head of the queue. This hopeful comes forward, thinking that Mr. Lee is going to conduct him into his private office. Mr. Lee takes him by the arm, leads him into the passageway, says, "I'm sorry, I can't do anything now," and steers him out through the extra door and into the waiting room again. This maneuver is known in the trade as the Shubert brush-off.

Nothing confuses Mr. Lee more than to be caught without anything to do. "It just happens you catch me at a time when everything is very quiet," he will apologize, scratching his head energetically with a paper cutter. When his embarrassment becomes extreme, he scratches himself under the armpits and behind the ears. "You should have seen it yesterday. I didn't have a minute to myself." On summer afternoons when there are only a few persons waiting to see him, he has been known to sneak out of his office, go downstairs to his limousine, and so off to the baseball game, returning when a queue of more flattering length has formed. "Business won't wait," he says when reproached for spending most of his time in the vicinity of Shubert Alley even during the dog days. During intervals of quiet, Mr. Lee often plays rummy with Peters, his valet. If Harry Kaufman, the ticket broker upon whom Mr. Lee relies for companionship as much as for advice, is available, they change the game to three-handed pinochle. Peters reads Mr. Lee's personal correspondence as a matter of duty and answers it. Mr. J.J. sometimes refers to Peters as "the Crown Prince."

Mr. Lee's insistence upon running all the Shubert theaters himself, even down to the smallest detail, is a carry-over from a period when theater treasurers and house managers consistently robbed their employers. Larceny was considered a perquisite of their jobs. The house manager would issue "complimentaries," and the treasurer would sell them. It was the Shuberts who devised the present method of accounting for tickets. Under this system, there are separate racks for unsold tickets, for the stubs of tickets that have been paid for—known in the trade as "the hardwood"—and for stubs of complimentaries, or "deadwood." Every seat in the house must be accounted for in one or another of the racks; by deducting unsold seats and deadwood from the house capacity, the theater owner knows exactly what should be in the cash drawer. The only subordinate who can issue complimentaries in the whole Shubert organization here is the publicity chief, Greneker, and he is exceedingly frugal with them. Most passes to Shubert shows are signed by Mr. Lee himself. Many Shubert employees have been with the elderly Syracuse boys for a long time. Mr. Lee has faith in them but can't get over his distrustful nature. Some years ago, he recalls, he was standing in Shubert Alley when a Negro walked up carrying a pair of shoes. The Negro asked him for a wardrobe woman who worked for the Shuberts. The Negro complained that the woman had sold him the shoes, which he was returning because they were misfits. They were Shubert shoes. The incident proved to Mr. Lee that a man of property must be on the alert all the time.

Just as the Shubert empire has two chiefs, so it has two heirs apparent. One is Mr. J.J.'s son, John, who, the father likes to remind Lee, is "the only direct-line Shubert of his generation." On Mr. Lee's side of the firm, the young hope is Milton Shubert. Milton, however, is not "direct line." He is a nephew who adopted the avuncular name for business reasons, and he is the only member of the family who has shown any interest in moving pictures. He used to be head of the Shubert dramatic department in New York, but now spends most of his time in Hollywood, where he is helpful in directing Shubert affairs on the West Coast. Milton's mother was a sister of Mr. Lee's and Mr. J.J.'s; his father was named Isaacs. John, who is very tall for a Shubert—five feet ten inches—is thirty-one and lives at the Hotel Astor in a suite overlooking Shubert Alley. Milton, short and small, is forty-two; he stays at hotels when he is in New York. John is supposed to take charge of Shubert interests in New York when both Mr. Lee and Mr. J.J. are out of town, but this has happened only once since John left the University of Pennsylvania twelve years ago. His regency lasted for two weeks. At least twenty other Shubert relatives, of various degrees of consanguinity, are employed in lesser jobs in the organization.

Because of their fear of assuming responsibility, Shubert employees in general are the most literal-minded attachés of the American theater. Their attitude has given rise to some famous yarns of niggardliness. When the cast of *You Can't Take It with You* was rehearsing in the Booth Theatre, the supply of drinking cups at the house's water cooler gave out, and Sam Harris, producer of the play, called for more. He got them, with a bill for $1.15. A representative of the Shubert auditing department pointed out that the contract of rental did not specifically obligate the Shuberts to provide drinking cups. Harris wrote an indignant letter to Lee Shubert, who had gone to considerable effort to get *You Can't Take It with You*, a prospective hit, into a Shubert house. He reprimanded his underling for sending the bill. "Before doing a thing like that," Mr. Lee said, "you should consult me!" Of a piece with this story is the one about Noel Coward. He was playing in *Point Valaine* at the Barrymore Theatre, and asked to have the paint in his dressing room freshened up. He got a bill for seven dollars for the painting job, again apparently from an auditor drunk with power. Coward vowed never to play another Shubert theater. Even among men who dislike Mr. Lee, few believe him guilty of these small, miserly touches. They are not in his style. "I paid Sarah Bernhardt eighteen hundred dollars a night," Lee says. "Do you think I need a couple of dollars?" When he is particularly vexed, he sometimes bursts into tears. "How could you do this to me?" he will ask the person who has displeased him. "I would rather have given you fifty thousand dollars."

Despite such demonstrations, well-trained Shubert subordinates continue at every opportunity to save money for their bosses. There is an interlude in *Hellz a Poppin*, a show which will probably earn over a million dollars for the Shuberts, in which all the lights go out while members of the cast pepper the audience with dried beans. Olsen and Johnson, the stars of the show, introduced this subtle bit of business long ago, when they were managing their own company in vaudeville. From the beginning, Olsen and Johnson bean throwers had used large paper cups holding half a pint of beans. Shortly after the show opened in New York the comics were approached by the company manager. "If we used ordinary drinking cups to throw the beans out of," he said, "we would get the cups cheaper, because we buy them in such large quantities for the theaters. Also, with the smaller cups we would use less beans. Altogether, I figure, we would save at least a dollar a week."

• No Suave Inflections •

On the day that *Hellz a Poppin*, the refined revue which began its run at the Forty-sixth Street Theatre, was scheduled to move to the larger Winter Garden, Ole Olsen and his partner, Chic Johnson, loitered sadly in front of the Fulton Theatre. The Fulton is also on Forty-sixth Street, and *Oscar Wilde* was playing there that season. "It will be a terrible thing for that show when we move," Olsen said with a wave of his hand. "They been living on our overflow." Johnson nodded in agreement. Both men were quite serious. This overweening modesty has carried Ole and Chic through twenty-four seasons of show business—as entertainers in a Chicago rathskeller, as a two-act on the Pantages and Orpheum time in vaudeville, and latterly as the proprietors of a "unit show" which has toured the country every year as regularly as *Uncle Tom's Cabin* used to in the eighteen-eighties. Vaudeville has been dead for a decade, but Olsen, the thin partner, and Johnson, the fat one, have never known enough to lie down.

An Olsen and Johnson unit show used to carry about forty people, including musicians and a line of twelve girls. There was always a quartet, members of which doubled in bits of slapstick; there were always a couple of specialty acts, and there were always Olsen and Johnson themselves, working like mad through the duration of the piece, just as they do now in *Hellz a*

Poppin. A unit ran seventy minutes, approximately half the length of a musical comedy, and there was no intermission. Olsen and Johnson and their assistants in the unit would play four or five shows a day, depending on business in the movie palaces where they were booked. When business was good, the house manager would ask the partners to speed up their show so that he could get more customers in and out of the seats. Olsen and Johnson would then rush the performance through in sixty minutes. When the unit was teamed with an unusually short feature picture, the partners would sometimes be asked to extend their running time to eighty minutes. Those actors in the present Winter Garden show who have worked with Olsen and Johnson on the road have found it difficult to overcome the habit of asking, "Long or short version tonight?" when they hear the opening chords of the overture. They are just beginning to realize that they are now working on a fairly static schedule. The first half of *Hellz a Poppin* is, with a few emendations, the unit show which Olsen and Johnson opened in Fort Wayne, Indiana, in July 1938. The second half is made up of material from the unit show with which they opened in Denver several years ago. Lee Shubert, their financial backer, saw the first half of *Hellz a Poppin* at a moving-picture theater in Philadelphia, but the partners had a hard time explaining the second half to him because they had no script. Olsen and Johnson carry on by ear, and it seems unnecessary to dwell upon their obvious relation to the *commedia dell'arte*. In order to copyright their present show after it became a hit, they had to have a stenographer sit in the wings and take down the dialogue in shorthand.

From the beginning of their career, Olsen and Johnson have been surefire between Cleveland and California. Intimate acquaintance with their art, which New York has tardily recognized, induces a patronizing bonhomie among the Western visitors who swarm backstage at every performance of *Hellz a Poppin*. These out-of-towners, frequently accompanied by their wives or nieces, casually invade the partners' dressing rooms in such numbers that the hospitable comics, crowded out by their visitors, have to change their trousers on stair landings. Olsen's room usually fills first because he has long been the front man and speechmaker for the team. His room presents the greatest cross section of inland America to be found anywhere on Manhattan outside the lobby of the Hotel Taft. "The boys have been big stars for the last twenty years out where I come from," said Stephen F. Chadwick, a National Commander of the American Legion, during one of his frequent visits to New York. The commander lives in Seattle. Olsen is constantly inviting callers from Spokane to shake hands with callers from Green Bay, Wisconsin, and prominent executives from Akron to shake hands with prominent executives from Columbia, Missouri. Most of his visitors, in fact, belong to that nebulous but exalted class, the American executive. Olsen and Johnson themselves are honorary members of the Executives' Club of Portland, Oregon, and Olsen is fond of executive turns of phrase. "My thought on this matter is . . ." he says frequently before advising Johnson to hit a stuffed skunk with a hammer instead of his hat or to use a dressed turkey instead of a dressed chicken for a hunting bit.

The partners are honorary members of the Gyro Club of St. Paul and Minneapolis, the Gray Gander Club of Seattle, the International Association of Police Chiefs, and the Chicago Police Lieutenants' Association. They belong to the Yellow Dogs Club and Ace of Clubs of Columbus, Ohio, organizations of downtown quarterbacks who live for the Ohio State football team. They also hold membership in the Couvert Club of Cincinnati, the Arnama (Army, Navy, and Marine) Club of Los Angeles, the Atey (80) Club of San Francisco, the Round Table of Spokane, and the Breakfast Clubs of Seattle, Portland, Los Angeles, and Denver. All of these are endemic variants of Rotary, Kiwanis, and the Lions. Olsen and Johnson are honorary Rotarians, Kiwanians, and Lions, too, and are aspirants to the Dutch Treat Club of New York City. They are Elks, and each has been made a Kentucky colonel twice, the second time by a governor who did not know that a predecessor had already commissioned them.

Through their perfect adaptation to the Midwestern terrain where they were born, Olsen and Johnson managed to survive and prosper there for years, preserving the art of hokum for its present brilliant revival. They prefer the word "gonk" to "hokum." "Gonk is hokum with raisins in it," they say. "Gonk is what we do." For a long while survival wasn't easy; Olsen and Johnson once rose at seven in the morning to ride sacred white Arabian stallions in a cattle roundup conducted by the Shriners of Sioux City, Iowa. They never missed an opportunity to play an Elks' smoker, even after having given their regular five shows that day. A glass eater who was with their act in 1929 complained that the benefit shows were ruining his digestion. Johnson convinced him that some chile con carne which he was in the habit of eating late at night was responsible. During one tour, Olsen sold 114 supercharged Auburn sport models for dealers along the route. Auburn salesmen in each town promised prospects a final demonstration by Ole Olsen, the matinee idol of the Northwest. In gratitude for Olsen's services, the Auburn dealers organized year-round Olsen-and-Johnson clubs. "It rendered the territory Olsen-and-Johnson-conscious," Olsen says.

Neither Ole nor Chic has the intrinsic comic quality of a Harpo Marx or a Frank Tinney. They were never as funny, individually, as Clark and McCullough, Duffy and Sweeney, or the members of half a dozen other gifted combinations, and Olsen and Johnson readily admit it. But they have worked for laughs with a grimmer determination than any of the others, and there is something in the forthright earnestness of their attack which is in itself pleasing. The chief comic asset of the team, considered merely as a team, is Johnson's face. It is a wide, lardy, fatman's face with bulging eyes that resemble poached eggs with pale blue yolks. These curious, anxious eyes belie the jaunty tilt of the derby he wears onstage; they are the eyes of a restaurateur watching a customer eat a bad egg. When the egg goes down without complaint from the customer, the face registers a vast and ingenuous relief. Johnson's expression oscillates between terror and insecure joy. It is impossible not to think about eggs when you think about him—he has a Humpty-Dumptyish personality. Olsen holds himself stiffly and is rather thin; only the wide, mobile mouth marks him as a comic. He is the straight man—glib, arrogant in a loutish way, but intermittently softening his arrogance with an ear-joining grin, like a circus clown. Olsen prepares the way for the laughs his stooges get—he is as much a ringmaster as a principal comedian.

One advantage the team possesses over contemporary combinations is its timing. Comedians who work in the films or before the microphone lose the sense of tempo which makes a vaudeville act click on the stage. Since Olsen and Johnson now are almost the only vaudeville team that has been working right along *as* a vaudeville team, they are among the few to retain this knack. An even more important asset when they are central figures in a show is their flair for contriving bits of comic business in which they utilize props and other actors. An exemplary Olsen and Johnson bit is the man who tries vainly to free himself from a strait jacket for practically the whole of *Hellz a Poppin* and winds up in the outer lobby when the customers are leaving after the show. Olsen and Johnson began using that bit in 1926. The timing of the escapist's repeated appearances makes each seem more comical. "The gag builds," Johnson says. "You have to know how to humor a gag like that." When the partners have an audience in their grip, they can make it laugh even at this sort of dialogue:

Q—What part of Ireland do you come from?
A—Staten Ireland.
Q—How old are you?
A—Sixteen.
Q—What do you want to be?
A—Seventeen.
Q—How much would you charge to haunt a house?
A—How many rooms?

"After a few more years," Johnson says of the final sally, "I think we will change that gag. I will ask, 'How much would you charge to sour some milk?' and the stooge will say, 'How many quarts?' "

"We don't go for suave inflections," says Olsen, the intellectual of the team. "We go for the ocular stuff. Suave inflections are poison in Youngstown, Ohio." It is his theory that if you once get a man laughing hard, you can keep him laughing all evening by talking fast. Babe Ruth never had to bunt. "To hell with chuckles," Johnson says. "Only belly laughs count."

Until *Hellz a Poppin* became a hit, producers and managers had considered this type of comedy too corny for present-day New York. "Corny" is a cultural term meaning crude, obvious, and the antithesis of what Noel Coward would do in a given situation. The corn taboo had been so fixed in Broadway minds by a succession of smart musicals, all the way from *The Band Wagon* through *I Married an Angel*, that the man who books acts for Loew's State Theatre, where there is a seventy-five-cent top, scorned the Olsen and Johnson unit. The partners were playing four shows a day in Philadelphia when the Loew's booker turned thumbs down on them. They were paying all the salaries and other expenses of their unit and would have been willing to bring it into New York for a price of five thousand dollars a week, out of which they would have taken a profit of around twenty-five hundred dollars. During the Philadelphia run, Olsen went to a night club for a steak sandwich and encountered Nils T. Granlund, a New York night-club operator who is a tenant of the Shuberts. Granlund thought the unit might have possibilities as a longer revue. He got Lee Shubert to come down from New York and look at the strange provincial charivari, and Shubert, who had several empty theaters in New York, rather dubiously agreed to back Olsen and Johnson in a full-length piece. "If I hadn't gone out for a steak sandwich and run into Granlund, we wouldn't be in New York today," Olsen says. "Big things always happen to us like that. We are creatures of destiny." The Shuberts did not invest much money in the show—probably something like fifteen thousand dollars. They provided it with a collection of sets from defunct Shubert musicals such as *The Show Is On* and *Hooray for What*, a smattering of secondhand costumes from their warehouse, and exactly three new sets of dresses for the chorus girls. Olsen and Johnson could have easily financed the production themselves, but they have always been frugal. "If we had had to buy everything new, it might have cost us twenty-five thousand dollars," Olsen says, "and that's not hay. The way it was, we figured that if the show folded in New York, we could open the unit in Baltimore the next week anyway, without having lost anything except our time."

The curious trade prejudice against a hearty laugh almost spoiled the opening at the Forty-sixth Street Theatre. The partners took especial pains to insure the success of their Broadway debut as author-actors. They had even provided a string trio to play in the men's lounge. On the old Orpheum circuit Chic Sale had been their only rival for popularity, and, like him, Olsen and Johnson have always specialized in smoking-room humor. They installed an intricate system of rubber tubing whereby stage-hands could blow air under the skirts of the women customers seated in the orchestra. No detail had been overlooked, and the audience laughed incessantly for three hours. This reassured Olsen and Johnson. As they waited up to read the record of their triumph in the morning papers, they kept telling each other that New York was just a department of the sticks. After all, they reasoned, Richard Watts, Jr., of the *Herald Tribune*, was a native of Parkersburg, West Virginia; John Mason Brown, of the *Post*, hailed from Olsen-and-Johnson-conscious Louisville; Brooks Atkinson, of the *Times*, from a small place in New England; Richard Lockridge, of the *Sun*, from Kansas City (a great Olsen-and-Johnson town), and John Anderson, of the *Journal & American*, from some place in Florida. The critics should have felt at home at *Hellz a Poppin*. It turned out that no one is so bashful in the presence of the corny as a fugitive from a cornfield.

Mr. Watts, of Parkersburg, wrote, "The greater part of it depended on the mere fact of its madness and didn't succeed in being funny." Mr. Brown, of Louisville, said, "Its lapses from taste are almost as frequent as its lapses from interest," and the Floridian Mr. Anderson called *Hellz a Poppin* "steadily vulgar and anesthetic." *Hellz a Poppin* seemed to embarrass the boys like a visit from a home-town cousin, and, among the Manhattan newspaper critics, only the native and uninhibited Walter Winchell dared to risk an outright plug for the show. Winchell plugged it so hard and so often that a rumor started that he owned the production. He didn't, of course, but when the show became a hit he began to think of himself as a major prophet. Olsen and Johnson are abjectly grateful, but it is probable that *Hellz a Poppin*'s success helped Winchell as much as Winchell helped *Hellz a Poppin*.

Life began for John Sigvard Olsen and for Harold Ogden Johnson when they met in the professional department of a music publisher's office in Chicago in 1914. They had existed, after a fashion, as individuals, but neither had as yet found his groove. Olsen and Johnson had come to the publisher's office in search of music for their respective acts. Olsen was with the College Four, a quartet of music-making comedians who played beer halls and rathskellers. He had been graduated from Northwestern, at Evanston, Illinois, in 1912 and was the only member of the College Four who had even been near a college. Ole played the violin, sang with illustrated slides, and did a bit of ventriloquism as his contribution to the act. Johnson was primarily a ragtime piano player, but he had a funny face. He was doing a two-act in small-time vaudeville with a girl named Ruby Wallace. Both the boys had had serious musical ambitions. Olsen's pattern, in his boyhood days in Peru (pronounced Pee-ru), Indiana, had been Jan Kubelik, the Czech violinist. Johnson had gone out into the world from Englewood, Illinois, to eclipse Paderewski. Olsen's parents were born in Norway, Johnson's in Sweden. Chic and Ole immediately saw each other as great men. "I knew as soon as I saw him that Ole was a genius," Johnson, the less articulate, says today. "He wore high yellow bulldog shoes that buttoned up the sides, and he was the first man I ever heard imitate a busy signal on the telephone. I knew I had to have him as a partner." Olsen experienced a similar recognition of destiny. "Chic had the most powerful right hand I ever heard on a piano," he says reverently. They could not sever their old associations right away, but they played a few dates together at the North American Café on State Street—violin, piano, ventriloquism, and harmony. They played together the following season and got a booking on the Pantages time. History does not record what became of Ruby Wallace or of Ole's three associates of the College Four.

Pantages shows were booked intact, a combination of five acts traveling together all season. Two of the four acts that traveled with Olsen and Johnson in their first year together were Victor Moore and Emma Littlefield, and William Gaxton and Anna Laughlin. A vaudeville act in those days grew gradually, the way a folk play or a legend does; it was not a static thing, like a play that a man writes on a typewriter. After the manner of a human body, it discarded dead cells and built up new ones. The more it was apparently the same thing, the more it changed. An act started with half a dozen gags; at the end of the first season, a couple of them might be dropped in favor of some experimental material. Some acts, while retaining their basic characters, changed all their material in the course of a few years. In others, one particularly strong comic bit would stay in for twenty or thirty years and become a kind of trade-mark. Olsen and Johnson still do a ventriloquist bit that was in their first act in vaudeville—the interlude in which Johnson sits on Olsen's knee. They dropped it for about fifteen years, then picked it up when Charlie McCarthy brought ventriloquism back. In their first act on the Pantages time, the curtain rose with Johnson seated at the piano, on which there was a telephone. The telephone rang, and Johnson, answering it, said, "Mr. Olsen? Is there a Mr. Olsen in the house?" Olsen entered and picked up the telephone. When he picked it up, the cord dangled free, and the audience could see that it was not connected. That was a sure laugh. Olsen sang into the telephone, "Hello, Frisco, Hello," with Johnson pounding the piano. Then Ole pretended to talk to someone on the telephone, producing the replies by ventriloquism. The bit included his immortal imitation of a busy signal. Olsen and Johnson got two hundred fifty dollars a week during their first season and then were booked on the Orpheum time, a more important circuit. The Orpheum was the Western division of the Keith-Orpheum system, the Big League of vaudeville, and their joint salary rose until it hit twenty-five hundred dollars. Orpheum acts that wanted to come East for the first time had to accept a cut in salary until they made themselves drawing cards here. The same thing was true of Eastern acts wishing to establish themselves in the West. So Olsen and Johnson stayed west of Chicago most of the time. Occasionally they accepted temporary cuts just for the glory of playing the Palace, but they never felt sure of themselves in New York. On one of their last Palace engagements, they brought along a 1912 Hupmobile with a Negro chauffeur. They would drive from the Palace to the Hotel Astor to buy a couple of cigars, and every time they got out of the old car the chauffeur would run before them and lay a ragged red Turkey carpet across the pavement for them to walk on. The Palace *cognoscenti* remained unimpressed by these high jinks, preferring the subtler comic style of entertainers like Frank Fay and Bea Lillie. When the great circuits cracked up and Olsen and Johnson had to take to the road at the head of their own units, they were compelled to widen their territory. Movie houses that will gamble on a stage show nowadays are sometimes far apart. Running out of big towns to play, Olsen and Johnson once tackled the one-night stands of the South, playing sixty-five nights, as Olsen elegantly expresses it, "in cow barns and illuminated outhouses." They made money. On a similar divagation from the beaten track, they acquired the title for their present show. The beaten track, for

Olsen and Johnson, includes Phoenix, Arizona, and while they were playing there in the fall of 1937, they were waited on by a delegation from Buckeye, Arizona, which is far afield, even for them. The delegation sought successfully to engage their unit as the chief feature of the annual Buckeye Cotton Carnival. This sagebrush Mardi Gras is always called "Helzapoppin," with one "l." The partners adopted the name of the Arizona festival for their 1938 unit, but they put a second "l" into it.

Offstage, Olsen and Johnson are serious types, resembling the European circus performers who reserve their eccentricities for the ring and remain solid *petits bourgeois* outside. The partners save their money; they rarely drink; they are good family men. They are in the European tradition, too, in that they make their enterprises a kind of family affair. Olsen has been married for many years and has a son, John Charles Olsen. He is a lank youth with cavernous cheeks and sad eyes, and he is quite the busiest stooge in the show. He acts as his father's dresser between his own cues. John Charles went to Ohio State and the University of Southern California, his father says, "in order to wind up as a shot offstage." He fires at least fifty rounds of pistol ammunition during the evening. Chic's wife, Mrs. Catherine Johnson, is the apparently suburban woman who wanders in the aisles of the Winter Garden during the show, yelling, "Oscar!" The Johnson were married twenty-one years ago and have a daughter who is an ingénue in Hollywood. Mrs. Johnson used to play in stock in St. Louis, and her husband says she can yell "Oscar!" better than any woman they ever tried in the role. The inspiration for the Oscar gag was a woman Johnson saw five years ago wandering up and down the aisles at a boxing match in Hollywood looking for her husband and getting in the fans' line of vision. Olsen has a home at Brentwood, California, near Hollywood, and another at Malverne, Long Island. He bought the Malverne house sixteen years ago, and it comes in handy now that he is working in the East. He lives there and commutes to the Winter Garden. Johnson has a house at Santa Monica, California, and a farm at Libertyville, Illinois, which he uses mostly for shooting. He likes to hunt and fish; he also likes to talk about his health and is addicted to chiropractors. "My health comes first," he often says. He has never missed a show on account of illness. In town, the Johnsons live at 25 Central Park West, an apartment house largely populated by successful actors.

Throughout the last ten or twelve years, Olsen and Johnson have managed to average forty weeks' work a year, earning about twenty-five hundred dollars a week between them. Since they have held on to a sizable share of this, both are well-to-do. The Shuberts now meet all the expenses of *Hellz a Poppin*, and Ole and Chic together collect eighteen per cent of the gross receipts. The show is drawing around thirty-four thousand dollars a week, so the partners split about six thousand dollars. Besides Olsen and Johnson's six thousand dollars, the show costs around ten thousand dollars a week to operate, stage hands' and electricians' salaries accounting for a good proportion of the total. This leaves a profit of almost eighteen thousand dollars a week for the producers. By risking a little of their own money, Olsen and Johnson might have kept the whole show in their hands, but Ole and Chic say they were never gamblers and profess to be well satisfied with the present arrangement.

In off hours the partners like to sit in Dinty Moore's restaurant at a table plainly visible from the street and there receive the adulation of the profession. If no actors are present, they gladly accept the adulation of the laity, for whom they write innumerable autographs. "It's the ham in us," Olsen cheerfully remarks. On days when there is no matinee, they sometimes spend all the afternoon in Moore's, drinking coffee and devising new bits of gonk. Or they may pass the time by speaking condescendingly of the hardhearted booker at Loew's State who refused to book *Hellz a Poppin*, or of Mr. Watts, the supercilious critic from Parkersburg, West Virginia, who is not yet Olsen-and-Johnson-conscious. Johnson looks in the full-length mirrors, picks his teeth, and spits on the floor. Olsen invariably wears a large spring of artificial flowers as a boutonniere. One of their favorite subjects of reminiscence is the offstage practical joke, a specialty of the firm, which brightened their dark years in the Rotary belt. One Christmas they sent pregnant rabbits to all the critics in San Francisco.

"No suave inflections," Olsen says when he tells the story of the rabbits, which is usually interrupted by convulsions of laughter.

"Sure," says the moon-faced Johnson, picking his teeth. "With us it's a belly laugh or nothing."

• The Boy in the Pistachio Shirt •

usinessmen like Baron Axel
Wenner-Gren, the Swedish
manufacturer of iceboxes and
anti-aircraft guns, and Bruce Barton, the advertising executive,
who know Roy Wilson Howard, head man of the Scripps-
Howard newspapers, think of him as primarily a Great Reporter. Howard frequently assures them that he would rather
cover a good story than do anything else in the world. Most of
the newspaper reporters who know Mr. Howard think of him as
primarily a Great Businessman, and this misconception, as he
terms it, pains him. "I'm still just a newspaper boy," Howard
democratically informed a former employee he met at the
Philadelphia convention of the Republican party. He was at the
moment waiting for Wendell L. Willkie, who had just been nominated, to pack a spare shirt and join him aboard the Howard
yacht, the *Jamaroy*, for a weekend voyage of relaxation. While
waiting, Howard called the ex-employee's attention to his green
hatband, made of the neck feathers of a rare Hawaiian bird.
"You can only use six feathers from a bird, and it takes two hundred birds to make one of these bands," he said with modest satisfaction. Abercrombie & Fitch sold a total of two or three of
these bands for one hundred fifty dollars apiece.

The *Jamaroy*'s fantail was draped in red, white, and blue for
the Willkie cruise, and Mrs. Howard, a plump, pleasant woman,

who looks a little like the first Mrs. Jimmy Walker, wore seagoing togs of the same colors. Howard stuck to an ensemble of bright green suit, shirt, tie, and hatband. He adopted loud clothes as a trade-mark when he first went to work nearly forty years ago, believing that they would prevent superiors from forgetting him. The clothes serve no practical purpose now, since he has no superiors, but they have become a habit. Barton, an old friend, explains them by saying, "When a product is going well, you don't change the package." Soon after Willkie arrived on the *Jamaroy*, newspapermen who came aboard with him to say good-by discovered that Helen Worden, a reporter on Howard's *World-Telegram*, was on the yacht as a guest. Fearing that Miss Worden might write a series of exclusive feature articles, possibly entitled "Wind, Waves, and Willkie," the other reporters kept complaining to the candidate until he gave in and ungallantly asked Howard to order her ashore, which the publisher did. Howard thought of this as one more instance of the unjust suspicion with which other journalists sometimes regard him. He is extremely sensitive.

One evening, during a particularly acrimonious phase of some negotiations with the American Newspaper Guild, the CIO union of editorial and business-office workers which now has contracts with fourteen of the nineteen Scripps-Howard newspapers, Howard learned that a Guild leader had spoken harshly of him at a meeting. Around midnight he called up a subeditor who lived in Yonkers and asked him to come to the Howard home in the East Sixties immediately. At about two o'clock the employee arrived. "Joe," the publisher shouted before the Howard butler had had time to take the man's hat, "tell me, am I a son of a bitch?" The man said no, and Howard seemed reassured. The same sensitiveness came to light after the passage of the lend-lease bill, which Howard and his editors had vigorously opposed. The Scripps-Howard chief telephoned to a number of acquaintances friendly to the administration and asked them if they thought he was an appeaser. "If you ever think I'm getting too far off base," he told one man, "I wish you'd call up and tell me."

Despite this concern over other people's opinions of him, the publisher frequently follows courses of action that strangers might consider dictated by self-interest. There was, for example, the time in 1937 when a Congressional committee was about to investigate loopholes in the income-tax law and, it turned out, to name Howard and several other Scripps-Howard officers, along with still other wealthy men, as having set up personal holding companies to cut down their taxes. Howard's particular device, entirely within the law, had saved him eighty thousand dollars in taxes on his taxable income of five hundred thousand dollars in 1936. For weeks before the committee met, Westbrook Pegler, Howard's favorite Scripps-Howard columnist, blasted away at the highhanded and inquisitorial methods of the government's income-tax men. Howard must have been tempted to ask Pegler, as a favor, to stop, on the ground that the world might think the excitement more than a coincidence, or to omit some of the Pegler columns from his newspapers. However, the publisher steeled himself against such tampering with the liberty of the press, and the columnist's opinions appeared.

Something in Howard's stature and carriage suggests a jockey, but he would be too big to ride in anything except a steeplechase. Howard blames the late Arthur Brisbane for spreading the impression that he is ridiculously short. "Brisbane once tried to get me into the Hearst organization," he says, "and he never forgave me for turning him down. After I got well known, he always referred to me in his column as 'little Roy Howard.' Arthur could never understand a man who wasn't interested in money."

Sometimes, to prove that he is not really small, Howard invites new acquaintances to stand up beside him in front of an immense mirror in his office. The publisher stands straight, lifts his chin, and waits for the caller's cheering assurance that he isn't such a very little fellow after all. He looks a trifle shorter than he is because his head, covered with gray hair that he parts in the middle, is large in proportion to the rest of him. He is five feet six.

Howard has a wedge-shaped face, broad at the temples and tapering toward the chin, and has a short, close-cropped, graying mustache. His face is youthful in a curious way, reminding one of a prematurely old boy. He is actually fifty-eight. One of Howard's characteristics is a high, banjo-string voice that plucks at a hearer's attention, dominates it, and then lulls it until, like the buzz of a mosquito returning from a swing around a room, the sound increases in intensity and awakes the listener again. He is acutely conscious of prolixity in others. He once telephoned a Scripps-Howard editor in Washington from New York to tell him of a long-distance conversation he had just had with Joseph P. Kennedy, who was in Boston. "That Kennedy talks your ear off," Howard complained. "I was paying the charges, and he had me on the phone for forty-five minutes." When Howard hung up, the editor looked at his watch. The publisher had been talking to him for just about forty-five minutes. Howard occasionally times his telephone calls with a stop watch so that he can later check his bills. Even with the expensive minutes fleeting before his eyes, he has the same emotional difficulty in hanging up a receiver that a fat woman has in waving away a tray of chocolate éclairs.

When Howard is on a local wire his pleasure is uninhibited by economic considerations, and there are days when he practically edits the *World-Telegram*, which is at 125 Barclay Street, from his own office at Scripps-Howard headquarters, on the twenty-second floor of 230 Park Avenue. On these days, Lee B. Wood, the executive editor of the *World-Telegram*, squirms at his desk in a corner of the newspaper's vast city room, holding the receiver against his ear and repeating "Yes, Roy," at irregular intervals until his voice sounds as mechanical as the clack of the news tickers. Wood, an extremely tall man, slides forward and down in his seat as such a day progresses, until finally he appears to be resting on his shoulder blades. Howard's voice sometimes seems to have a narcotic effect on the cerebral processes of his subordinates. An irreverent *mot* of the *World-Telegram* city room defines a Scripps-Howard editor as "a man who walks briskly, smiles a lot, and rearranges furniture." Top editors have an additional function: keeping down expenses. A good Scripps-Howard editor is never too tired to walk around a newspaper plant at the end of the day and turn out unnecessary lights.

This frugality is a heritage from the reign of Edward Wyllis Scripps, the founder of the newspaper chain, who was accustomed to go into towns where there was an established conservative newspaper and start an opposition sheet on a minimum budget. The Scripps entry would plump for labor as a matter of business principle. Its chances of survival depended on keeping expenses low. The Scripps formula, as expressed by a cynical veteran, was to "hire a shed down by the railroad station, put in a press that Gutenberg had scrapped and some linotype machines held together with baling wire, then put in a kid for twelve dollars a week to be editor and promise him one per cent of the profits as soon as the circulation hit a million." Scripps's thesis, as he himself expounded it, was that a heavy outlay on a newspaper put a publisher at the mercy of bankers and advertisers. Only a shoestring newspaper could afford to be pro-labor, he used to say, but if a pro-labor paper could survive for a while, it was bound to catch on. He once said that ninety-five per cent of all newspaper readers were not rich and would read a daily published in the interest of the have-nots. A profitable amount of advertising would follow circulation. Scripps remarked late in life that he had founded about forty papers on this shoestring basis and that a third of them had been great financial successes. When he died, in 1926, his newspaper chain was estimated to be worth forty million dollars. Since his death, there have been changes in the business concepts as well as in the editorial doctrines of the firm, but a vestigial frugality remains.

None of this frugality is evident in Howard's private office, which is a loud version of an Oriental temple in red-and-black lacquer and gilt, with a chandelier in the form of a Chinese lamp trailing red tassels. The walls are decorated with scrolls addressed to the publisher by admiring Celestials. They are long, vertical strips of parchment covered with large calligraphy, and Howard, who reads no Chinese but knows an English version of each of the texts by rote, likes to translate them for visitors. "The Chinese send them instead of autographed photographs," he says. "That one there, for instance, is from my old friend Tong Sho-yi, who was slated to be President of China if Wu Pei-fu had beaten the Kuomintang, but the Kuomintang beat Wu Pei-fu, and Tong Sho-yi was killed by hatchet men in Shanghai. He was a great friend of Herbert Hoover's. The scroll says, 'To make love to a young woman is like feeding honey to a baby on the point of a knife.' " In his house in the East Sixties, which looks something like a branch public library, he also has a Chinese room, and Mrs. Howard has a three-hundred-year-old Ning-po lacquer bed that was imported in a hundred and twenty-three pieces, with directions in Chinese for putting it together. "The only Japanese stuff in my house," Howard says, "is a dressing-table set of pigeon's-blood cloisonné that Mrs. Matsuoka gave Mrs. Howard." Until recently, Mr. Matsuoka was the Japanese Foreign Minister.

The surface of the huge desk at which Howard works in his office, and which looks long enough for him to sleep on, is so brightly polished that it mirrors his face, and a caller sitting across from him may have the sensation of being talked at simultaneously by two identical faces, one perched on Howard's neck and the other spread out on the desk. There is always a small bowl of dark magenta carnations on the desk, and Howard usually has a carnation of the same shade in his lapel, day or night. When he dines out, he has been known to wear patent-leather Russian boots, an evening cape, a red tie, a checked waistcoat, and a dinner jacket. His business suits are short-waisted and double-breasted, and have long, pointed lapels like the ears of an alert donkey. Although the suits in themselves are notable, people usually remember them only as accessories to his haberdashery. Beholders recall chiefly the wine-red shirts with large plaids of shrill green; the shirts of turquoise-and-gold squares; the orange, mauve, and pistachio shirts; the shirts of jade, rust red, and tangerine, lovingly picked out with electric blue, and, invariably, the matching bow ties and pocket handkerchiefs cut from the shirting. A fascinated colored washroom attendant who once observed him in the clubhouse at Saratoga stared for a minute and then said with awe, "All that man need is a gold horseshoe front and back and he have the prettiest racing colors in America."

Whenever Howard gets an idea he considers good, he walks into an office adjoining his own and tries it out on William W. Hawkins, chairman of the board of the Scripps-Howard newspapers, who has been his closest ally inside the organization since both were youngsters working for the Scripps wire service, the United Press, thirty years ago. Hawkins is a broad-bodied, placid, red-faced man who gazes at you benignly through gold-rimmed spectacles. There is nothing exotic about his office. It is traditionally American-executive in motif, and is adorned with a large portrait of Will Rogers by Leon Gordon. Howard owns 13.2 per cent and Hawkins 6.6 per cent of the stock of the E. W. Scripps Company, which holds over fifty per cent of the voting stock of each of the more than fifty separately incorporated Scripps-Howard enterprises. According to its financial statement for 1939, the E. W. Scripps Company's net worth was $43,161,753, making Howard's and Hawkins' stakes in it roughly $5,611,027 and $2,805,513, respectively. Its net earnings in that year were $1,530,000. The other 80.2 per cent of the stock is owned by the Edward W. Scripps Trust, which was established by the Scripps will. Robert Paine Scripps, last surviving son of the founder of the company, was sole trustee during his lifetime. The stock now is held by the trust for his three sons. The present trustees are Howard, Hawkins, and George B. Parker, the editor-in-chief of all the newspapers. The three are to be relieved of their duties in turn as Robert Paine, Jr., Charles Edward, and Samuel H., the three sons of Robert Paine Scripps, reach the age of twenty-five. Hawkins will retire as trustee in 1943, when the eldest boy reaches that age. Parker will yield his place to the second son in 1945. Howard is slated to remain until 1952 before giving way to the youngest Scripps son. Since Howard and Hawkins always vote alike, the arrangement leaves the two partners, as complementary and alliterative as a gentile Potash and Perlmutter, effectively in control of a property which includes nineteen newspapers, several newspaper syndicates, and the great United Press. Parker is a stern-looking, white-haired man, conspicuously decorated with a Phi Beta Kappa key. He was graduated from the University of Oklahoma in 1908 and is the cultural force of the triumvirate.

Until shortly after Robert Paine Scripps' death, Howard and

Hawkins had no share in the parent E. W. Scripps Company, but possessed large interests in several of the individual properties it controlled, particularly the *World-Telegram*. Since, as trustees of the Edward W. Scripps Trust, they might have been suspected of favoring certain subsidiaries at the expense of others, they exchanged their holdings for shares in the E. W. Scripps Company.

If Howard and Hawkins constituted a vaudeville team, Howard would be known as the star and Hawkins as the feeder. Flashy, mercurial, and enormously energetic, Howard, in conferences with Hawkins, characteristically walks around his seated partner like an ocean traveler circumambulating a deck. Hawkins intones only brief, bass responses to Howard's rapid tenor litany and speeds or slows Howard's gyrations by increasing or diminishing the degree of what seems to be apathy in his voice. Howard expresses great faith in his intuition, but he usually seeks reassurance from others before he acts on it. He doesn't expect to be contradicted, but he does gauge the intensity of an associate's approval. A couple of unadorned yeses from an editorial writer, for example, would indicate the man's deep conviction that Howard was wrong. Hawkins is actually four months younger than Howard, who was born on January 1, 1883, but he sometimes refers to his partner as "the boy." "We would have had the boy dressed up if we'd known you were coming," he once said to a visitor when Howard stepped into his office wearing a relatively subdued arrangement of suit, shirt, and tie all in a large black-and-white hound's-tooth pattern. Hawkins has an idea that Howard's yacht is bad publicity for the firm and does his best in conversation to make it sound like a dory. "It's really not much of a yacht," he says. "I don't know what the hell he wants it for." The *Jamaroy* is a 110-foot power vessel which once belonged to C. F. Kettering, a vice-president of General Motors.

Howard and Hawkins made their way up in the newspaper

world with the United Press, which the elder Scripps established in 1907 after buying out a news service known as the Publishers' Press Association. They both went to work there that year. Howard's flashier qualities got him off to a faster start than Hawkins, and they assumed their present roles in the combination almost instinctively. When Howard became president and general manager of the United Press in 1912, Hawkins became second in command. When Howard resigned in 1920 to become chairman of the board of the Scripps newspapers, Hawkins succeeded him as president of the United Press. Hawkins followed Howard to the Scripps-Howard main office in 1923. The current *Directory of Directors* lists Hawkins as an officer or director of fifty separate organizations, all within the Scripps-Howard group. Howard, possibly because of diffidence, is listed only forty-seven times.

Among the eighteen Scripps-Howard newspapers, aside from the *World-Telegram*, are the Cleveland *Press*, Pittsburgh *Press*, Cincinnati *Post*, Memphis *Commercial Appeal*, San Francisco *News*, Washington *News*, and papers in Birmingham, Indianapolis, and Columbus. Of these, the Cleveland, Pittsburgh, and Memphis papers are believed in newspaper circles to be extremely profitable and the others less so. The combined circulation of the nineteen papers is about 1,500,000, which is around three quarters that of the New York *Daily News* and approximately three times that of the New York *Times*. Howard and Hawkins have said repeatedly that the profits of the *World-Telegram*, despite its 400,000 circulation, have been negligible. On one occasion in 1935, Howard, addressing a group of editorial employees, said that Heywood Broun's salary of approximately forty thousand dollars was larger than the profits of the newspaper in the previous year. The United Press, a newsgathering organization that sells its news to 1460 papers in the United States, South America, and Japan, as well as to five hundred radio stations, has been said to earn a million dollars a year. There are also complementary organizations, like the Newspaper Enterprise Association, or N.E.A., a syndicate which sells newspaper features; the Acme picture service, which sells news pictures, and the United Feature Syndicate. Every Scripps-Howard paper pays a fee to the central office for "national management." Sometimes a paper which, considered as a single corporate enterprise, is just breaking even is actually a profitable Scripps-Howard property because of this fee and the fees it pays as a customer of the Scripps-Howard syndicates.

Howard says that he has not been in an office of the United Press for years and that its policy is controlled entirely by Hugh Baillie, its president, who has a much larger financial interest in that organization than either Howard or Hawkins. The E. W. Scripps Company, which Howard runs as an officer and trustee, although he owns only about thirteen per cent of its stock, holds over half of the stock in the United Press. Baillie has worked for the United Press for thirty years. It now has fifteen hundred full-time correspondents and fifty-five thousand contributing part-time correspondents. The subscribers include a hundred and fifty-one papers in twenty-one Latin-American countries, the Japanese-government news agency, the Osaka *Mainichi* and Tokio *Nichi-Nichi*, which are two of the most widely circulated newspapers in the world, and a cluster of customers in Europe, including thirty-three papers in Germany.

Howard and Hawkins are less inseparable in social life. This may be because Howard tries to regulate the big-bodied Hawkins' intake of food and drink for what he considers Hawkins' own good. He takes a maternal interest in the private life of everybody he knows. A United Press correspondent, explaining a fondness of his employer's for Orientals, once said, "Roy likes to teach them how to use chopsticks." Another time, when Howard was on a cruise ship, the vessel's social director fell ill, and the publisher spent a satisfying week introducing apathetic men to patently antagonistic women and making people play deck tennis when they didn't want to. Not long afterward he bought the *Jamaroy*, on which he could be social director officially. He is never happier than when he has guests on his yacht to organize. Merlin H. Aylesworth, former president of the National Broadcasting Company, who was an important Scripps-Howard official for about two years after he left the radio corporation, says he once saved a leading Howard columnist from being killed by the publisher's solicitude. "Roy wanted him to go on the wagon," Aylesworth says, "and I told him, 'Roy, if that fellow goes on the wagon, he'll die.'" The columnist is still in good health.

The publisher freely volunteers advice to political candidates, plans complete careers for young women he has known three minutes, and for a year tormented a Russian portrait painter he knew with instructions for the improvement of a left eye in one of the painter's works. The maddened painter finally turned on him and shouted, "Yah, and I know who designs your shirts! The Congoleum Corporation of America!" As a matter of fact, Howard has them made for him by Walter-McCrory, on West Forty-sixth Street. Howard's willingness to run things sometimes rises to the international plane. Matsuoka, whose wife sent Mrs. Howard the cloisonné, was chief of the Japanese delegation to Geneva at the time Japan withdrew from the League of Nations. Howard was also in Geneva then. "Matsuoka never could sell me on the idea of taking Japan out of the League of Nations," Howard says, "but he tried like hell." Another Japanese project of which Howard disapproves is the appointment of Wang

Ching-wei as puppet President of China. "I am personally acquainted with Wang Ching-wei," he says, "but I do not think he would make a good president."

Howard prefers as friends men whom he considers leaders in their field. This includes not only businessmen like Barton, Bernard M. Baruch, and Bernard F. Gimbel but Howard Chandler Christy and Leon Gordon, the artists; Lowell Thomas, the broadcaster; Rex Beach, Rupert Hughes, John Erskine, and Hendrik Willem van Loon, the writers; and Kent Cooper, general manager of the Associated Press. Of the entire group, Baruch is the only one who might be called a representative of finance capital. Howard grew up in Indiana with a pious, Midwestern fear of Wall Street. In general he finds the Eastern or pseudo-English type of rich man a bit stiff and prefers the company of transplanted Midwesterners like himself. Many of his friends are members of the Dutch Treat Club, a sort of Kiwanis of the arts. Howard likes the Rotarian congeniality of the club and doubtless approves of the house rule that every man pays for his own lunch. He has a feminine reluctance to part with money for anything except clothes. Sometimes he tries to make this characteristic amusing, saying blithely, "I'm Scotch," as one of his employees pays the fare for the taxi in which they have been riding or picks up a check for drinks. On other occasions, in restaurants, he determines the tip by dividing the amount of the check by ten and leaves the exact tithe, down to the penny. "The so-and-so gave us the worst service I ever saw in my life," he is likely to say afterward.

The event in his life to which Howard most frequently refers in ordinary conversation is the time he had an audience, in 1933, with Hirohito, Emperor of Japan. This privilege, as the United Press was careful to explain in sending out Howard's account of the meeting, had never before been enjoyed by an American newspaperman. Howard was unfortunately unable to quote the

Emperor in his newspapers, because court etiquette forbade it. However, his account of the colloquy, which ran on the front pages of all Scripps-Howard papers, left no doubt that the publisher had favorably impressed the Emperor. Howard often dates events by the momentous day. "That was two and a half years before my interview with the Emperor of Japan," he will say to a woman he meets at a dinner party, while discussing almost anything, and one associate unkindly says that Howard thinks of the Christian era as something that began 1933 years before the historic encounter.

According to Howard's own story of the interview, Matsuoka, who, after maneuvering the Japanese out of the League of Nations at Geneva, barnstormed the United States in a dignified fashion, explaining Japan's position, suggested that the publisher come to Tokio sometime and meet the Mikado. One gathers that, having business there a few months later, he dropped in on Matsuoka casually and the statesman practically dragged him through the palace gates, insisting that Hirohito would be offended if he didn't call. Newspapermen who were stationed in Tokio at the time are wont to state openly that however easy it had been for Howard, it hadn't been much of a cinch for Miles Vaughn, the United Press correspondent there, who had gone through months of diplomatic toil arranging the audience. Howard was not permitted to write much more than such general statements as "Japanese-American friendship, understanding, and cooperation are of the utmost importance to peace not only in the Far East but in the world, in the opinion of His Imperial Majesty Hirohito, Emperor of Japan." As one looks back, it is doubtful if the interview can be considered a milestone in the old endeavor of the Occident to understand the Orient.

Howard, in some moods, likes to deprecate the importance of his scoop as a journalistic accomplishment, although it is naturally impossible to deprecate anything without mentioning it. He does not wish it to obscure other achievements. "Nobody ever says anything about my knowing anything about Russia," he often complains. "I interviewed Stalin too." The Stalin interview was in March 1936. The publisher submitted a written list of questions before the interview, and the dictator was ready with prepared answers which were read off by an interpreter. Stalin spoke harshly of Hitler and the Japanese. "The interview was devoid of forensics and dramatics," Howard wrote. ". . . the informality and ready humor which characterized the conversation are silk gloves covering an often-demonstrated iron will." Although Stalin didn't divulge much information, Howard felt that his time had not been wasted. He believed that he had a clearer understanding of the Russian situation. On his return to New York he told ship-news reporters that Russia had the kind of government the people wanted and that any businessman could see that it was going to last, a statement he has since referred to as illustrating his open-mindedness. "Stalin is a little fellow," he told the ship-news men, "not as tall as I am."

Howard also had an interview with Hitler in 1936, but his impression of him was not so happy. "I only got a chance to say four or five words," he says. "Every time I said something to the interpreter Hitler let loose with an oration in German." It was one of the rare occasions in Howard's life on which he has been talked down.

II—The Pax Howardiensis

Early the morning after last Election Day, a message went out on the wires of the United Press, the Scripps-Howard news service, to editors of the nineteen Scripps-Howard papers scattered over the United States, saying, "Kill Talburt Cartoon Out at Third—R. W. H." The cartoon, drawn by Harold Talburt, an artist employed by a Scripps-Howard feature syndicate, showed Franklin D. Roosevelt in baseball togs sliding for a base marked, with the usual Scripps-Howard subtlety, "Third Term." The third baseman, marked "American People," was, presumably upon Scripps-Howard advice, tagging him out. The precautionary message was a typical tribute from Roy Wilson Howard to the alertness and intelligence of his editors. He wasn't taking any chances. A few weeks after this, Howard paid a friendly call on Mr. Roosevelt at the White House. Ever since the first Wednesday of last November, a sign above the desk of the President's secretary, Stephen T. Early, has proclaimed, "We ain't mad with nobody." It is unlikely that any other critic of the President as acrid as Howard took the sign literally so soon.

As Howard left the President's office after the interview, reporters from the press room in the White House gathered around him on the chance of picking up a few quotations. The publisher waved the newsmen away with a twanging "Nothing to say, boys." As he headed for the door, somebody called out, "Mr. Howard, did you call to report another armistice?" "Who said that?" Howard asked. Nobody answered, and the publisher hurried on with his short, quick stride. The anonymous voice had recalled the most gigantic *gaffe* in newspaper history, the false-armistice report Howard sent over from France on November 7, 1918. The fellow who had asked the question may have reflected on the possibility that the false-armistice episode was the clearest proof in Howard's career of his ability to survive experiences that would have proved mortally discouraging to other men.

The report that set the country to celebrating the end of the first World War on the afternoon of November 7 was received by the United Press in New York and said, in the customary newspaper cablese: "URGENT ARMISTICE ALLIES GERMANY SIGNED ELEVEN SMORNING HOSTILITIES CEASED TWO SAFTERNOON SEDAN TAKEN SMORNING BY AMERICANS." It was signed "HOWARD SIMMS." Howard, then president of the United Press, was supposed by his subordinates here to be in Paris. William Philip Simms, now foreign editor of the United Press, was then the organization's manager in Paris, and it was a rule that all United Press messages from France had to bear his signature. When Howard sent the cable, he was not in Paris but in Brest, where he had just finished having a chatty lunch with Vice-Admiral Henry B. Wilson, commander of the American naval forces in France. According to Howard's subsequent account of the affair, he had concluded that the World War was about washed up and had obtained permission to return to America on a transport scheduled to sail from Brest on November 8. Armistice was in the air. The German government had appointed a delegation to meet with representatives of the Allied powers and receive terms. The two delegations were due to come together sometime on November 7, but Howard did not know the exact hour. When he met Admiral Wilson, the naval officer told him that he had just had a telephone call from a friend in the United States Embassy in Paris. The friend had told Wilson that the armistice had been signed. Howard promptly wired this interesting item from Brest, which was the cablehead of the transatlantic cable. The Brest censors were in the streets celebrating the armistice rumor, which had spread rapidly from the officers of Admiral Wilson's staff to American sailors and from them to the inhabitants. The telegraph operator assumed the censors had passed Howard's dispatch and simply transmitted it. Howard had added Simms's signature *ultra vires* as Simms's boss, and because of Simms's name the United Press office in New York assumed that the message came from Paris via Brest, instead of directly from Brest. Simms, if consulted, might have advised his superior to double-check his information, a naïve procedure habitual among journalists of lower voltage.

Newspapers in the United States passed the news along to the public under headlines like the New York *Journal*'s "GERMANY GIVES UP, WAR ENDS AT TWO P.M." and the *Evening Post*'s "REPORT ARMISTICE SIGNED; CITY IN WILD DEMONSTRATION." Factory whistles blew; church bells rang, and office workers began throwing paper out of windows. It cost New York eighty thousand dollars to clear the debris of the celebration off the streets. The State Department issued a statement in the afternoon denying that the war was over, but the public refused to be balked. The Associated Press, older and more conservative rival of Howard's pushing organization, denied the report from the first, but newspaper editors suspected that it was covering up its own lack of enterprise. An angry crowd tried to wreck the office of the Associated Press at 51 Chambers Street, shouting that it was a nest of German spies. Outside the headquarters of the United Press in the Pulitzer Building, an air-raid siren, vintage of 1918, shrieked at one-minute intervals.

During the twenty-four hours that followed the publication of Howard's report, other, lesser American correspondents in France were desperately chivied by their editors, who plaintively cabled, "CAN YOU CONFIRM WAR END?" A *Times* man at the headquarters of the American Second Army received twenty-seven messages from Carr Van Anda, his managing editor. The correspondent kept asking Major General Robert L. Bullard, the army commander, if the war had ceased, and Bullard kept insisting it hadn't. Each denial, when cabled to America, apparently made Van Anda more suspicious. The *Times* headlines on November 8 furnish a concise chronicle of the previous day: "FALSE PEACE REPORT ROUSES ALL AMERICA," "CITY GOES WILD WITH JOY," "SUPPOSED ARMISTICE DELIRIOUSLY CELEBRATED HERE AND IN OTHER CITIES,"

"Crowds Parade Streets," "Jubilant Throngs Reject All Denials and Tear Up Newspapers Containing Them," "Judges Close the Courts," "Mayor Addresses Crowds at City Hall," "Saloons Closed at Night to Check Disorder," and "United Press Men Sent False Cable."

The afternoon newspapers on November 8, particularly those that had been taken in the day before, attacked the United Press. A Brooklyn *Eagle* editorial, typical of the milder approaches to the subject, began, "The United Press, its news dupes, and the French censors must get out of this muddle as best they can." The *Post* deplored the heavy loss of working hours incurred when shipyard workers knocked off to celebrate. The *Sun* said, "The responsibility is serious in the extreme." The *Globe* wondered, "Will the public dare to rejoice over the real news when the armistice comes or will the celebrations be an anticlimax?" During the following week, United Press news disappeared almost completely from the pages of American papers.

All through the false-armistice excitement, William W. Hawkins, Howard's phlegmatic second-in-command, who was in charge at the New York United Press office, fought to defend the Howard message. Hawkins had collaborated with Howard from the first year of the United Press's existence and was two years later to succeed him as president of the organization. Five or six hours after the State Department's denial of the story, Hawkins, at his office in the Pulitzer Building, said that the United Press would stand by the report until it was disproved. The State Department said that German and Allied delegates to a conference on armistice terms had not even met at the time the report was released. Hawkins replied that it was lucky Howard had got his story past a momentarily relaxed censorship. Twenty-four hours after the false report, the United Press sent out another dispatch just received from its president, saying, "URGENT BREST ADMIRAL WILSON WHO ANNOUNCED BREST NEWS-PAPER ARMISTICE BEEN SIGNED LATER NOTIFIED UNCONFIRMABLE MEANWHILE BREST RIOTOUSLY CELEBRATING. HOWARD SIMMS." Subsequently it sent out a message from Admiral Wilson admitting that the report had originated in his office. Years afterward, when the *Tribune* had been taken in by a fake report of a fleet of gambling palaces off the Atlantic coast, Howard, playing golf on a Westchester course, shouted to a *Tribune* man named Montague, who was playing near by, "Where did you get that scoop?" "Admiral Wilson told us," Montague answered. Howard was struck dumb for five or six seconds.

The signing of the real armistice on November 11 saved Howard and the United Press from any prolonged humiliation. Americans were too pleased with the real thing to stay angry over the false. Howard ordinarily thinks of the incident light-heartedly. In 1928, on the first anniversary of his acquisition of the New York *Telegram*, a purchase which marked Scripps-Howard's entry into the New York newspaper field, the editorial staff held a beefsteak dinner at Cavanagh's Restaurant. The publisher acted as master of ceremonies. Francis Albertanti, a sports writer, heckled Howard freely. At last, Howard happily yelled, "Shut up! I once stopped a war and I can stop you!"

The false armistice and its aftermath did nothing to estrange Howard from Edward Wyllis Scripps, the odd old man who owned fifty-one per cent of the stock in the Scripps newspapers and the United Press and had been Howard's employer for thirteen years. The way Howard bounced back after the nightmare of November 7 increased Scripps's respect for him. Scripps, in his spare time, used to dictate for his own amusement notes he called "disquisitions" on anything that came into his mind. He had already dictated one on Howard in 1917. Howard, then thirty-four years old, had been president of the United Press for five years. "Right from the start, Howard's self-respect and self-confidence was so great as to make it impossible for it to increase," Scripps had said. "Doubtless to himself his present situation in life, his successes and his prosperity, all seem to be perfectly natural, and to be no more nor less than he expected." Describing the young man at the time of their first meeting, Scripps dictated, "His manner was forceful and the reverse of modest. Gall was written all over his face. It was in every tone and every word he voiced."

Scripps never tried to build a large metropolitan newspaper. He remained true all his life to a formula of establishing liberal, shoestring newspapers in towns so much alike in their outlook that the publications could have practically interchangeable parts. The national policies of the papers were determined at annual conventions of Scripps editors held at French Lick, Indiana, where Scripps would berate them all on general principles. The editors could determine their own local policies, provided they favored labor. In the eighties, Scripps, as a young man, had tried to run a newspaper in St. Louis and had found Joseph Pulitzer's *Post-Dispatch* too well intrenched in the liberal field in that city. He had thereupon decided that he was destined to be a newspaper Woolworth rather than a Tiffany. Except for St. Louis and Chicago, where he launched a small-scale experiment with an intentionally adless newspaper just before the World War, Scripps tried no city larger than Cleveland. There, in 1878, he founded the enormously profitable *Press* with an initial investment of $12,500. Howard, while he worked under Scripps, was a liberal too. He was frantically adaptable.

The town of Gano, in southwestern Ohio, where Howard

was born in 1883, is so small that it does not appear in an ordinary library atlas. Howard usually refers to himself as a Hoosier because his family moved to Indianapolis seven years after he was born. William Howard, his father, was for several years a railroad brakeman and later became a conductor. Railroad pay was low in the last century, and the Howards had a harder time than most railroad families, even though Roy was an only child. William Howard was tubercular, and a good part of his income went for medical care. When a friend a few years ago made fun of Howard for tipping a Paris taxi driver only fifty centimes, the publisher declared solemnly, "If my father had had a thousand dollars saved up, he could have gone out to Colorado and been cured." Howard sometimes speaks appreciatively of the railroad labor brotherhoods, because, he says, his father's pay and working conditions were terrible in those old non-union days. Roy went to Manual Training High School in Indianapolis, and became the school correspondent for the Indianapolis *News*. William Howard died during his son's senior year, and after the boy graduated he went to work as a reporter on the city staff of the *News* at eight dollars a week. He soon transferred to the *Star*, the opposition paper, where he became sports editor at twenty a week. Supporting his widowed mother, the boy, small, tense, determined to get on, adopted his now well-known uniform of gaudy shirts and patent-leather shoes as an outward disclaimer of his inward forebodings.

On the Indianapolis *News*, Howard met several men who became more or less fixtures in his life. Among them was the late Ray Long, a slightly older Hoosier, who was already city editor of that paper. Long, about Howard's size, was shallow, quick, energetic, and hedonistic. Howard always admired him as a pattern of worldliness and *savoir-vivre*. For twenty-five years, from

1910, when Long left Indianapolis to be a magazine editor, until 1935, when he committed suicide, he and Howard were inseparable companions after working hours. During that period Long edited *Red Book, Cosmopolitan*, and other magazines. Another friend Howard made in Indianapolis was a reporter named Lowell Mellett, a Hoosier born in the Elwood that Wendell L. Willkie subsequently made famous. Mellett, present director of the Office of Government Reports in Washington, is one of Franklin D. Roosevelt's principal advisers on public relations. Men who worked with Howard in Indianapolis remember most his eagerness and the neat manner in which he always draped his jacket on a hanger before sitting down at his typewriter. An older man on the *News* named Charles Stewart, who liked Howard, presently got a job as telegraph editor of the St. Louis *Post-Dispatch* and took the cub with him as assistant. Howard's mother rented a house in St. Louis, and Stewart boarded with the Howards. When Ray Long became managing editor of Scripps's Cincinnati *Post* a couple of years later, he sent for Howard to be news editor, and mother and son moved to Cincinnati. Mellett also joined the *Post* staff. Scripps's Midwestern papers were then known as the Scripps-McRae League; the McRae was Milton McRae, a junior partner who owned a relatively trifling amount of stock. Howard, who had been reading O. Henry, was eager to move on to New York and become a New Yorker. Long managed to have him appointed New York correspondent for the Scripps-McRae League, and Howard took the train for the big city. When he became proprietor of the New York *Telegram* twenty-one years later, he put notices on the bulletin board in the city room that said, "Remember! New York is Bagdad on the subway." O. O. McIntyre, when he eventually began writing his column, seemed to Howard the only authentic interpreter of the New York scene.

The twenty-three-year-old Howard who came to New York with an assured thirty-eight-dollar-a-week job, a beginning most of his colleagues would have envied, had already acquired a species of bantamweight dignity. "When you're my size," he sometimes says, "you can't afford to be a comedian." Newspapering, despite urgent prodding from schools of journalism, has always lagged behind the learned professions on the march to seemliness. Lawyers wrestled and played practical jokes on each other in Lincoln's time, but newspapermen continued to rough each other up for many decades thereafter. Howard, small, obstreperous, and glossy, had had to put up with an unusual amount of mauling during his Indianapolis and St. Louis days. One contemporary remembers seeing him tossed across the city room of the *Star* by a fat-headed giant giving a demonstration of jujitsu. Another time a colleague on the *Post-Dispatch* playfully touched a lighted match to the nape of the cub's neck. Howard, unfortunately, had that morning drenched his hair with a tonic that contained alcohol. A blue flame flickered over him, and for a moment he resembled a crêpe Suzette *flambée*. He never entered into the spirit of these high jinks, and finally his special brand of dignity came to be respected.

The Hoosier *boulevardier* was just beginning to settle into his role as the Babylonian correspondent of the Scripps-McRae League when Scripps, in 1907, acquired the Publishers' Press Association, a decrepit news-gathering service which he made the nucleus of a new agency he called the United Press. The Publishers' Press, which had its headquarters in New York, cost Scripps about $180,000. The Associated Press has always been a cooperative enterprise which will issue no new franchise on its telegraphic news service in a city where there are member papers unless the members consent. Since at that time there was no other large-scale telegraphic agency in the country, a non-member paper was at a tremendous disadvantage. Scripps said that the U.P. would buck the A.P. and sell news to anybody who would pay for it. He considered it his greatest contribution to a free journalism, and it proved to be one of his most profitable accomplishments. Shortly before his death he wrote, "Perhaps the greatest reason, however, for my objecting to becoming an integral part of the Press Association [the A.P.] in the crisis was that I knew at least ninety per cent of my fellows in American journalism were capitalists and conservatives. In those, my youthful days of pride, I swelled up with vanity at the thought that I was to be the savior of the free press in America. Of course, I have learned since that it requires more than one man to guarantee such freedom." Howard decided, soundly enough, that he would have more future as an executive with the new organization than as the solitary correspondent in Gomorrah of a group of Ohio newspapers.

The first president of the United Press was John Vandercook, a former Cincinnati *Post* official who knew Howard. Howard made his interest in the U.P. known, and Vandercook hired him as New York district manager. Mellett soon came on from Cincinnati, too, and for a while the two Indianapolis boys, both thin, shared a single bed in the apartment he and his mother rented. Hawkins came on from Louisville, where he was working on the *Courier-Journal*. The United Press was guaranteed against loss in the first few years by dues Scripps levied on the score of papers he controlled to cover the news agency's operating costs. Scripps, following his custom, reserved fifty-one per cent of the stock for himself, giving an option on twenty per cent to Vandercook and an option on another twenty per cent to Hamilton B. Clark, the business manager. Minor executives had chances to acquire smaller blocks of stock. The executives were to pay for their stock out of the profits of the new venture, if profits developed. This was a system Scripps had developed for giving executives of his newspapers an extra incentive. Even today Scripps-Howard executives of importance usually have an agreement with the management that they call "a deal," which means that they are rewarded with stock in the corporation employing them, if the corporation shows a profit. When an executive leaves one Scripps-Howard corporation for another, or for the outside world, he is compelled to surrender his stock at a price fixed by an "appraisal board" of other Scripps-Howard brass hats. His successor then has a chance to acquire the same stock. Vandercook, a newspaperman of great ability, died suddenly just as the United Press profits began to come in. Howard, already conspicuous for his push, begged for a chance at Vandercook's job. Gilson Gardner, Scripps's secretary, has described Howard as "busy as a wasp trying to get through a windowpane." Clark backed the youngster. Scripps was at Miramar, his California ranch. He spent most of his time there because he didn't like other rich men and couldn't abide poor people, he once told one of his associates. The old man had never seen Howard, but Scripps's wife and Howard's mother had been chums as girls, and Scripps had heard a good deal about him. "I was surprised at being urged to let Howard be tried out," Scripps later wrote. But he gave him the job. "My fancy was tickled with the idea," the old man continued; "my propensity to try experiments demonstrated itself again. However, Howard made good. Howard continued to make good. The United Press . . . began to grow into a property that had an actual value." Soon Howard got a chance to buy Vandercook's twenty-per-cent share of the company's stock, and did so. Clark resigned to found a Philadelphia paper, and Howard also picked up his twenty per cent. In 1909, Howard made a trip abroad to report to Scripps on the foreign-news-gathering arrangements. Some time before, he had met a young freelance newspaperwoman named Margaret Rohe in New York. Miss Rohe, tiring of letters, had gone to London in the cast of an American show called *The Chorus Lady*, in which she had a small speaking part. Howard met her again in London and married her. Howard's mother took a second husband a few years after her son's marriage and moved to the Pacific coast, where she died in 1931.

The United Press started off with the same independent Left Wing slant for which the Scripps-McRae newspapers were known. That was because, in the beginning, most of its clients were members of the chain. In its handling of the strikes of the Danbury hatters in 1912 and the Paterson silk workers in 1912 and 1913, the U.P. was noticeably more pro-labor than the Associated Press. The contrast gradually disappeared. Howard was not slow to recognize that a news service has a market unlike that of a newspaper. Scripps had once remarked that ninety-five per cent of all newspaper readers are not rich even though ninety per cent of the publishers are "capitalists and conservatives." When, in 1912, Howard was made president of the United Press and was in a way to become a rich man, old friends in Indianapolis considered him a great success in the East. In New York, unfortunately, there was no Scripps paper and nobody seemed to know him. As an ambitious young man of twenty-nine aspiring to take his place as a prominent metropolitan figure, he was pained scarcely less that few New Yorkers had ever heard of E. W. Scripps, either. He indicated a feeling that Scripps's indifference to Broadway showed a blind spot.

The first World War brought the United Press the big newspapers of South America as customers. Before the war they had been clients of Havas, the agency subsidized by the French government. Also, during the war, newspapers all over the United States felt the need of more wire service, and the United Press, which was selling its service to five hundred clients in 1914, had seven hundred newspapers on its list in 1918. Howard's false armistice had no effect on his fortunes, which unexpectedly improved further when Scripps quarreled with his eldest son, James, publisher of the Seattle *Star* and several other Western papers. James gained control of the stock of these papers and broke with his father. James's death in 1921 came before a reconciliation was possible. A second son, John, died in 1914. James's defection in 1920 left only Robert Scripps, twenty-five years old and profoundly uninterested in the newspaper business, as an heir. The elder Scripps had to pick a practical newspaperman as a running mate for his son, and since most of the editors who had helped him build his newspapers had short life expectancies, Howard was the logical choice. Old Scripps made him chairman of the board of the Scripps-McRae newspapers in 1920. Howard resigned as president of the United Press in order to accept the new job. McRae, the second barrel of the Scripps-McRae name, was already out of the firm. The following year Howard's name replaced McRae's on the mastheads of all the papers in the chain, which added to Howard's prestige. The resplendent young news-service man was nevertheless looked upon with some suspicion by the older set of Scripps's followers among newspaper publishers, Midwestern liberals who thought Howard had been corrupted by his residence in the East. Scripps gave up active direction of the Scripps enterprises in 1924, but retained a controlling financial interest.

The combination of Howard and Robert Paine Scripps, who together took over the direction of the news empire when the elder Scripps retired, was once compared by a company eulogist to "the two blades of a pair of shears." It was an accurate metaphor only if the writer was thinking of a tailor's shears, which has one flat and one cutting blade. Robert Scripps was the flat blade. Originally planning to be a nature poet, he had been drafted into the newspaper business because his father believed in keeping his properties in the family. Robert Scripps used to say, "I hate to make decisions. Roy loves to make them. So I let him." E. W. Scripps died aboard his yacht, *Ohio*, off the coast of Liberia on March 12, 1926, at the age of seventy-two. He left his newspapers, valued at a total of forty million dollars, to his son and three grandsons in a trust which would be dissolved upon the death of the last surviving grandson. Eleven months later, Howard acquired the New York *Telegram* for the Scripps-Howard chain. At last, by stretching a point, he could call himself a New York publisher. It was a little like the gesture of a turf-struck movie actor who buys a lame old horse for the sake of wearing an owner's badge. Ever since he had come to this city, Howard had wanted a New York paper, but E. W. Scripps had forbidden him to buy one. The *Telegram* was literally a museum piece. Frank Munsey had willed it along with the *Sun* to the Metropolitan Museum of Art, which had sold both to William T. Dewart. Dewart kept the *Sun*, which he still owns, and sold the *Telegram* to Howard for $1,800,000. The *Telegram* was housed in a rat-infested old barracks at Washington and Dey streets, where its personnel was strictly forbidden to smoke lest the Fire Department condemn the building. The paper, founded in 1876 by James Gordon Bennett as a raffish afternoon running mate to his morning *Herald*, had a circulation of 195,000, which depended chiefly on the racing news and Tammany political gossip that it published. It had been adopted by Tammany as a kind of house organ and got considerable political advertising. Howard was so impatient to own a New York newspaper that he closed the deal before he persuaded Robert Paine Scripps to string along with him. Young Scripps acceded to the *fait accompli*.

Howard, having restlessly kibitzed the New York newspaper business for twenty-one years while working for the United Press and Scripps-Howard, had a number of ideas about what a metropolitan newspaper should be. He completely revamped the character of the *Telegram*, although he retained several members of the staff, and started out to show New York a supercharged version of, say, the Evansville *Press*, with trimmings from *Smart Set*. The publisher believed that news stories in New York papers were too long. Shorter, crisper stories would be more widely read, he told his editors. The space saved on news stories could be devoted to feature articles with the accent on fine writing. The first effect of Howard's doctrine was a reduction almost to the vanishing point of news matter in the paper. The second was a mass invasion of New York by fine writers, recommended by Scripps-Howard editors in twenty-five cities, including Albuquerque, New Mexico; Youngstown, Ohio; and Covington, Kentucky. They wrote in a style which has been classified by historians of English literature as Oklahoma Byzantine. Since they were unacquainted with the gags that press agents had sold to previous generations of feature writers, the *Telegram*'s pages began to look like a retrospective show of publicity wheezes. Some of the young men were encouraged to shine in the high aesthetic line, while others wrote, for the first page of the second section, in-the-know biographies of sterling Wall Street characters, most of whom subsequently jumped bail. Howard's first managing editor was a man named Sturdevant, who once had been happy as the editor of the Youngstown *Telegram*. Sturdevant was followed in office by Ted Thackrey, present executive editor of the *Post*, who was then fresh from Cleveland. Lee B. Wood, who had made a name in Oklahoma City, eventually displaced Thackrey. None of them could do anything to make Howard's venture profitable, and the *Telegram* finally declined to the point of losing a million dollars a year. It was steadily losing readers, too, many of them people who had developed hallucinations from reading its prose and were dragged from subway trains slapping at adjectives they said they saw crawling over them. This did not shake Howard's confidence in himself. He can take a beating and come back with the undiminished aplomb of an actress blaming her last flop on an unsuitable vehicle.

He made his first spectacular move toward establishing the new *Telegram* by hiring Heywood Broun in the spring of 1928. Broun was at liberty because, after a long wrangle with the late Ralph Pulitzer, publisher of the *World*, over his columns on the Sacco-Vanzetti case, he had written an article for the *Nation* which Pulitzer considered "disloyal." The first sentence of that article was "There ought to be a place in New York City for a liberal newspaper." Howard gave Broun a two-year contract at twenty-five thousand dollars a year. By hiring him, Howard got a name for broad-mindedness and at the same time gave a large number of people one reason for reading the *Telegram*. Broun was the best-known columnist in the country, with the exceptions of O. O. McIntyre and Arthur Brisbane. The glory reflected on the employer of a public figure pleased Howard, and he began to be seen in speak-easies with Broun, wearing a grin, like the minstrel men who used to sing, "I've Got a White Man Working for Me Now."

III—An Impromptu Pulitzer

Edward Wyllis Scripps, founder of the Scripps newspaper empire, was content to create the second- or third-best newspaper in each of a couple of dozen cities. When Roy Wilson Howard, chairman of the board of the Scripps-Howard newspapers, bought the Pittsburgh *Press* in 1923 for $6,200,000, *Editor and Publisher*, the trade magazine of the newspaper industry, observed that this purchase of a ready-made daily marked a change in a Scripps policy almost fifty years old. Howard bought the paper and announced its acquisition while old E. W. Scripps, who had retired from active supervision of the chain, was on his yacht *Ohio* somewhere in the South Seas. Robert Paine Scripps, his son, was with him. The younger Scripps had succeeded his father as titular head of the Scripps-Howard newspapers, but Howard was generally permitted to do about as he pleased. Colonel Oliver S. Hershman, who had published the *Press* for twenty-three years, wanted to retire but drove a hard bargain for his paper. Howard and a retinue of other Scripps-Howard executives, including William W. Hawkins, his administrative alter ego, checked into a Pittsburgh hotel, secretly, in order to mask their movements from possible competitive bidders, about a week before the deal was closed, all the executives registering under the names of their secretaries. They bargained with Colonel Hershman and his lawyers almost continuously for a week, and finally reached a point where Howard's offer was within twenty-five thousand dollars of Hershman's asking price. Hershman flipped a coin to decide who would pay the difference, borrowing a quarter from Howard for this ceremony. Howard called and lost.

As Howard's control of the Scripps-Howard interests became more nearly complete, he continued this policy of buying going papers. In making an acquisition of this sort, he sometimes had to go to a bank for money. Old Scripps had a horror of borrowing from a bank, a practice which he feared might affect a paper's editorial independence. Howard feels that his own integrity is superior to such considerations. The *Press* has paid heavy dividends on the Scripps-Howard investment. A couple of other

Howard purchases, like the Denver *Rocky Mountain News* and the Denver *Times*, which he bought and merged in 1926, and the Buffalo *Times*, which he got in 1929 and discontinued in 1939, turned out to be heavy losers. There were twenty-five Scripps-Howard newspapers when E. W. Scripps died in March 1926. Howard added four to the chain within the next year. Since then the number has declined to the present nineteen. In the same period the total number of dailies in the United States has dropped from 2333 to 1998. Howard's fourth addition to the chain after E. W. Scripps's death was its first New York newspaper, the *Telegram*, acquired in 1927. He paid something less than two million dollars for this property. When, in 1931, he made a bid for the New York *World* with a view to merging it with the *Telegram*, the gesture seemed slightly presumptuous. It was as if the Knott hotel chain had offered to take over the Waldorf-Astoria.

The *World, Evening World*, and *Sunday World* were properties of the Press Publishing Company, of which almost all the stock was held by the estate of Joseph Pulitzer. Pulitzer's will forbade the sale of the Press Publishing Company stock "under any circumstances whatever." He had written, "I particularly enjoin upon my sons and my descendants the duty of preserving, perfecting, and perpetuating the *World* newspaper (to the maintenance and upbuilding of which I have sacrificed my health and strength)." Ralph, Joseph, Jr., and Herbert Pulitzer were directors of the Press Publishing Company, as well as trustees of their father's estate, but the will had assigned a six-tenths interest in the newspapers to Herbert, the youngest son, so in a pinch he could outvote his brothers. The papers earned a handsome income for sixteen years after the senior Pulitzer's death in 1911, and the profits were distributed among his sons and the other beneficiaries of the estate. By 1931, these included fifteen Pulitzer grandchildren. Pulitzer, perhaps in the belief that the papers would make money *every* year, had neglected to provide for a reserve fund. Money flowed from the newspapers into the estate, but there was no way of getting it back from the estate again. When, after a succession of business mistakes, the Press Publishing Company lost the relatively small sum of $474,000 in 1928, Herbert Pulitzer and his brother Ralph, who was editor of the *World*, became alarmed. Joseph Pulitzer, Jr., was giving all his energy to another Pulitzer paper, the St. Louis *Post-Dispatch*. Ralph retired as editor of the *World* in 1930, and Herbert took charge. When the company's balance sheet for 1929 showed a somewhat larger deficit, Herbert began looking for exits. At the *World* papers' lowest ebb, the *World* had a circulation of 320,000, the *Evening World* had 285,000, the *Sunday World* had 500,000, and their joint annual revenues were in excess of twelve million dollars. However, Herbert Pulitzer was neither a gambler nor a newspaper enthusiast. Howard was behind seven million dollars in his operation of the *Telegram* and in the position of a poker player so far in the hole that his best chance of pulling out was to double the stakes. He had a dream of acquiring the competing *Evening World*, the *Sunday World*, and the *World*, and of then scrapping the last two and absorbing the first into the *Telegram*.

Howard had met Ralph Pulitzer aboard the *Paris* on a transatlantic crossing in the summer of 1928. The publishers had talked half jokingly of swapping the *World* for the *Telegram* and then merging the *Telegram* and *Evening World*. A year later, in New York, Herbert Pulitzer had promised Howard not so jokingly that if the brothers ever wanted to sell out they would tell him before anybody else. Pulitzer kept his word in January 1931, and on January 31 a contract of sale with Howard was signed. Howard promised nothing more definite than that he would continue the *World* papers "in spirit." It is not certain that Herbert Pulitzer gave a hoot. The deal became public only on February 24, when, as trustees of the Pulitzer estate, the brothers asked permission of the Surrogate's Court to go through with the sale. On such short notice it was almost impossible for other potential buyers to prepare competitive offers for the property, but the 2867 employees of the *World* papers, their jobs threatened, banded together to make a cooperative offer for it. They held a mass meeting at the Astor, a few pledging their savings and all promising to turn back a portion of each week's salary to the paper if the cooperative plan went through. At a hearing before Surrogate Foley, Howard argued that any delay would have a bad effect on the *World* staff's morale and that the paper's good-will asset would depreciate. Wearing a wasp-waisted, double-breasted brown suit, the publisher appeared at his most incisive. Upholding the Pulitzers' right to sell, the surrogate blandly ruled that, notwithstanding Joseph Pulitzer's own lucid words, "the dominant purpose of Mr. Pulitzer must have been the maintenance of a fair income for his children and the ultimate reception of the unimpaired corpus by the remaindermen, permanence of the trust and ultimate enjoyment by his grandchildren, as intended." This, naturally, would have been obvious to any surrogate. Foley added that he had no right to instruct the Pulitzers whether or not to accept the Howard offer, because in selling the Press Publishing Company they were acting not as trustees but as directors of the Press Publishing Company selling its assets. This would have been equally obvious to any good legal mind. Howard's offer was a definite three million dollars and the possibility of an additional two million. The money was to be paid a half million down, a half million in ninety days, and two million in eight payments of two hundred and fifty thousand dollars, to begin in 1934. The final two millions were to be paid out of the profits of the new paper, the *World-Telegram*, if and when it earned any profits.

"No one possessed of a drop of the milk of human kindness could view with disinterest the situation of the many employees of the *World* who face at least temporary unemployment," Howard said in a prepared statement after the transaction was closed. He had Lee Wood, managing editor of the *Telegram*, set up a registration office in the ramshackle Telegram Building on Dey Street for survivors of the *World* publications.

In the first issue of the new *World-Telegram*, Heywood Broun, the *Telegram*'s columnist graduate of the *World*, wrote, "It is my sincere belief that the Scripps-Howard chain is qualified by its record and its potentialities to carry on the Pulitzer tradition of liberal journalism." His optimism was based on his own relations with the *Telegram* before the merger. For several years, Broun, like a star pitcher with a last-place baseball club, had been allowed a flattering latitude of opinion in his column. The *Telegram* circulation had risen only infinitesimally in four years of hard pulling with Howard as coxswain, but it was probably true, as the publisher said, that a new set of readers had replaced the old ones who had bought the *Telegram* for the racing news and Tammany items. The new *Telegram* readers were people willing to pay three cents to see what Broun had to say.

The *World-Telegram*, which made its first appearance on the day after the merger, resembled a colored houseman wearing some of his dead massa's old clothes. Rollin Kirby, Denys Wortman, and Will B. Johnstone, the cartoonists, were retained from the *World*, along with Harry Hansen's book column and J. Otis Swift's nature notes. On the whole, it was an amorphous publication that looked like the result of physically telescoping two totally different newspapers. It bulked large because Howard had taken over the *Evening World* advertising contracts. Since the advertising rates had been based on a circulation of less than three hundred thousand and that of the merged paper hovered for a while around a half million, the *World-Telegram* lost money on every advertisement printed. When Howard later raised the rates in proportion to the new circulation, many advertisers quit. They have had to be wooed back over a stretch of years, a factor which some critics contend has had a perceptible influence on the newspaper's policy. Within a few months after the merger, the *World-Telegram* had returned to the appearance and editorial formula of the Scripps-Howard *Telegram*, except for the three new cartoonists, and Swift, and Hansen. A number of *World* reporters and sports writers hired at the time of the merger were not with the new paper long. That summer, the *World-Telegram* moved into a new building at 125 Barclay Street. At about the same time, Howard, finally the important and full-fledged New Yorker he had long looked forward to becoming, with a major local paper of his own, gave up his suburban home, which was on Pelhamdale Avenue in Pelham, and moved into the heart of town. The Pelham house had seventeen rooms and five baths; the one he took on the East Side, near Central Park, has sixteen rooms, six baths, and an elevator. The elevator is not quite high enough for a tall man to stand upright in. The diminutive publisher enjoys seeing his tall executives, such as Lee Wood, stoop when they ride in it.

When Howard had bought the *World*, he had told the press that the transaction meant not "the death of the *World* but its rebirth." However, the *World-Telegram* made no serious effort to carry on the *World* tradition. The foreign staff of the *World*, which even in the paper's last years included such correspondents as John Balderston and William Bolitho, went out of existence.

The *World-Telegram* rarely sent members of its own staff farther out of New York than, say, Hopewell, New Jersey, mostly relying on the Scripps-Howard United Press and out-of-town Scripps-Howard newspapers to cover it on more distant assignments. The Scottsboro, Alabama, trials, for example, were described for the *World-Telegram* by a reporter on the chain's Birmingham *Post*. The great droughts, the West Coast shipping strike, and the trial of Al Capone got the same modest attention. The feature writers gave the paper a façade of knowingness. The feature men's most important work appeared on the first page of the second section, known in shoptalk as the "split page." Every week one of them wrote a series of articles on such topics as Powers models, soldiers of fortune, voodoo rites, and prison reform. Howard decreed that there should also be a feature story about a woman, with accompanying photographs, on the third page of the first section every day. He said that people were interested in women. The *World-Telegram* consequently published daily a story about a woman who made powder compacts out of flattened tomato cans or was making good in some Broadway show, which usually closed by the end of the same week. The only requirement was that the subject should be as good-looking as a muskrat, and this was frequently waived. Appearing on the split page along with the polychromatic prose of the feature men were Broun's column and Alice Hughes's shopping notes. It was on the split page that Howard eventually developed one of his major contributions to newspaper strategy, the practice of letting columnists more or less express a paper's editorial policy while the editorial writer *en titre*, whom comparatively few people read anyway, remains free to hedge at the publisher's discretion. In the beginning, however, the page resembled the continuous entertainment at a pretentious Coney Island restaurant.

There had been slight rifts at the *Telegram* between Howard and Broun in the first years of the depression. The publisher, for example, had asked Broun not to devote so many of his daily columns to *Shoot the Works*, a cooperative musical revue the writer had put on with unemployed actors. Commercial producers, who paid for their advertising, were complaining. In the summer of 1930, Howard, in a *Telegram* editorial, had chided Broun for running for Congress on the Socialist ticket. The *Telegram* had backed Norman Thomas for mayor in 1929, but in 1930 Howard seemed to imply in his reproof to Broun that a few decent people were beginning to read his paper. Neither of these quarrels lasted long, since *Shoot the Works* soon ran out of audiences and Broun failed by a wide margin to get elected. The strain between the two men increased after Howard merged the *World* with the *Telegram*. Howard's paper was no longer an outsider trying to attract attention but an insider trying to hold on to everything it had suddenly fallen heir to. Broun, instead of being a magnet to draw readers from the competing *Evening World*, was now merely an employee who might say something to offend the advertisers. He could not possibly draw readers from the conservative *Sun*, and the *Evening Post*, as run by the Curtis-Martin Newspapers, was crumbling to powder without outside assistance. Liberal readers in New York had to take the *World-Telegram* because they had no alternative.

Most successful New York newspapers began their runs from the liberal position that the *World-Telegram* now held almost by default. James Gordon Bennett, when he founded the *Herald* in 1835, was labeled a scurrilous radical. Joseph Pulitzer cast himself in the same role in 1883, when he began to edit the *World*. Hearst made his first impression here as an imitation radical. The *Daily News*, the most profitable newspaper of our period, has from the first been on the whole the city's most forthright champion of social legislation. Howard abandoned his strategic ground as casually as he had attained it. The *World-Telegram* differed from the *Herald*, the *World*, and the *Journal* in one important historical respect. It turned conservative *without* making big money.

The sole form of liberalism that Howard thought it safe to emphasize in New York was something called Fusion, which is somehow usually popular with large taxpayers. Fusion furnished Howard with his one opportunity to feel like a kingmaker. The king he indisputably helped make was Fiorello H. LaGuardia, who was elected Mayor in 1933, the *World-Telegram* furnishing his only outspoken newspaper support. The tone of numerous Howard-inspired editorials in the same paper has since suggested that the Mayor is not sufficiently grateful. Likewise, Howard has given LaGuardia numerous pointers, which are generally conveyed to him through the *World-Telegram*'s City Hall reporter. To these LaGuardia has paid little attention. Whenever the publisher sends an emissary to tell him how to run the city, the Mayor lectures the City Hall man on editorial policy. La-Guardia asks for the heads of reporters with the same assurance that Howard asks for those of city commissioners. The two little men obtain equally negative results and are in a fairly constant state of reciprocal exasperation.

The *World-Telegram* split page rose to journalistic eminence side by side with the United Feature Syndicate, a Scripps-Howard subsidiary organized in 1921 principally for the purpose of marketing weekly articles by David Lloyd George. As the first World War receded in public memory and Lloyd George in prominence, the articles became more difficult to place. A United Press man named Monte Bourjaily was delegated to take charge of the syndicate. He hired Benito Mussolini, Camille Chautemps, and a now nearly forgotten German statesman named Wilhelm Marx to write monthly letters about European politics and offered the fourfold service to non-Scripps Sunday newspapers. The syndicate feature sold moderately well. Upon the accession of Pius XI, Bourjaily obtained the American newspaper rights to an authorized biography of the new Pope by an Italian cardinal. This feature sold extremely well, and the cardinal used his share of the payments to rebuild a church. United Feature later bought the American newspaper rights to Charles Dickens' *The Life of Our Lord*, an unpublished manuscript that his heirs made available for publication in 1931. *The Life of Our Lord* earned a quarter million dollars for the Scripps-Howard syndicate. Bourjaily next bought the rights to Napoleon's letters to Marie-Louise, until then never published. This feature did not go well, apparently because few newspaper readers knew who Marie-Louise was. A competing syndicate scored handsomely by dressing up Napoleon's letters to Josephine with illustrations and selling them to more newspapers than bought the letters to Marie-Louise, although the letters to Josephine had been in the public domain for a century.

Bourjaily also tried to sell Broun's column to newspapers outside the Scripps-Howard chain, but never with great success, because, from fifty miles outside the city limits, Broun in those days assumed the aspect of a gin-drinking Communist with loose morals. United Feature entered the syndicated columnist field in a serious way in December 1933, with the launching of Westbrook Pegler. This writer had some years earlier worked for Howard, almost totally unremarked, as a reporter, a war correspondent, and finally as a sports editor of the United Press. He had then switched to the Chicago *Tribune* syndicate as a sports columnist, and his work had been sold to a number of other papers, including the *Post* in New York. In 1933, Colonel Frank Knox, publisher of the Chicago *Daily News*, who wanted Pegler's stuff for his own paper, suggested to Howard that the *News* and the *World-Telegram* combine to engage Pegler as an essayist on general subjects. Howard agreed, and Pegler was signed up at a salary of thirty thousand dollars a year and half of all syndicate sales in excess of sixty thousand dollars. Pegler, as a sports writer, had been philosophical rather than technical, presenting the wrestling and boxing businesses as a sort of parable of *Realpolitik*, which had only a slight literal relation to anything that would interest a sports fan. As an essayist, Pegler was assigned a spot on the split page with Broun.

Pegler wrote several practice columns to prime himself for his new job, and showed them to Howard. They included one approving the lynching by a mob in San Jose, California, of two men charged with kidnaping. The publisher thought that this was about right for a new columnist who wanted to attract attention. The lynching column was the third to appear under Pegler's by-line in his new column. It drew a great deal of indignant notice, which was just what Howard had wanted. One of the hottest reactions was Broun's. He asked, in his neighboring column, "Is this to be the measure of justice in California? Men with blood and burnt flesh on their hands are to be set free. Mooney must remain in jail. Freedom for the guilty. Punishment for the innocent." It was generally conceded that a rave review of a lynching represented a fresh point of view.

Howard's own writing is undistinguished. In Pegler, he evidently grew to feel, he had found his voice. Pegler was to Howard what Jenny Lind had been to Barnum. Some years ago a volume of Pegler's columns was published under the title of *The Dissenting Opinions of Mister Westbrook Pegler*. By a rare phenomenon, he almost always dissents from the side where the money isn't. In the last presidential campaign, for example, Pegler fearlessly dissented from the majority of his fellow citizens by plumping for Wendell Willkie. It was a happy coincidence that eighty-one per cent of the newspaper publishers who buy columns were on the same side. Dorothy Thompson, whose candidate won, lost about fifty per cent of her syndication during the campaign. Pegler is a courageous defender of minorities—for example, the people who pay large income taxes. Just the same, he has devoted around twenty columns to attacking the American Newspaper Guild, which Howard loathes. Pegler's idea of a demagogue, to judge by his columns on Senator Wagner, is a senator who favors labor laws. One of the columnist's favorite irritants is a character known as "the boss-hater." On the other hand, Pegler may dislike sycophants but he never writes any columns against them. He has written thousands of words about labor-union officials who employ violence or have criminal records, but he has never touched on the incidence of criminality among company guards or strikebreakers. During the last campaign he wrote several columns about the godlike virtues of Hoosiers, without mentioning specifically either the Republican candidate or Howard. In January, shortly after Willkie split with Howard over the question of giving aid to England, Pegler wrote a column denouncing Willkie as a fake Hoosier. This was the case of dissent from himself.

Howard, in addition to sensing the ideological kinship between himself and Pegler, found in Pegler one who sympathized with his belief that ignorance is an endearing quality. This is the basis of the Artemus Ward school of humor. There is nothing, except perhaps Mrs. Roosevelt, on which the columnist can grow more bitterly satirical than the subject of college professors, who, he implies, are parasites on society and had better keep their noses out of public business. He calls psychoanalysts "Viennese head feelers," and once wrote a column voicing his suspicion that Einstein was a fraud since he, Pegler, couldn't follow Einstein's reasoning. His top effort in this line was a column last summer fearlessly deploring false sympathy for Paris. Paris, Pegler wrote, was a city famous only for naked women.

Howard's second important addition to the split-page menagerie was another United Feature discovery, Brigadier General Hugh S. Johnson, a Reserve officer who had been administrator of NRA for the first sixteen months of its existence. General Johnson, who had finally broken with the President, brought away from Washington a conviction that Mr. Roosevelt had fallen among evil advisers, along with a vocabulary culled from among the ruins of the *Decline and Fall of the Roman Empire*. The enterprising Bourjaily read a speech that General Johnson had made before a group of businessmen and went to see him at the Hotel St. Regis, where he was then living. Bourjaily told Johnson that the speech, properly cut up and pasted together again, would have made five syndicate columns and that it was uneconomical to give the stuff away. The General was pleased to learn he could sell what he had to say. He signed a contract with United Feature which gave him an advance and fifty per cent of the money received from the syndication of his articles. As a columnist, the General warmed up slowly, with the thesis that the President was a possibly honest fellow who had been kidnaped by Stalinist janissaries. This was too mild to appeal to most publishers, and it was not until the General got down to painting Mr. Roosevelt as a he-witch hurrying the nation to a massacre that the column became a really popular number in the syndicate salesmen's line. By the time the Supreme Court fight was at its hottest, Johnson's share of the syndicate sales had risen to forty thousand dollars a year. The King Features Syndicate hired Johnson away from United Feature early this spring for a flat guarantee of fifty thousand dollars a year, but the column is still appearing in the *World-Telegram* and in Howard's Washington *News*, without, however, any mention of the fact that the General is now working for Hearst.

The most incongruous member of the split-page collection is Mrs. Roosevelt, still another Bourjaily literary find. Mrs. Roosevelt had, when her husband became President, accepted the editorship of a new Bernarr MacFadden magazine called *Babies, Just Babies*. The proceeds from her contract had gone to a couple of her favorite charities, but, all in all, the venture had not been happy. Bourjaily suggested that she write a column in the form of a daily letter to a woman friend relating the events of her day. He then signed her to a ten-year contract. The feature, at the last report, was grossing about eighty thousand dollars a year, of which forty thousand dollars is retained by United Feature and forty thousand dollars goes to Mrs. Roosevelt, who turns it over to a number of charities. Mrs. Roosevelt is not only a business asset for Howard but also, in his frequently expressed opinion, a proof of the *World-Telegram*'s impartiality. "If I were such a hell of a Tory as people say," he protests, "I wouldn't have Eleanor there, would I? But I don't think she ought to write about politics."

When the split page began to attract notice, Broun's column, "It Seems to Me," appeared in the upper right-hand corner of the page, that position being considered the most prominent. Later, Broun was shifted to the left side of the page, and Pegler, the new arrival, received the place of honor at the right. As Howard accumulated columnists, he began to pack them into layers, like Chinese in an opium den. They were all stacked together in a tier on the left side of the page, and their relative levels indicated the importance the management attached to their output. Pegler, for economic and symbolic reasons, has been from the beginning of this arrangement what racing men would call the top horse. He brings in the most money, about one hundred and fifty thousand dollars yearly. Broun, who once wrote, "The underdogs of the world will someday whip their weight in wildcats," at first ran directly under Pegler. Broun complained that his pieces were often shortened, sometimes by the excision of sentences or clauses that he considered vital to continuity, and was told that this was done not from malice but because it was necessary to make the tier of columns come out even at the foot of the page. Johnson had the third position from the top, and Mrs. Roosevelt, possibly because she was an avowed Democrat or because Howard felt a lady should have a lower berth, occupied the nethermost position. As differences between Broun and the publisher developed, the heavyweight columnist's specific gravity appeared to pull him toward the bottom. When the day came that Howard moved Johnson above Broun, a memorandum informed all Scripps-Howard editors, "General Johnson is a columnist of increasing importance, as indicated by the change in his relative position on the page."

IV—Once Again She Lorst 'Er Nime

A series of articles which appeared in the Philadelphia *Record* and the New York *Post* last winter referred to Roy Wilson Howard, head man of the Scripps-Howard newspapers, as "the mastermind of appeasement." This irritated Howard but scarcely astonished him. He ascribed it to the *Post*'s desire to take away the *World-Telegram*'s department-store advertising. Howard also said that Robert S. Allen, the author of the articles, was angry at him because he had never run Allen's daily column, "Washington Merry-Go-Round," in the *World-Telegram*.

William R. Castle, Under-Secretary of State during the Hoover administration, and General Robert E. Wood, chairman of the board of Sears, Roebuck and national chairman of the America First Committee, two of the country's outstanding and least apologetic appeasers, are among the few prominent citizens with whom the publisher does not admit close acquaintance. "Why, I only met Castle once in my life, and that was about eight years ago on a beach in Hawaii," Howard recently said. As the Senate debate on the lend-lease bill was nearing its close in March, he said, "I wouldn't know General Wood if I saw him." Nevertheless, Howard wrote a first-page editorial on the lend-lease bill in which he made verbatim use of one of the mail-order General's most narcotic arguments: "If six million men, well trained and well equipped, cannot cross twenty miles of water and conquer 1,500,000, how could they possibly cross three thousand miles and successfully invade the United States?" The first part of this proposition implied that Great Britain was safe from invasion, the second that the larger the expanse of water to be defended by a given force was, the easier the defender's task would be. Howard introduced Wood's double-barreled paralogism with the casualness of a teacher making an allusion to accepted truth. The editorial was a retreat from Howard's all-out opposition to the bill; its thesis was that since the measure was bound to pass anyway, the country should support the President. The *World-Telegram* then eased into a campaign of opposition to convoys and reproof to detractors of Charles A. Lindbergh. While Howard has made no frontal attack on aid to Britain in principle, he has fought a continuous delaying action against every concrete proposal of aid. Of the thirty-one members of the America First national committee who first appeared on its letterheads last winter, three—General Hugh S. Johnson, John T. Flynn, and Major Al Williams—were Scripps-Howard columnists. Howard said at the time that it was a coincidence. Feverishly isolationist senators like Burton K. Wheeler of Montana, Gerald P. Nye of North Dakota, and Robert R. Reynolds of North Carolina are treated with conspicuous respect in the Scripps-Howard press. The collective efforts of this group of senators, so faithfully cheered on by Howard, delayed the passage of the cash-and-carry bill of 1939 for two months. They held up the Selective Service Training Act until the end of last summer, which caused a still longer delay in the expansion of the army, since men could not be sent to training camps in fall weather until barracks had been built for them. Howard, however, has never joined forces with the isolationists. He calls his procedure "maintaining detachment." In a parallel manner, from 1935 through 1937, he called himself a supporter of the President but opposed many of his specific projects and said he hoped Roosevelt wouldn't get a large majority of the electoral vote in 1936 because too much power is bad for anyone. Similarly, last fall, while Howard was in agreement with Wendell L. Willkie in principle, Westbrook Pegler and General Johnson, in their Scripps-Howard columns, seemed to develop a temporary attack of non-partisanship every time Willkie refused a Howard suggestion about campaign strategy. Whenever Willkie complained, Howard explained that the most effective support was the least obvious.

Howard's position on the country's foreign policy has possibly been influenced by a feeling that the President has never taken him seriously enough. He once related with some indignation part of a conversation with the President at the White House. He had told Roosevelt that a certain stand he had taken was a serious mistake, and the President had replied, "Horsefeathers, Roy, horsefeathers!" The publisher's attitude toward the war, like that of some of the America First leaders, is possibly affected by the simple fact that he is a wealthy man who does not wish to be disturbed. In addition he regards himself as intuitive and a repository of confidential information. If he were a race-track plunger, he would never look at horses or form charts. He would put his faith in his hunches and conversations with dopesters. Some of the dopesters he has listened to, like Al Williams, have a high opinion of German prowess and may have influenced him to put a bet on isolationism. Munich, in Howard's estimation, was good business sense. He has said that Neville Chamberlain has not yet been fully appreciated. Howard visited Europe in the summer of 1939 and filed a series of dispatches to his papers belittling the danger of war. Some people accused him of acting, like Senator Borah, as if the world crisis were a political gimmick rigged by Roosevelt. It usually takes Howard, on a foreign reporting tour, around four days to learn the truth about a major power, but he can fathom a nation of less than twenty-five million inhabitants in one afternoon. Before going on such a trip, Howard, who tells new acquaintances that he is "primarily a reporter," bashfully asks his subordinates if they think it worth while for him to cable some stories. They invariably think so.

It is impossible to imagine Howard playing Harun-al-Rashid on the Bowery, as hulking Captain Joseph Medill Patterson, publisher of the *Daily News*, sometimes does. Howard's contacts with the people are generally those he makes on Pan American clippers, at de luxe hotels, and at dinner parties. One acquaintance who made a considerable impression on him in the thirties was Baron Axel Wenner-Gren, the Swedish industrialist, who is heavily interested in the Electrolux and Servel corporations and whose European holdings include timberlands, paper mills, and munitions factories. Wenner-Gren was at the time a friend of Edward VIII, Mrs. Simpson, and Von Ribbentrop, then German

Ambassador to London. He had also known Hermann Göring during the German's sojourn in Sweden after the first World War. Wenner-Gren's viewpoint, as recorded in the *World-Telegram* and elsewhere, seemed to be that though there were labor unions in Sweden they knew their place, whereas in Germany and Italy the workers, by insisting on too much, had made necessary a totalitarian revolution, and that he feared the same thing might happen in the United States. Whenever Wenner-Gren was coming to New York, Howard was apt to have a reporter sent to meet his ship, with advice on what opinions to look for in the statement the Baron had not yet made. The Baron believed that Germany and the United States could get along beautifully with the right people running both countries. Senator Wheeler was another whose interviews were frequently "front-office" assignments. Not only such officially protected game as Wenner-Gren and Wheeler but almost all *World-Telegram* interviewees wearing suits that cost more than one hundred dollars would begin by asking the reporter, "How is Roy?"

In the years between his purchase of the *World* and the beginning of the second World War, Howard succeeded in becoming a fairly well-known New York figure, although he never got to be a celebrity *du premier plan*, like Jimmy Walker or Walter Winchell or Dutch Schultz. He is certainly the only publisher of a New York newspaper except William Randolph Hearst whose photograph would be recognized by the average newspaper reader. Captain Patterson, Ogden Reid, Arthur Hays Sulzberger, and William Dewart are men without faces as far as the public is concerned. Returning to his hotel from one of the sessions of the Democratic convention in Chicago last summer, Howard and a few of his employees, unable to get a taxi, climbed aboard a crowded streetcar. A large, sweaty fellow in work clothes looked down at the small, iridescent publisher and snarled, "Say, you look like that so-and-so Roy Howard." Howard seemed thoroughly pleased. In the early years of his career as a publisher, he often accepted appointments to public bodies; he was once, for instance, on the board of judges in a Camel-cigarette essay contest. Now, while he is more conservative, he is still receptive to the right kind of appointment. It was the belief of several political writers during the last campaign that he would have liked to be Willkie's Secretary of State. He does not allow his name to appear in the society columns of his own papers, because, he says, "Shucks, I'm not society," but he is constantly interviewed by other papers climbing in and out of planes, and he used to be a minor staple for ship-news reporters. Mrs. Howard, a tranquil, friendly woman, does not appear at all the gatherings he attends. The schedule would be too rigorous for almost any woman. The Howards have two children, a son and daughter. The son, Jack, was graduated from Yale in 1932 and is now president of Scripps-Howard Radio, Incorporated, which operates two broadcasting stations in Memphis. Jane, the daughter, is married to Lieutenant Albert Perkins of the United States navy.

Howard has paid less and less attention to his out-of-town newspapers in recent years. The national headquarters of the chain are in New York, instead of in Cleveland, where they were in E. W. Scripps's day, and editorial conventions are now held in Washington more often than in French Lick, the traditional site. Old-timers say that the programs at these get-togethers are quite uniform. One of the officers makes a speech denouncing the Reds; another complains about taxes, and a third delivers a rousing plea for more concentrated, punchy writing. After that, everybody plays poker.

The chain's papers have become increasingly orthodox, and they no longer reveal any of the Scripps crotchets about the dangers of monopoly or the right of labor to organize. When Scripps-Howard bought and merged the Denver *Times* and the *Rocky Mountain News* in 1926, Howard announced that the chain had come to Denver "to correct a sinister journalistic situation" which was caused by the domination of the Tammen and Bonfils *Post*. Three years later he told the Denver Chamber of Commerce he was in town primarily to sell advertising. When the chain acquired the Memphis *Commercial Appeal*, a rich, conservative newspaper, a few years ago, it retained the *Appeal*'s make-up, typography, and syndicate features, as well as its traditional editorial policy and, as a consequence, its advertisers. The Scripps-Howard San Francisco *News* has supported a referendum proposition to make the franchises of a traction company perpetual. So it goes, more or less, with other Scripps-Howard papers.

One of the publisher's amusements is hunting. "Roy loves to shoot a moose," William W. Hawkins, the second man in the Scripps-Howard organization, says. Howard democratically plucks the birds he shoots on Bernard M. Baruch's estate in South Carolina and takes pride in the way he dresses a rabbit. Even as a hunter, he is financially conservative. He went to New Brunswick with a group of his associates a couple of years ago, and their guide showed them fine sport. The other huntsmen gathered in the Scripps-Howard offices the day after their return to decide what to send the guide as a mark of appreciation. They had just about settled on a rifle when Howard entered the conclave. "Now, wait a minute, boys," he said. "Let's not be so splendiferous. Let's call in one of our artists from N.E.A. and have him draw a picture of a moose's head crying big tears. Then we'll all sign it and send it to Jean so he can hang it in his cabin." The guide got the picture.

Howard's present political course was determined in 1937,

the year Franklin D. Roosevelt began his second term in the White House. That year the publisher broke with his old friend Lowell Mellett, the editor of the Scripps-Howard Washington *Daily News*, who had been something of a final link with the Scripps days. Mellett saw the New Deal as an expression of the old Scripps progressivism. In the early twenties he had written a series of articles denouncing what he called "government by the courts," and limitation of the power of the Supreme Court had become almost a Scripps copyright theme. When, in 1937, Howard wanted the *News*, like the other papers of the chain, to campaign against Roosevelt's scheme to reorganize the Court, Mellett resigned, giving up an income of twenty-five thousand dollars a year to take a government job at eight thousand dollars. That same year Howard broke irrevocably with Broun. The precipitating cause was a document in the form of a letter "to a famous newspaper publisher," which Broun contributed to the *New Republic*. Broun, addressing his purportedly fictitious publisher as Butch Dorrit, wrote:

> Do you honestly think that the great American public is all steamed up about your income tax? Take off the false whiskers. There's nothing immoral or unethical in your espousing the conservative side all along the line, but doesn't that pretense of progressivism sometimes cleave to your gullet? All your arguments are based upon the premise that you're a great success. You've scrapped some great papers and what have you got to show for them? What's left is an eight-column cut of the Quints asking permission to go to the bathroom.

This last sentence was a reference to the full-page layouts of pictures of the Dionne Quintuplets with which the *World-*

Telegram had been embellishing itself about once a week. The Newspaper Enterprise Association, a Scripps-Howard feature syndicate known as the N.E.A., had triumphantly obtained exclusive American rights to newspaper photographs of the sisters. Perhaps more cutting was Broun's allusion to Howard's tax affairs. Broun's contract still had two years to run, but after this incident he and Howard did not make even a pretense of mutual tolerance. "I wouldn't pour water on Broun's leg if he was on fire," the publisher once said to some *World-Telegram* men. The Bureau of Internal Revenue, in an attempt to illustrate loopholes in the tax law, had named Howard and several of his associates, along with other wealthy men, at a hearing by the Congressional Joint Committee on Tax Evasion and Avoidance, as creators of personal holding companies. The Treasury subsequently maintained that the choice of names was accidental, but some observers thought the accident well planned. The testimony, they figured, was aimed to forestall a Scripps-Howard newspaper campaign for downward revision of the surplus-profits tax. A newspaper owner who was already taking full advantage of a wide gap in the law would make an awkward figure as crusader for further tax reductions.

Old Scripps had anticipated an economic revolution within a hundred years and had been accustomed to say that it was up to people of wealth to make the change painless. Howard once said, "I wonder if the old man would have been such a liberal if he had had a pistol up against his belly the way I have." Howard was referring to the American Newspaper Guild. Broun was one of the founders and the first national president of this union of newspaper editorial and business-office workers. The coming of the Guild to the Scripps-Howard papers brought a general rise in minimum wages and the establishment of severance pay in proportion to length of service. The Guild also protected the forty-hour week established by NRA. These changes cost the newspaper chain about a million dollars a year. Restrained editorial support, in the old days, of unions in other industries had cost precisely nothing, and Scripps himself might have balked at paying this much in cash for his franchise in the friend-of-labor business.

In 1934, when Broun's original contract with the *World-Telegram* expired, the Guild, which had not yet arrived at the *World-Telegram*, had still seemed innocuous. It had not yet joined even the American Federation of Labor, from which it later seceded to affiliate itself with the CIO. Westbrook Pegler, who had been placed on the famous "first-page second-section," or "split page," with Broun toward the end of 1933, had not yet established himself as more than a side dish, and the older columnist remained the *World-Telegram*'s chief claim to prestige. During the honeymoon months of the first Roosevelt administration, Broun even began to look a little like a prophet. There was a popular enthusiasm for the sort of governmental innovations that would have been called radical a couple of years earlier. Business in general showed signs of improvement, and William Randolph Hearst, foreseeing a period of commercial expansion, began a campaign to hire away his competitor's editorial assets. Broun was getting about five hundred dollars a week, but Hearst's King Features Syndicate offered him a contract at twelve hundred dollars and a cash bonus of twenty-five thousand dollars if he would sign it. Howard offered Broun a contract at seven hundred dollars a week, which, with the columnist's share of his rather modest syndicate sales, would bring his annual income to forty thousand dollars. The idea of working for Hearst was not pleasant to Broun, so he took the Howard offer even though it was lower.

When the Guild joined the American Federation of Labor in

1936 and started its campaign to get the *World-Telegram* to sign a contract with it, Howard told the Guildsmen that the public would have no confidence in reports of labor disputes by writers who belonged to unions. Broun argued that the public had no confidence in journalists who had to reflect the views of anti-labor publishers. Howard always treated as coincidental, extraneous, and without importance the fact that in general the level of salaries on the *World-Telegram* was far below that on the *Daily News*, whose management welcomed union organization. Around that time a favorite anecdote in the *World-Telegram* city room was about a depressed and impoverished reporter who in 1934 scooped the entire country by obtaining facsimiles of the signatures on the Lindbergh-kidnaping ransom notes. Lee B. Wood, the *World-Telegram*'s executive editor, told the reporter that in recognition of his coup the paper had decided to reward him with a due bill on a chain clothing store entitling him to a thirty-dollar suit of clothes. The reporter went to the store, got a suit, and, when he looked in the glass, acquired enough confidence to try to find another job. He landed one at two and a half times his *World-Telegram* salary.

Howard issued a long statement to the *World-Telegram* staff in 1936 saying that he would never negotiate with the Guild, although he would welcome a company union. The following year, however, he signed a contract with the Guild, which had become powerful enough to make him eat his words. Even without the Guild, Howard, at fifty-eight, might today be a well-established conservative, but the fight probably speeded up his natural metabolic changes.

In 1928, Howard, overruling the Scripps-trained editors like Mellett, had his papers back Hoover for the presidency when most liberals supported the Democratic ticket of Alfred E. Smith and Joseph T. Robinson. Howard argued that Hoover was a great progressive in disguise. The depression did not make Howard change his mind. Moreover, since it enabled him to absorb the competing *Evening World* and to pick up a few shreds of the morning *World*'s prestige at bargain rates, he had no cause to be heartbroken, and in his enthusiasm he was probably inclined to believe the bankers when they predicted that prosperity might return almost any week end. He said, however, he felt that the voters would demand a change of administration and that he wanted a safe one. He went to the Democratic national convention in Chicago in 1932 to collaborate with John F. Curry of Tammany and John McCooey, the Democratic leader of Brooklyn, in a stop-Roosevelt drive. Tammany was angry at Roosevelt because while he was Governor of New York State he had forced Mayor Jimmy Walker out of office. Howard, whose editorial writers had howled for Walker's removal, evidently now felt that he was nearer to Tammany than to Roosevelt. The *World-Telegram* announced that it favored the nomination of Al Smith. A widely accepted theory held that Howard figured Smith would block Roosevelt, after which, with the convention in a deadlock, the publisher could effect the nomination, as a compromise, of Newton D. Baker, Secretary of War under Woodrow Wilson and then, incidentally, general counsel for the Scripps-Howard newspapers. This apparently boyish attempt to name a President of the United States amused James A. Farley, who was managing Roosevelt's campaign. "Howard thought he could take off a few afternoons from his newspaper duties to nominate a presidential candidate," Farley wrote in his memoirs. "The game is somewhat more complicated."

After the Republicans had renominated Hoover, the Scripps-Howard editorial convention at French Lick endorsed him. The

publisher showed no warmth for Roosevelt until the summer after the inauguration, when "New Deal" had become a password
to popularity. He then threw himself on the President's neck with
all the shyness of a hostess in a navy café. "Roy is a fellow who
likes to climb aboard a band wagon," one politician said awhile
ago, "and then gets mad if the fellows who were on first won't let
him drive and play the bass drum at the same time."

Howard's infatuation with the President ended with the
"breathing-spell" letters they exchanged in the summer of 1935.
Alarmed by the administration's tax program and quietly relieved by the Supreme Court decision which terminated the
NRA, Howard proposed to Stephen Early, the President's secretary, that Mr. Roosevelt grant him an exclusive interview. The
President was to furnish prepared answers to a questionnaire
previously submitted by Howard. The affair was to be on the
grand scale. There would be photographers, newsreel camera-
men, and probably a broadcast, and the purport of the President's answers would be that recovery had already been achieved
and that reform was something business might thenceforth cease
to worry about. The President demurred, but agreed to answer a
letter from Howard and permit publication of the letter with his
reply. The publisher wrote that large-scale industry, harassed by
taxation which it considered "revengeful," felt there should be "a
breathing spell and a recess from further experimentation until
the country can recover its losses." The President answered,
"The 'breathing spell' of which you speak is here—very decidedly so." He also said, "The tax program of which you speak is
based upon a broad and just social and economic purpose—this
law affects only people who have incomes over fifty thousand
dollars a year." Howard published Roosevelt's reply, but his editorials soon indicated that he thought the President had trifled

with his affections. "I was never so thick with the President as people said," he now remarks modestly, and adds, rather defiantly, "and I'm not so thin with him now as some people would like to have you think."

In the 1936 presidential campaign, Howard gave nominal support to the administration. George Morris, a shrewd old political writer whom he had inherited with the *Telegram* when it was a wardheelers' Bible, assured him from the start that Landon would carry only two states. The publisher nevertheless took occasion during the campaign to visit Landon on his special train in Buffalo to pay his respects. "Our bark is worse than our bite," he told the Republican candidate. The fight over the Supreme Court made the division between Howard and Roosevelt definite. In the course of this struggle, the *World-Telegram* expressed extravagant admiration for Governor Herbert H. Lehman of New York, who helped beat the President's proposals. The praise bounced back in Howard's face in 1938, when Lehman ran for reelection against Thomas E. Dewey, the publisher's favorite adolescent Republican. A typical *World-Telegram* editorial of those days might begin with some such statement as "The State is indeed fortunate to have a choice of two such equally remarkable candidates" and then go on to the end praising Dewey. After Lehman's reelection, Howard may have felt that both men owed him gratitude, but the Governor refused a request of his to remove the Brooklyn district attorney from office. This proved that Lehman was no more to be depended on than Roosevelt or that earlier ungrateful protégé, LaGuardia.

The great German offensive of 1940 may well have annoyed Howard, as it practically insured the President's nomination for a third term. The publisher, who had looked to 1940 to deliver him from the insubordinate Roosevelt, suddenly found himself in the dilemma of a racing trainer who has to beat something with nothing. Dewey, whose prestige had steadily declined since his defeat by Lehman in the gubernatorial campaign, was too callow for a crisis President. Senators Taft and Vandenberg had demonstrated a remarkable knack of inspiring apathy. The kingmaker was standing on a corner waiting for a hitch on a band wagon when Oren Root, Jr., and Russell W. Davenport, Henry R. Luce, and a group of other men on the staffs of *Time* and *Fortune* came along with Wendell L. Willkie. Howard's wooing of the large, talkative Indianan was tempestuous. He appeared so consistently at the same dinner parties Willkie attended that Willkie, trapped once into playing a free-association parlor game and suddenly presented with the word "Howard," answered, "Soup." "Howard wore those nineteen newspapers in his lapel with that red carnation," a member of the original Willkie group has said. "He talked about them as if he were going to give them to us." Howard now says that he is sorry the election provided no clear-cut test of public opinion on intervention in the war. When Howard went to the Republican convention in Philadelphia as one of Willkie's most vociferous rooters, Willkie had already declared himself for full aid to Great Britain, but Howard, like many other Willkie admirers, may well have believed that Willkie was not really in earnest. One close friend has said, "Roy doesn't believe anything that is not told to him confidentially." At any rate, Howard seemed to think of the candidate's later demonstration of consistency as one more betrayal. As in the case of Roosevelt, Howard saw the first sign of ingratitude when he moved to help take charge of his new protégé. Davenport, Root, and Luce, discoverers of the new white hope, refused to cut Howard in for a big enough piece. Howard, the *Time-Fortune* people say, seemed to think that about ninety-eight per cent would be right. Howard encouraged General Johnson to make a trip to Colorado Springs, where the candidate was resting, to write Willkie's acceptance speech for him. This was a mistake, because if there is one thing Willkie is sure he can do, it is write. The clash of literary temperaments was intensified by Johnson's insistence that Willkie include a plan for farm relief the columnist had thought up and that he should mention the Virgin Mary someplace in his speech. The Elwood, Indiana, stylist felt hurt, and said so. Johnson returned to the East and wrote a couple of columns calling Willkie's advisers political amateurs. Howard, boarding the campaign train soon after Willkie's first tour had started, remained enough of a businessman to complain that the candidate was timing his speeches to break in morning papers (eighteen of the nineteen Scripps-Howard newspapers appear in the evening). As a political expert, he also gave some constructive criticism about the setup of the train and the itinerary.

Meanwhile, Pegler and Johnson, after the General had recovered from his irritation, wrote columns in boiling oil, invoking the wrath of a just deity who had destroyed Sodom and Gomorrah upon the subversive activities of Mrs. Roosevelt, who belongs to the American Newspaper Guild. They discussed the third term in a clinical style that reminded readers of the *Daily News* campaign against syphilis. The General fumed over the appointment of Elliot Roosevelt to a captaincy in the army. For comic relief, he went on the radio and told funny stories in Jewish dialect, a lapse which brought a disclaimer of responsibility in the *World-Telegram*. Howard, talking recently about the activities of his columnists during the election, said that they had run away with him. "You know, I would not interfere with any man's freedom of expression," he said solemnly, "but I thought they were very unfair to Franklin." Among the columnists, Raymond Clapper, the *World-Telegram*'s accredited liberal, in a relative sense, remained almost neutral until near the end of the campaign. Finally he came out for

Willkie, too, like the white horse in the circus chariot race who loafs along behind the others until the last lap. "When I looked in the paper and saw that Clapper had come over too," Howard says, "I said, 'Oh, my God!' It made us look partisan."

In his experience with public men, Howard has been betrayed so many times that he sometimes must feel like the cockney girl in the song "Once Again She Lorst 'Er Nime." Last January, when the administration began to propose a lend-lease bill, Howard telephoned to Willkie at his home, asked him to prepare a statement attacking the bill, and indicated that this was a chance to make up for the mistakes he had made during the campaign. "All the other boys are going to jump all over this bill, Wendell," Howard said in effect, "and I don't want you to get left at the post. I have a reporter with Tom Dewey writing his statement for him now, and I'm having lunch with Hoover tomorrow." (Howard has always had a tender spot for Hoover. He has given unlimited publicity to all the Hoover projects for sending food through the British blockade, despite the possibility of embarrassing the administration, which has tried to coordinate its foreign policy with Great Britain's.) Willkie told Howard that he could not decide until he had read the bill. The next day, after he read it, he said he would be for it if minor changes were made in it. The publisher and the ungrateful candidate had a resounding argument later at a dinner party given by John Erskine. It wound up by Howard's telling a blackface story to Willkie. The punch line of the story was "Wait till I get my razor on you tomorrow!" Willkie, more ingenuous than a LaGuardia or a Roosevelt, was astonished at such disrespect. "A man like that is too flippant to have so much power," he told friends later. He has as large a capacity as Howard's for feeling that his affections have been trifled with. Immediately after Willkie's return from England,

Howard sought a reconciliation. He succeeded in getting Willkie to come to dinner at his house, but their twanging wrangle continued all through the intended love feast. "To tell you the truth," Howard afterward remarked to a friend, "as long as one of them had to be elected, I'm glad it was Roosevelt. Willkie is a fellow you can't depend on."

• "Pull His Whiskers!" •

Few American industries have suffered so spectacular a decline as wrestling, which had its happiest days during the early years of the general depression. In the winter of 1931–32 ten wrestling shows were held at Madison Square Garden, and drew an average gate of twenty-four thousand dollars. These indoor shows merely served to prepare the wrestling public for outdoor bouts at the Yankee Stadium and the Garden Bowl, which occasionally drew sixty thousand dollars. The last match in the Garden was promoted on March 30, 1938, by an old acquaintance of mine named Jack Pfefer, and it attracted less than five thousand dollars' worth of patronage. If a promoter tried to rent the Yankee Stadium or even Ebbets Field for a wrestling show this summer, sporting people would think he had been overcome by the heat. Pfefer, however, is still conducting wrestling matches in a small way, and feels that from an artistic point of view they are superior to those of the great era. The trouble, according to him, is that the moneyed clientele has ceased to believe in wrestling as a sport and has not yet learned to appreciate it as a pure art form, like opera or classical dancing.

Pfefer holds shows in neighborhoods like Ridgewood, in Queens, and the region just south of the Bronx Zoo, and they draw fairly well at a general admission of a quarter or forty cents.

Several nights a week he leads his wrestlers out of the state to places like Jersey City and Bridgeport. Pfefer's wrestlers do not make big money, but most of them work five times a week even in summer. The promoter has been celebrated for years as the most unrelenting foe of the English language in the sports business. "You never heard it of an unemployment wrestler, didn't?" he asked me when I visited him awhile ago in his office on the tenth floor of the Times Building. "For wrestlers is no WPA."

In the trade, Pfefer is believed to have retained money despite the debacle. He was one of the four partners who controlled the wrestling business in New York in the golden era, and when the money was rolling in he lived frugally. His present enterprises, although on a very small scale, are often mildly profitable. He is a tiny, slight man, weighing about a hundred and twenty pounds and possessing the profile of a South African vulture. His eyebrows rise in a V from his nose, and he wears his hair in a long, dusty mane— a tonsorial allusion to a liking he has for music. On the walls of his office, among pictures of wrestlers, he keeps a death mask of Beethoven and signed photographs of opera singers.

He never opens a window in this office and wears a vest even in summer. In the street he always carries an ivory-headed cane presented to him by an Indian wrestler named Gafoor Khan. Pfefer's entire office staff consists of a worried, middle-aged ex-newspaperman named Al Mayer, at one time a successful manager of prize fighters. When the wrestling business was in its majestic prime, the partners in the local syndicate, besides Pfefer, were the late Jack Curley, a promoter named Rudy Miller, and a former wrestler called Toots Mondt. Miller and Mondt are among the little man's competitors. In the good days, it was Pfefer who had charge of the department of exotica—he was responsible for such importations as Ferenc Holuban, the Man without a Neck, Sergei Kalmikoff, the Crashing Cossack, and

Fritz Kley, the German Corkscrew. Most of the foreigners were built up into challengers of Jim Londos, the syndicate's perennial champion, who would throw them with his spectacular "airplane whirl."

Pfefer blames Londos' rapacity for the decline of the wrestling industry. After the syndicate had for several years informed the public that Londos was the greatest wrestler on earth, the Greek began demanding most of the gate receipts. The promoters had but two equally unpleasant alternatives. They could become virtual employees of Londos or destroy the edifice of legend they had built around him by declaring he was not much of a wrestler after all. They chose the second course. Within a year the country swarmed with champions, each group of wrestling promoters recognizing its own titleholder. At last reports, there were in different parts of the United States fifteen wrestling champions, including Londos, who has been performing for at least twenty-five years. The New York State Athletic Commission acknowledges no world's champion, and for that matter refuses to admit that wrestling is a competitive sport. The commission refers officially to all wrestling bouts as "exhibitions," and will not allow them to be advertised as contests. Pfefer says he is glad the commission doesn't permit a champion, because it saves hard feelings among his wrestlers. When they perform, they know it is just a night's work and they can concentrate on their histrionics.

I went up to Pfefer's office late one Wednesday afternoon a couple of summers ago, having made a date by telephone to go out to the Ridgewood Grove Arena with him and see his current band of wrestlers in action that evening. He was in a bad mood when I entered. A rival promoter had hired a wrestler to hit Pfefer in the jaw on the previous evening, as Jack sat in a restaurant on Forty-fourth Street. Evidently, to judge by the absence of facial wounds, Pfefer had been able to fall down before being seriously damaged, but it wasn't the blow that had hurt—it was the insubordination the blow had implied. "A wrestler should hit a promoter!" Jack wailed. "Because they don't like me, those loafers are breaking the wrestling business down to little pieces!" The chief reason for the bitterness between Pfefer and his rivals is his agreement with the Athletic Commission that wrestling is a form of show business. "A honest man can sell a fake diamond if he says it is a fake diamond, ain't it?" he yelled, appealing to me. "Only if he says it is a real diamond he ain't honest. These loafers don't like that I say wrestling is all chicancery—hookum, in other words."

There are three small rooms in Pfefer's suite of offices. While he was telephoning to a couple of city editors who, he felt, had underplayed the news of the assault upon him, I went into one of the outer rooms and talked to two wrestlers who were sitting there. They were looking at their own pictures in a copy of *Ring*. Both of them were in their middle twenties, a couple of solid young men wearing slacks and sports shirts. Both had the fantastically mangled ears which mark their trade. They were heavily tanned, because, one of them explained, they were living at Coney Island for the summer and exercised on the beach every morning. One introduced himself as the Italian Sensation. He came from up Boston way, he said, and had started wrestling ten years ago in the Cambridge Y.M.C.A. "The girls like these ears," he said self-consciously. The other wrestler, blond and jolly-looking, said he was the Mighty Magyar. He came from St. Louis and had begun wrestling in a boys' club there. "Both my parents were born in Hungary, though," he said.

People of foreign birth provided the chief support for wrestling during the pre-Londos era, before the general public became interested. It was a popular form of vicarious suffering in Europe before boxing was known there. Now that the public has abandoned the industry, it again depends largely on the foreign-born, and to excite the small clubs a performer must claim some European affinity. "You can't get rich wrestling nowadays," the Mighty Magyar said, "but you can afford to drive a car." After a while the boys went out to eat. I was to see both of them wrestle later in the evening.

Not long after the Italian Sensation and the Mighty Magyar left, Pfefer said it was time to start for Ridgewood. Al Mayer, Pfefer's factotum and publicity man, came with us. Mayer, a short, plump man with graying hair and mustache, carried a large framed picture of a wrestler named King Kong, the Abyssinian Gorilla Man, which was to be hung in the lobby in Ridgewood. The picture restored Pfefer's spirits. "Look at him," he said to me, pointing to King Kong with his cane, "a great funny maker!" King Kong wears a full black beard, and the picture showed him in a kind of regal robe, with a crown on his head, looking a little like Haile Selassie. "He's a Greek," Pfefer said, "but during the Fiopian war I made him for a Fiopian." We took the B.M.T. under the Times Building and rode down to Union Square. En route, I asked Jack how the wrestlers knew who was supposed to win each bout. Jack Curley used to evade this question with a grin. Mr. Pfefer, however, is forthright. "I tell them," he said. "I treat them like a father, like a mother beats up her baby. Why should I let some boys be pigs, they should want to win every night yet?"

Pfefer said that the Italian Sensation, whom I had met in the office, was to wrestle in the feature event of the evening against a fellow known as the German Superman. They would divide ten per cent of the house, which on a warm night like this would probably mean twenty-five or thirty dollars for each of them. In the next show, Jack said, they would both wrestle in preliminaries, while two other members of the troupe appearing in preliminaries tonight would meet in the feature attraction. Performers in supporting bouts receive ten dollars each, a minimum fixed by the Athletic Commission. A wrestler working five nights a week, including one feature exhibition, can count on about sixty-five dollars. Ridgewood is a neighborhood where a great many German-Americans live, so the card for the evening stressed the Axis powers. Besides the German Superman, the program listed a German Apollo and a German Blacksmith, and in addition to the Italian Sensation, it included a Hollywood Italian Moving-Picture Star and an Italian Idol. Pfefer, Mayer, and I changed to the Canarsie line of the B.M.T. at Union Square, and as we walked down the ramp connecting the two platforms a big shirt-sleeved fellow rushed up to Pfefer and squeezed his arm. "Hollo, Jack!" he shouted. "Got work for me soon?" Pfefer told him to drop around to the office. The promoter explained that the big fellow was the Siberian Wolf, who now had a job in a Brooklyn shipyard but liked to pick up extra money at his old trade. Pfefer and Mayer left me at the door of the Ridgewood Grove Arena, a low, widespread, wooden building, and I walked over to a German saloon on St. Nicholas Avenue and had my supper.

When I returned, the crowd was beginning to arrive at the Grove. Most of the men were in shirt sleeves, and about half of them wore stiff straw hats. They moved forward heavily, with the experienced air of men going to church on Sunday and prepared to criticize the sermon. There were a good many women with them, most of them shapeless and wearing house dresses.

Pfefer had given me a working-press ticket, which calls for a seat directly at the ringside. The ushers looked surprised when I sat down there. No newspaperman had covered a wrestling show at the Grove for years. The only other person in the first row at my side of the ring was one of the judges, an old boxing referee whose legs have gone bad. Although the Athletic Commission concedes that wrestling exhibitions are not contests, it insists on the presence of two licensed judges and an inspector, as well as a referee and a doctor. The referee gets fifteen dollars and the others ten dollars each.

The first exhibition brought together the Polish Goliath, a vast and bulbous youth who, according to the announcer, weighed 310 pounds, and the Italian Idol, a strongly built fellow weighing a mere 195. As soon as the Goliath appeared, wearing a dingy bathrobe with a Polish eagle sewn on the back, the crowd began to boo. This was partly because he had such an advantage in weight and partly because of Poland's anti-German foreign policy. When the bout began the Italian Idol clamped an arm lock on the Goliath's left arm and started to twist it. The Goliath contorted his face in a simulation of agony. A fellow in the crowd shouted to the Italian Idol, "Break it off!" Soon the rest of the audience took up the chant, "Break it off! Break it off!" The Italian Idol seemed to put a great deal of pressure on the arm, but when the Goliath merely waved his wrist the Idol not only lost the hold but fell flat on his back. From what I could recollect of a few painful experiments in college wrestling, this seemed a remarkably easy way to break a hold, but it convinced a man behind me. "Jeez, he's strong!" the man exclaimed in an awed tone. I could hear variations of the same comment all over the hall. But the Pole seemed as stupid as he was powerful. He just stood there glaring at the prostrate Idol instead of pouncing on him. Then he turned to the audience, raised one fat fist, and solemnly thumped it against his nearly hairless chest. The crowd exploded in fury, booing and whistling. The Goliath turned toward the Idol and waddled slowly forward. He put his feet together and made as if to jump on the Idol. The Italian wriggled out of the way and got to his feet, and the referee, a lively young man, shook a finger warningly at the Goliath. The putative Pole demanded loudly, "What's the matter with that?" He said it in good clear Brooklynese, for, as I later learned, he is a native of South Brooklyn. But the crowd, convinced in spite of their own ears that a Polish Goliath talks with an outlandish accent, shouted back mockingly, "Vot's der mottur vit dot?"

While the Goliath was talking to the referee, the Italian Idol, miraculously revitalized, rushed across the ring and butted his opponent in the rear. The Goliath fell partly through the ropes. When he disentangled himself, he turned to the referee. "Why don't you watch that, ref?" he bellowed. The fans shouted in unison, "Vy don't you votch dot, ref?" It was a kind of litany. The wrestlers repeated the arm-lock routine three times, and then the Goliath got both arms around the Idol's head, pulled him forward and pushed his head down. The Goliath's face reflected an ogreish pleasure. The Idol stamped as if in acute pain. I looked up under the ropes and saw the Idol's face, which was invisible to the crowd. He was laughing. The sympathetic fans shouted, "Referee! Referee! Strangle hold!" One fellow screamed, "We had a good referee here last week, you butcher!" Then the man behind me yelled, "Step on his feet!" The Italian Idol promptly stepped on the Pole's feet, and the Goliath let him go. One of the Goliath's most effective gestures for inciting boos was to stand back, place his hands on his large, womanish hips, and puff out his chest and stomach. Another was to put his left hand on the Italian's right ear and then, with his right hand, twist his own left thumb. This looked as if he were twisting the Idol's ear off. After about fifteen minutes of such charades, the Goliath grabbed the Idol by the hair on top of the head and threw him over his left shoulder. I thought the Idol must have cooperated in this maneuver, but the crowd took it literally. The Idol lay as if stunned, and the Goliath fell on him. The referee slapped the Goliath on the back to signify victory. The fans booed angrily, but there was a note of anticipation in their howls, as if they knew that sooner or later they would have the pleasure of seeing the Goliath ground in the dust. In the meantime they would continue to come to the shows whenever he was billed.

The principals in the second exhibition were the Irish Wild Man and the German Apollo. In some neighborhoods, Irish athletes are presented in an endearing light, but not in Ridgewood. This was immediately apparent when the Irish Wild Man refused to shake hands with the German Apollo before they came to grips. The man behind me yelled, "Make it short and snappy, Fritz! He wouldn't shake hands with you!" The Wild Man, a stocky fellow with a considerable paunch, evidently had been in the navy or a side show, for he was almost covered with tattooing. Soon after the bell rang he hit the Apollo on the jaw with his fist and knocked him down. From my seat, I could see that the blow had really landed on the Wild Man's own left hand, which he had carefully placed on the Apollo's neck before swinging his right. The crowd booed frantically, because hitting with the fist is a foul. The Apollo got up, staggering. The Wild Man knocked him down again, with a terrific blow that missed him. The referee intervened and held the raging Wild Man away while the Apollo got up and walked around the ring, apparently in quest of consciousness. Then, when the referee turned the Wild Man loose, the Apollo hit the villainous Irishman a ferocious punch on the breastbone. The Wild Man went down with a crash, which he produced by kicking the mat with his heels. The fans shouted triumphantly. "How do you like that, you mick?" the man behind me cried.

When the Wild Man got up he immediately started to run away from the Apollo, who followed him relentlessly. Every time the Wild Man got into a corner of the ring, he would turn and hold both arms wide, as if disclaiming evil intent. Occasionally he would hold out his hand to shake, but the Apollo, who played his role straight, would disdain the proffered clasp. Then the Wild Man would jump out of the ring and stay outside the ropes until the referee argued him into returning. The referee pleaded with the Apollo, who finally nodded a majestic forgiveness. The Wild Man held out his hand again in friendship, and the guileless German reached to grasp it. Instantly the Wild Man hit him on the jaw again. I saw his fist pass behind the Apollo's head, but anyway the German fell down. The Wild Man loosed a peal of depraved laughter and then started to kick the Apollo's prone form. The Apollo sat up moaning and rubbing his groin. A lynching seemed imminent. Suddenly the Apollo, galvanized by righteous anger, jumped up, seized the Wild Man by the head, and threw him down. Then he began to twist the Wild Man's left foot, to the accompaniment of a cadenced chant of "Break it off!" in which all the lady spectators joined with shrill fervor. The Irish Wild Man rolled his eyes and groaned, rather incongruously, "Ach! Ach!" He pounded the mat with his hands, but got no sympathy. Shortly afterward the Apollo pinned the Wild Man's shoulders to the mat, amid hosannas of Teutonic triumph. Mr. Pfefer had slid into a seat beside me and was observing the Wild Man's *moues* with the intent appreciation of a McClintic watching a Cornell.

"A nice boy, the Wild Man," the promoter said as the Irishman climbed down from the ring, shaking his fists at the crowd.

"He got five children, and he's so good he couldn't hurt a fly on the wall. But in the ring he acts like a wildcap. He is a good villain, the dope. In every match must be a hero and a villain or else a funny maker. The villains and the funny makers are the hardest ones to develop."

Both of my acquaintances of the afternoon, the Italian Sensation and the Mighty Magyar, appeared to fall within the hero category. The Magyar threw the Hollywood Italian Moving-Picture Star, a large gentleman who seemed to me a poor reflection of the Polish Goliath, employing the same comedy technique but less effectively. The Italian Sensation lost to the German Superman. Of all the wrestlers on the card, the Superman, a recent *émigré*, seemed the one most puzzled by the proceedings. When he grabbed the Sensation and the latter came off the floor as lightly as the woman in an adagio team, the Superman was obviously astonished. But he did the only thing feasible—he let the Sensation fall with a crash. This produced an impression of boundless strength. "He'll learn," Pfefer said. "He'll be someday a wonderful funny maker."

Earlier in the evening, I had turned around to look at the vociferous man in the row behind me, and had been surprised to recognize in him an outwardly cynical waiter from the Gaiety Delicatessen near Longacre Square, a place I go to occasionally. As the principals in the final exhibition climbed into the ring, I stole another glance at the waiter. He was white with emotion, and his tongue protruded between his lips. He stared at the Abyssinian Gorilla Man with the horror that suggestible visitors to the Bronx Zoo reptile house sometimes show before a python. As the exhibition was about to begin, the waiter plucked at the arm of the man next to him. "That man's a murderer," he said. "I seen him wrestle before. It shouldn't be allowed—not with a human being."

The Gorilla's opponent in the closing turn was the German Blacksmith, a creamy-skinned, blue-eyed, and golden-haired youth who could have posed for an illustration in a Hitler primer. The Gorilla Man dragged this Aryan god toward the ropes and pretended to rub the Blacksmith's eyes out against the top strand. The referee tore the Gorilla Man from his prey. The Gorilla Man made a motion to strike the referee. The Blacksmith held his arm over his eyes. The fans expected to see a couple of bloody sockets when the arm dropped. But his eyesight had been miraculously preserved. The Gorilla Man treacherously extended his hand. The fans shouted, "No, no! Don't shake!"

The Gorilla Man then sneakily got behind the Nordic and began to strangle him. The referee made him release his unfair hold. The Blacksmith coughed desperately to indicate the degree of strangulation. The Gorilla Man grabbed him from behind again. It seemed unlikely that he understood the referee's English. He was an untrammeled savage. "Stop it!" my friend the waiter shrieked. "For God's sake, stop it!" The German did not seem to know what to do. Suddenly my friend had an idea. "Pull his whiskers!" he shouted. The German Blacksmith appeared to hear. He reached behind him and pulled at the Gorilla Man's long black beard. The Gorilla Man let out a wild scream and released his hold. He jumped up and down in the center of the ring clutching his whiskers. Then, with another shout, he leaped at the Blacksmith again and got another strangle hold. But now the fans had the answer. "Pull his whiskers!" they shouted joyfully. The Blacksmith pulled; the Gorilla danced and then took another hold. "Pull his whiskers!" came the chorus. The sequence was repeated four more times. At length the Blacksmith butted the Gorilla Man in the stomach. The latter fell down, still holding his whiskers, and the Blacksmith pinned his Graeco-

Abyssinian shoulders to the mat. On the way to the nearest exit I caught up to my friend the waiter and greeted him. He looked at me a trifle sheepishly and said, "How did you like the show? I never take it serious." Mr. Pfefer, at my other elbow, said, "We did only about six hundred dollars, the bums."

The Broadway Library of Larceny

The Library of Larceny is a collection of books about—and sometimes by—people who exploit public confidence for their own personal monetary gain. Some of them are thieves pure and simple. Some are get-along types who just happen to be standing nearby with pockets flapping when spoils are divided. And some are con artists—with equal stress on the second word of that formula—men and women who do not steal, exactly, and certainly never employ violence or strong-arm tactics, but who extract sums by means of a sort of psychic jujitsu from pigeons who are often all too willing to be plucked. These books fall into the true-crime genre, but that genre (once dominated by pipe-smoking sleuths) has lately been given over almost entirely to depressing psychopathology and gore for gore's sake. The Library of Larceny proposes instead to restore property crime to its full, glorious stature. It is, after all, a portion of the inheritance of this Land of Opportunity.

The books in the series highlight the ingenuity of their subjects, their delight in the aesthetics of their profession, their artisanal pride in a neatly turned score, and, not incidentally, their pleasure in language. For whatever reasons, swindling seems to awaken in its perpetrators a gift for vigorous, highly colored language, with accompanying dead-pan humor. The metaphors so often come from the natural world—a victim is a "doe" or an "apple"; he or she is "lop-eared"; a dollar bill is a "fish" or a "bumblebee"—that it is as if we were listening to lions and tigers discussing their jobs. Add to all this an inside view of a world of poolrooms and racetracks and bars and brothels, the raffish world of professional leisure. The books will span the past century, stretching from the time after the West had been won—and the wildlife that had evolved along the way sought new outlets for its talents—right up to the present era of corporate malfeasance, by way of the hectic, wised-up city life of the cocktail age. The books, many of them long out of print, will appeal to a wide range of readers, young and old: hipsters, pirates, roués, scalawags, poets, armchair psychologists, advertising strategists, cultural theorists, promoters, touts, sibyls, and bon vivants everywhere.

Luc Sante
Series Editor

About the Author

A. J. Liebling joined the staff of *The New Yorker* in 1935 and stayed there until his death in 1963. His many books included *The Earl of Louisiana*, *Back Where I Came From*, *Between Meals*, and *The Sweet Science*, which was recently voted the finest sports book of all time.

About the Series Editor

Luc Sante is a renowned writer and critic and author of the classic book on the raffish, violent, and criminal side of New York, *Low Life*. He also wrote the introduction for Anchor Books' reissue of the David Maurer classic, *The Big Con*. An authority on the history of photography, Sante is now a professor at Bard College.